Catholic Problems
in
Western Canada

Also from Westphalia Press
westphaliapress.org

The Idea of the Digital University

Dialogue in the Roman-Greco World

The History of Photography

International or Local Ownership?: Security Sector Development in Post-Independent Kosovo

Lankes, His Woodcut Bookplates

Opportunity and Horatio Alger

The Role of Theory in Policy Analysis

The Little Confectioner

Non-Profit Organizations and Disaster

The Idea of Neoliberalism: The Emperor Has Threadbare Contemporary Clothes

Social Satire and the Modern Novel

Ukraine vs. Russia: Revolution, Democracy and War: Selected Articles and Blogs, 2010-2016

James Martineau and Rebuilding Theology

A Strategy for Implementing the Reconciliation Process

Issues in Maritime Cyber Security

A Different Dimension: Reflections on the History of Transpersonal Thought

Iran: Who Is Really In Charge?

Contracting, Logistics, Reverse Logistics: The Project, Program and Portfolio Approach

Unworkable Conservatism: Small Government, Freemarkets, and Impracticality

Springfield: The Novel

Lariats and Lassos

Ongoing Issues in Georgian Policy and Public Administration

Growing Inequality: Bridging Complex Systems, Population Health and Health Disparities

Designing, Adapting, Strategizing in Online Education

Pacific Hurtgen: The American Army in Northern Luzon, 1945

Natural Gas as an Instrument of Russian State Power

New Frontiers in Criminology

Feeding the Global South

Beijing Express: How to Understand New China

The Rise of the Book Plate: An Exemplative of the Art

Catholic Problems
in
Western Canada

by George Thomas Daly

Preface by Most Reverend
O. E. Mathieu

WESTPHALIA PRESS
An Imprint of Policy Studies Organization

Westphalia Press
An imprint of Policy Studies Organization
1527 New Hampshire Ave. NW
Washington, D.C. 20036
info@ipsonet.org

ISBN-13: 978-1-63391-669-2
ISBN-10: 1-63391-669-3

Cover design by Jeffrey Barnes:
jbarnesbook.design

Daniel Gutierrez-Sandoval, Executive Director
PSO and Westphalia Press

Updated material and comments on this edition
can be found at the Westphalia Press website:
www.westphaliapress.org

Catholic Problems

in

Western Canada

By
George Thomas Daly, C.SS.R.

With preface by the Most Reverend O. E. Mathieu,
Archbishop of Regina

TORONTO: THE MACMILLAN COMPANY OF
CANADA. LTD., AT ST. MARTIN'S HOUSE

Permissu Superiorum

ARTHUR T. COUGHLAN, C.SS.R.,
Provincial.

Imprimatur

† EDWARD ALFRED LEBLANC,
Bishop of St. John, N.B.

St. John, N.B., December 8th, 1920.

RESPECTFULLY DEDICATED
TO
THE CATHOLIC HIERARCHY
OF CANADA.

CONTENTS

[6]

CONTENTS

PART 2.—EDUCATIONAL PROBLEMS

PART 3.—SOCIAL PROBLEMS

PREFACE

*Letter of the Most Reverend O. E. Mathieu,
Archbishop of Regina, to the Author*

REVEREND G. DALY, C.SS.R.,
St. John, N.B.

Dear Father,—

QUEBEC Province claims you as her son.
There you lived for many years; there you
learned to admire the peaceful life and to appreciate the genuine happiness of our patriarchal
families; there you were an eyewitness of the
"bonne entente" and noble rivalry which exist between the ethnical groups that go to make up its
population.

At various times your sacred ministry has
brought you in touch with the other Eastern Provinces of our broad Dominion. A keen observer,
you readily grasped existing conditions and the
mentality of the various elements of our Canadian
Population.

The year 1917 found you laboring in our beloved Province of Saskatchewan, as Rector of our
Cathedral. For three years you lived with us.
The possibilities of our great West soon appealed
to your enthusiastic heart. The various problems
which here engage the attention of the Church
fired your soul with noble ambition. I shall never

forget the good you have done in the parish committed to your care. I shall be ever grateful for the zeal with which you devoted yourself, heart and soul, to the guidance of those under your charge. You found your happiness in making others happy, remembering that kindly actions alone give to our days their real value. Your priestly heart understood that when one is in God's service he must not be content with doing things in a half-hearted way or without willing sacrifice.

But the voice of your Superiors called you to another field of action, and with ready obedience you hastened to the Eastern extremity of the Dominion. I can assure you, dear Father, that, though absent, your memory is still fresh among us. Your old parishioners of Holy Rosary Cathedral, and others with whom you came in contact through missions and other work throughout the Province, have kept a fond and faithful remembrance of your Reverence. The citizens of Regina who are not of our Faith still remember the noble efforts you always put forth to promote good will and concord in the community at large. Your charity proved to them that we were not born to hate but to love one another. It affords me great pleasure to see that since you left the West you have continued to have its welfare at heart, its problems ever present in your thought. For you tell me that you are just about to publish a book on "Catholic problems in Western Canada."

The West, you have known, studied and loved. The tremendous obstacles, as well as the great possibilities which there face the Church at this critical hour of our history, have left on your mind a lasting impression. You fully realize, dear Father, that our Western problems are not sufficiently known by the Catholics of the East. Were the importance of these issues fully appreciated by all, a greater interest would be taken in regard to their immediate solution. Catholics throughout the Country, you rightly state, are obliged to further the influence of Holy Mother Church in our Western Provinces, which will certainly be called upon within a very near future to play a most important part in our Dominion.

To draw the attention of Catholics to the critical issues which conditions, during the last decade or so, have created in our great West, and to offer solutions which will be beneficial to the Church, are the noble motives that have prompted your important work and guided you on to its completion.

Even though some may not fully share your views, or see eye to eye with you on the means of action you suggest, you will have nevertheless attained your object. You will have, I am confident, awakened interest in our Western problems which, I repeat, are unfortunately not known, or at least, are not fully appreciated by too many of our own.

There is a saying that the heart has reasons

which the mind does not fully grasp. I feel sure that the many hours you have spent in the composition of your book, coupled with the strenuous work of the missions, to which you have consecrated yourself with unrelenting zeal since your departure from our midst, have been calculated to weaken your health. But your heart, unmindful of self, did not consider time and fatigue so long as your fellow-man was being benefited. Your love for God and His Church induced you to undertake this work and carry it through to completion. Your book, I am sure, is destined to produce happy results. This will be your consolation and your reward. Asking God to bless your work and wishing you to accept this expression of my constant gratitude and sincere friendship, I remain as ever,

Devotedly yours,

†OLIVIER ELZEAR MATHIEU,
Archbishop of Regina.

ARCHBISHOP'S HOUSE,
REGINA, November 21st, 1920.

INTRODUCTION

Praesentia tangens. . . . . .
                    Futura prospiciens.

PROBLEMS characterize every age, sum up the complex life of nations and give them their distinctive features. They form that moral atmosphere which makes one period of history responsible and tributary to another. And indeed, in every human problem there is an ethical element. This imponderable factor, which often baffles our calculations, always remains the true, permanent driving force. For in the last analysis of human things, morality is what reachest furthest and matters most.

Problems may vary with the times and the countries, and yet, the moral issues involved never change; for, right is eternal. To detect this ethical element amid the ever restless waves of human activities has ever been the noble and constant effort of true leaders. Like the pilot they are ever watching for the lighted buoy on the tossing waves.

This moral element underlying all our national problems is what affects Catholics as such, or rather the medium through which Catholics are called to affect them. No period should prove more interesting to Catholics than our own, for the very principles of Christian Ethics are now being questioned and vindicated in the lives of nations, either by the benefits accruing from their

[13]

application, or by the evils consequent upon their neglect.

Our neo-pagan world is learning by a cruel and sad experience that Religion is the foundation of morality, and morality that of true legality. "For unless certain things antecedent to conscience be granted and firmly held, 'conscience' becomes synonymous with 'sentiment.' "

Mr. Lloyd George himself, addressing a religious gathering in Wales on June 9, 1920, recognized Religion as the only bulwark able to resist the rising tide of anarchy. "Bolshevism is spreading throughout the world," said the British Premier, "and the churches can alone save the people from the disaster which will ensue, if this anarchy of will and aim continues to spread." The task of the churches, he continued, was greater than that which came within the compass of any political party. Political parties might provide the lamps, lay the wires and turn the current on to certain machinery, but the churches must be the power stations. If the generating stations were destroyed, whatever the arrangements and plans of the political parties might be, it would not be long before the light was cut off from the homes of the people. The doctrines taught by the churches are the *only* security against the triumph of human selfishness, and human selfishness unchecked will destroy any plans, however perfect, which politicians may devise.

This period of history, to quote Gladstone, is "an agitated and expectant age." The world is travelling fast into a new era. The modern social fabric, built on the shifting sands of selfishness and injustice is rocking on its foundations. Amid accumulated ruins nations are searching for the basic principles of true Reconstruction. This period of unrest is in itself a challenge to Christianity, to the Church. But the vitalizing force of Christianity can solve these problems of a decrepit civilization just as it solved the problem of tottering Rome. Problems therefore must be faced and solved. Every Catholic has his place in this world-wide work. If our religion does not make its influence felt in every phase of our life's activities, it is—as far as our life and its influence on others is concerned—a gigantic fraud. Bishop Kettler understood this pressing obligation when, breaking away from a too conservative programme of action, he was the first in the Church to give an impetus to the study of the modern social problem. His policy and action were said to have prompted the celebrated letter of Leo III, *Rerum Novarum.* The words of this great democratic Bishop still bear his timely message to Catholics of to-day, "To save the souls of countless workmen entrusted to her by Christ, the Church must enter the field of Social reform, armed with extraordinary remedies. She must exert herself to the utmost to rescue the workmen from a situation which constitutes a real proximate occasion of sin for them, a situation which makes it morally impossible for them to fulfill their duties as Christians."

"The Church is bound to interfere *"ex caritate,"* as these workmen are in extreme need and cannot help themselves. Otherwise, the unbelieving workingman will say to her: "Of what use are your fine teachings to me? What is the use of your referring me, by way of consolation, to the next world, if in this world you let me and my wife and my children perish with hunger? You are not seeking my welfare, you are looking for something else."

Our fair and broad Dominion has not escaped from that spirit of unrest. Spasmodic eruptions in the East and in the West indicate the same central fires of the universal volcano upon which the world now sleeps uneasily. Yet, various reasons have urged us to limit our investigation and reflections to Western Canada. The predominating interests of the West have of late become more and more evident in the economic and political life of our country. Lord Salisbury, when trouble was brewing on the far-flung border of India, gave to the people the famous warning "Look at big maps." To get a just appreciation of our mighty West we may well follow that same advice and "look at big maps." The sudden and rapid growth of our Prairie Provinces particularly, the unlimited and perennial resources of their fertile soil, the progressive spirit of the population have made of the West the land of great possibilities and mighty problems. The future of our Country, the peace and prosperity of the nation depend to a great extent on the reasonable and just exploitation of these resources and on the adequate solution to these problems.

There is no place in Canada where problems develop more rapidly and meet with more radical solutions than in Western Canada. This is the case in every young and prosperous country. No dead are behind the living, to link the past to the future with the steadying influence of tradition. Who has not heard of "The Spirit of the West?" Broad in its vision, sympathetic and ambitious in its plans, over-confident in its powers and most aggressive in its policies, that spirit grips you as you pass beyond the Great Lakes into the unlimited horizons of the rolling prairies. Those who have never experienced its secret influence, will never fully understand its tremendous power. J. W. Dafoe, of the Manitoba Free Press, welcoming to the West the Members of the Imperial Press Conference (1920), assured them that they would observe in the West evidence "of a newer Canadianism, the Canadianism of to-morrow; not hostile to the East, but, we think, a little better."

As the West has forced itself on the attention of our economic and political world, so also have its Religious problems loomed up many and

great on the horizon of the Church. The Catholic
Church, there, as in many mission countries, is in
process of formation: immense fields await the
scythe of belated reapers. Yet, notwithstanding
this state of imperfect organization, the Church
stands out as one of the great moral factors which
outsiders are the first to respect, and politicians
too willing at times to exploit. Through her
teachings and her children, she is bound to make
the beneficial influence of her presence felt, even
by her enemies. Her teachings indeed create for
her loyal children issues which have to be faced
squarely and unflinchingly. The influence of the
Church on Society depends on the manner Catholics understand their social responsibilities and
translate into action her doctrine. We may well
apply to the life of the Church in a country this
biological truism: "life consists in adaptation to
environment." From a Catholic viewpoint Our
West will be vitalized only in as much as the
Catholics in Western Canada, thoroughly patriotic
in their aspirations and thoroughly Catholic in
their ideas and feelings, will bring their influence
to bear on our national life. Their example and
their influence will lead to the silent and "pacific
penetration" of the Society in which they live.
And the Catholics throughout Canada cannot
stand aloof, disinterested in the upbuilding
of the Western Provinces, where the Canada
of to-morrow is being created. There indeed

the clash of ideals is more marked, the fermentation of thought is stronger, issues are more vital. Our national life, to a great extent, will depend on how these conflicting elements are absorbed into the blood and sinews of the Country.

The problems on which we dwell are, in our humble estimation, of paramount importance and should arrest the attention and elicit the co-operation of every Catholic alive to their seriousness. No doubt we have been sleeping at our posts. Red lights spot the darkness of the future and speak of danger ahead if the problems upon which we dwell are not pressed home with constancy and energy, if some concerted action is not agreed upon. Behind these problems lurk mighty issues. They strike at the very foundations of Christianity and Christian civilization, and cannot be disposed of by Parliament-Laws or Orders-in-Council.

We are a minority, some may say, and without influence. Yes, we are a minority, but were we a militant minority, our ideas would make their way. "Small as the Catholic body was in England," said H. Belloc, "it knew what it thought; it had a determined position. That was of enormous importance. A minority which was logical, reasonable, and united was a very much stronger thing than its mere numbers would suggest." Did not the ideas of a few Oxford men revolutionize the Church of England and bring on a movement the results of which we still witness throughout the English-speaking world. The men who see clear and far, who feel keenly and deeply will necessarily be leaders. The hand that leads is always governed by a warm heart and a clear eye. "Devotion is the child of conviction," said Lord Haldane.

The non-Catholic may be inclined to look upon our exposition of these Western Problems as a merely sectarian viewpoint, and therefore, of no value to him. He may even look upon our work as an open challenge.   I would answer in Newman's words: *"Our motive for writing has been the sight of the truth and the desire to show it to others."*

The serious minded non-Catholic, whose soul has not been wholly warped by prejudice, will at least consider the Catholic Church as one of the great moral factors in the nation. He will naturally wish to know the mind of the Church and the reasons for its stand in many problems common to all Canadians. Our candid explanation will help to give him a better understanding of facts and a better appreciation of our position on issues to be faced by us all. We are prompted by a sincere love for our Country in offering these solutions for the various issues with which we are confronted. "Preconceived opinions and inherited prejudices, particularly in religious matters tend to make men either blind or indifferent to the merits of systems other than their own." We do not expect our non-Catholic readers to see eye to

eye with us in the discussion of the various problems under examination.   Our viewpoint is naturally the Catholic one.   But we do believe that the
broad-minded Westerner is open to conviction and
willing to take an argument on its face value.
'Give us a hearing' . . . . this is the burden of our
message to our non-Catholic countrymen.   This
book is not written in a spirit of controversy.
Were some to see it in this light, then I would
claim for the author what Birrell said of Newman: "He contrived to instil into his very controversy more of the spirit of Christ than most men
can find room for in their prayers."   Moreover,
we are persuaded that the great war has mellowed
the minds of men and made them more receptive.
The contact with other countries has softened the
contours of certain controversies and given to all a
broader outlook.

However, should our arguments fail to prove
satisfactory or should they give rise to contradiction, we would repeat here what Newman wrote
in his Preface to "Difficulties of Anglicans."
"It has not been our practice to engage in controversy with those who felt it their duty to
criticise what at any time we have written; but
that will not preclude us under present circumstances, from elucidating what is deficient in them
by further observations, should questions be asked,
which, either from the quarter whence they proceed, or from their intrinsic weight, have, accord-

ing to our judgment, a claim upon our attention."

The problems we touch upon are of a general character. They are not new, but the war and the loose and hysterical thinking which has accompanied and followed it, have forced them into startling prominence. We have grouped them under three headings: *religious, educational,* and *social.* We do not pretend to present an exhaustive treatment of the matter. To do so, would be on our part a stroke of temerity and for the reader, an assured deception. Human problems are ever the same. The surface may be somewhat changed, the handling a little different, but the principles upon which depends their solution do not change. Our effort is to throw a new light on old subjects.

To be of service to the Church, and, through Her to our Country, is the sole ambition we have had before us in gathering together in book-form stray sheaves of thought, published here and there, during the course of the last few years. We are quite convinced that a clear vision of the problems facing the Church in Western Canada will awaken a sense of the responsibility which they entail for every Catholic in the land.

Our views and suggestions in the matter are but those of a humble soldier who belongs to the rank and file of the great Catholic army. But often a private in the firing line can suggest a plan of action which, when corrected or modified at headquarters, proves to be of some benefit to his battalion. This explains the dedication of our humble effort to the Hierarchy of Canada. For in problems which affect the Church, we would not lose sight of this supreme truth: "The Holy Ghost has placed the Bishops to rule the Church of God, which He has purchased with His own blood."—

(Act XX, 28)

St. Peters Rectory,
St. John, N.B.

On the Feast of the "Immaculate Conception," December 8th, 1920.

PART I

RELIGIOUS PROBLEMS

"It is surprising how at the bottom
of every political problem we always find some theology involved."
—(Proudhom)

CHAPTER 1

THE CALL OF THE WEST*

A Call from the West

WHO has not heard the call of the West?
Like the blast of the hunter's horn in the
silent forest, its thrilling and inviting sound has
awakened the echoes throughout the land. Springing from the granite heart of our mighty Rockies,
that call comes through their valleys, is heard over
the "Great Divide" and whispers its way to the

---

*This Chapter formed the matter of a series of articles pub-
lished in the "Catholic Register" of Toronto. The Catholic Church
Extension Society republished them in pamphlet form with the
following introduction by Archbishop McNeil.

"The author of this pamphlet has lived in the West and has
felt—I was going to say—the need of Catholic co-operation, but
that falls short of the reality. Co-operation among Catholics is
more than a means to a missionary end. It is an essential part of
Catholic life. Boundaries of jurisdiction are conveniences and
means to an end. In the first centuries of the Christian era it was
centres rather than circumferences that marked divisions of work
and of jurisdiction; but, in any case, administrative divisions were
never intended to be divisions of brotherhood. In places where
we are well established we are inclined to look upon Christian
brotherhood in an abstract way. In the West they feel it as a
necessity of Catholic life, not only as a source of financial help, but
as brotherhood in sympathy, interest, and mutual helpfulness. The
West can help the East by its growing influence, and Catholics in
the West can do their part in defence of Catholic ideals and Catholic
institutions. The more we do for them the more they can do for
us. Father Daly describes the Call of the West, and it is fittingly
through Catholic Extension that the call is now made and will be
answered."

foothills.   Soft as the evening breeze, strong as the
howling blizzard, we hear it across the prairie,
gathering as it were, on its triumphal march to the
East, something of the immensity of the plains and
freshness of the lakes.

In the din of our manufacturing cities, in the
quietness of our towns and villages, by the rivers
and winding bays of our Maritime Provinces,
along the peaceful shores of the St. Lawrence, the
call of the West has been heard.

Its alluring sound has cast a spell upon our
youth, the hope of the country.   Faces flushed
with the bright hues of life's dawn, eyes sparkling
with the fires of early youth, instinctively turn to
the West.   From all points of Eastern Canada
young men and young women are leaving for that
mysterious land of brilliant promise and great
possibilities.

The Call of the West!   All Canada is eager to
hear its message.   Has not the merchant his ear
to the ground, listening to the throbbing of the
growing harvest on our Western prairies?   He
knows that in the furrows of that rich loam lie the
wealth and prosperity of the country at large.   The
Eastern manufacturer anxiously scans the daily
paper to be posted on crop conditions in the West.
They regulate to a great extent the activities and
output of his plant.   And when college and university days are over, where does the young professional man turn his eyes?   To the West.   West-

ward, with the sun, he travels; its fiery course is an invitation to and a harbinger of his bright career.

The Call of the West! Across the ocean it has gone and awakened the dormant energies of old European nations. Settlers of every race and creed have rushed to our shores, like the waves of "the heaving and hurrying tide."

The attraction of the Canadian West has become general, at home and abroad. Nothing can stop this onward march to the land of promise. A new Canada is being created beyond the Great Lakes.

A very small fraction of the Western fertile soil is under cultivation and already the phenomenal yield has prompted the nations at large to call the Prairie Provinces "the granary of the world." Already in Canada the industrial, commercial, and to a great extent, the political world hinges on the Western crop. It is the great source of Canada's national wealth. For, the prodigious resources of our mines and forests, and the annual yield of our harvest are the two poles upon which revolves the credit of our country abroad. But the growing value of the West to the economic and national life of Canada is a mere shadow of its increasing importance in the religious world. Above the hum of the binders and loud clatter of the threshing machines, above the sharp voice of the shrieking steel rail, counting, as it were, one by one, the freighted cars on their way to the Eastern ports, above the clamor of commerce and industry, ring out the voices of immortal souls. The West, for the Church of God also is the land of great possibilities and brilliant promise. The waving sea of its wheat fields calls to mind the words of the Master: "Lift up your eyes and see the countries ready for the harvest. . . . The harvest is great indeed but the labourers are few. . . ."

On his return from a visit to our Canadian West Cardinal Bourne, in the course of conversation, spoke of Canada with almost exclusive reference to the Western Provinces. Some one remarked to him, "Your Grace is referring to conditions in the West?" "Yes, the West, the West is Canada!" he replied.

No one can over-estimate the importance of the West from a Catholic standpoint. It is a new empire that is being formed beyond the Lakes, an empire with tremendous and perennial resources, with ambitious ideals and progressive policies, with forward-looking people and youthful leaders. There the ultra-conservatism of the East has been brushed aside and space made for a new democracy. The question of paramount importance for us is: "What will be the condition of the Church in that coming part of Canada? What share will She have in the solving of the social, educational and economic problems of that new domain?"

Every Catholic should be interested in this vital issue. The call of the West for a Catholic is the call of the Church, the call of a Mother to a loyal son. She has a right to a hearty response from every Catholic throughout our broad Dominion. It is, therefore, a duty of conscience for every son of the Church in Canada to come to the assistance of his mother, to take her honor to heart. At the present hour this duty is most imperative, this obligation most pressing. There is nothing in the wide sphere of our Catholic social duties so immediate in its urgency or so far reaching in its consequences. The Church depends on the loyalty of her children.

To bring this call of our Western missions to the attention of every individual Catholic, to make every soul a co-operator in the extension of God's kingdom in Canada, to develop that sense of responsibility which makes one consider the Church's business his own business, to rally our disbanded forces, to unite our sporadic efforts around the great work of the "Catholic Church Extension Society of Canada"—such is the object of these few pages. To place facts before the reader, and suggest remedies; to sound the call of the West, loud and sonorous as the bugle pealing a great *"reveille,"* strong and clear as the trumpet blast that stirs the blood; to prompt a timely and generous response in the East, by uniting the Church of Canada in a crusade of prayers and sacrifices for our

Western Missions: this is our aim and hopeful ambition.

The Call of the Catholic Church in the West

The call of the Church in the West is a cry for help. Great indeed are the pressing needs of the Western Church, for numerous and various are the difficulties with which Catholics have to contend on the prairie and in the small towns.

The first barrier to surmount is *distance*. The very layout of the country is to a great extent a hindrance to the efficient working of a parish. The survey of the land has been made from a strictly economic point of view. Large farms,—vast wheat fields—were the final object of the survey. The social, educational, and religious phases of the situation are in the background. This renders church and school problems particularly difficult to solve, as was outlined in Dr. Foght's report of the educational survey in the Province of Saskatchewan (1918). This difficulty—let us not forget—will persist for years to come in Western Canada. According to competent authorities wheat growing, being essentially a large unit undertaking, demands extensive farming. This statement is very important, for its consequences in Church organization are far-reaching.

The planless settling of the Catholic homesteaders here and there on the prairie, has also created for the Church one of its greatest difficulties. Living often 30, 40 and 50 miles from a Catholic chapel, these settlers drift away from the authority, teaching and sacraments of the Church. To form self-supporting parishes in the sparsely settled districts is often an impossibility.

To this barrier of immense distances are added for long months, *unfavourable climatic conditions*. The very severe cold, the high winds which have such a sweep on the boundless prairies, the terrific blizzards of the long winter months, will always remain great obstacles to an intense Catholic life in rural parishes. Many Sundays, from December to March, it is a real impossibility for those who live at any distance to go to Church.

And who are those who have settled on our Western plains? This is not the place to discuss the immigration policies of the past. We are dealing with facts. We have the *most cosmopolitan population* one could imagine. The most divergent factors go to make up the racial composition of our western population. We know of a city parish that counted 16 different nationalities within its boundaries. During the first and second generation, during what we would call the period of Canadianization of these various national elements, the Church has to face a most difficult and complex situation.

Diversity of nations means *variety of ideals, differences of customs and traditions*. The disassociation from former relations and the sudden transfer to new conditions of life, have proved to be such a shock to many settlers that they fail to readjust their lives to the arising needs. "Separated from the influences of his early life the immigrant is apt to suffer from disintegrating reaction amid the perplexing distractions, difficulties and dangers of his new environment. Frequently it happens that old associations are destroyed and there is no substitution of the best standards in the new environment. A vacuum is created which invites the inrush of destructive influences." How many foreigners have been lost to the Church because the teachings of their Faith were no longer handed down to them, wrapped up, we would say, in the folds of their national customs and celebrations! The oriental and southern mind is more particularly susceptible to the influence of this national tinge with which religion itself comes to them.

The fusion of so many ethnical groups and their adaptation to new surroundings are the result of a very delicate and slow process, especially in rural communities. "You cannot play with human chemicals any more than with real ones. You have to know something of chemistry," said Winston Churchill. Thousands of foreigners have been lost to the faith because many of our own, clergy and laity, did not know the first elements of "human chemistry." The great leakage from the Church in the West is among Catholic immi-

grants.   Unscrupulous proselytisers on the specious plea of "Canadianization" have weaned
them from the faith of their fathers.   This nefarious process is still at work, especially in the
Ruthenian settlements.

The number of languages complicates still more
this ethnical problem.   Not hearing the Catholic
doctrine in his own language and crippled by that
instinctive shyness and extreme reserve which seem
to grasp him as he steps on our shores, the foreigner
often loses contact with the Church.   Like a transplanted shrub in an uncongenial soil, he languishes
for years in his faith and its practices.

The very atmosphere of the West is another
great cause of defections among the faithful.   You
must live for some years "out West" to appreciate
the full meaning of this statement.

Moral atmosphere is to the soul what air is to
the lungs; it is health and life.   Two elements
constitute that factor which plays such a vital part
in our religious life—tradition and environment.
Tradition links the past to the present and gives to
the soul a certain stability amidst the fluctuations
of life.   It is made up of details if you wish, but,
like the tossing buoy, these details betray where
the anchor is hidden.   This absence of the past has
a great influence on our Western Church.   People
hailing from all points of Eastern Canada, of the
United States and of Europe, have not yet formed
religious traditions which are to the Catholic life

of the family and of the parish what roots are to
a tree.

And what *environments* surround our scattered settlers on the prairie?   Only those who
have come in close relation with the lonely
homesteader can understand how much he is de-
barred from the influence of Catholic life. Very
often not even a chapel is to be found for miles
and miles. A chapel, no matter how humble it
may be, is in the religious world of a community
like the mother-cell; in it life is concentrated;
from it emanates activity. Mass is now often said
in a private house, a public hall or a school house.
Children who have not known the beauty and the
warmth of Catholic worship will hardly appreciate
its lessons.

Moreover, *social relations* often bring our
Western Catholics in very frequent contact with
the different Protestant churches and their tremendous activities. *Mixed marriages* are the outcome
of these circumstances. God alone knows how
many of our Catholic boys and girls have been lost
to the faith through "mixed marriages" and marriages outside of the Church.

.   .   .   .   .

These various obstacles, *geographical* (distance
and climate), *ethnical* (race and language), *religious* (absence of Catholic tradition and surroundings), are the ever open crevices through which a
tremendous leakage has been draining the vitality

of the Church in Western Canada. So the call of
the West is like the frantic S.O.S. on the high
seas, that snaps from the masts of a ship in danger.
It is the cry of thousands of Catholics sinking into
the sea of unbelief and irreligion. In the wreckage
there is still a gleam of hope. Great numbers yet
cling to a remnant of the old faith of their fathers;
it will keep them afloat until helping hands come
to their rescue.

The Call of the Church in the West is a call
of distress. Has the Church in the East heard it?
What is its response?

The Response of the East

Has the Church at large in the East heard the
call of the West? Has that cry of distress gone
through the ranks of our Catholics like the shrill
blast of the bugle call? Has it awakened our
Catholics from their torpid lethargy and quickened
their sense of responsibility? Has the call been
answered, or has it gone out like a cry in the wilderness, lost in the noise of our busy world, stifled by
the clamour of other voices, smothered under other
diocesan and parochial claims?

In the Church of Canada there have always
been generous and noble souls for whom the missions of the West have had a mysterious attraction.
Who can read without emotion of the heroic deeds
of the first Jesuits who followed the explorers and
courreurs-des-bois in their perilous adventures?

What tribute of admiration and gratitude do we not owe to the Oblate missionaries who lived and died with the wandering children of the plains, who have kept the fires of Faith burning, from the banks of the Red River to the Pacific Coast, from the winding shores of the Missouri and Mississippi to the everlasting snows of the Arctic. Their lives of heroism furnish a bright splash on the rather drab and bleak landscape of what was known as the Northwest Territories. The Church of Canada will ever remain indebted to these noble pioneers of the cross, apostolic bishops and priests of the first hour; their saintly lives are forever emblazoned on the pages of Canadian history; the western trails murmur their names in gratitude and the children of the prairie still bless their memory by the dying fires of their camps.

Indeed the Province of Quebec for years sent her money to help the struggling schools of Manitoba. The Catholic Church of Canada has pledged itself in the Plenary Council of Quebec to help the Ruthenian cause; the Catholic Church Extension Society of late years is enlisting the sympathies of Eastern Catholics for our Western missions. With the help of their motherhouses our various sisterhoods have dotted the West with convents, schools, hospitals and charitable institutions. We all recognize the beauty and the heroism of their Catholic charity and apostolic zeal. Notwithstanding these noble efforts, can we safely state that the Church of Eastern Canada, as a whole, is deeply interested in the Catholic welfare of the West? Have we kept pace with the changing conditions the last decade has brought throughout our Western Canada? *No. And this is our national sin.* The Church as a whole, has not awakened to its responsibility. As individuals, as parishes, as dioceses, Catholics here and there have nobly done their duty. As a body, as a living Church of Canada, we have failed to help the struggling West as we should have done. We have not thrown all the energies of our great living, organizing Church into this missionary work. The Catholics of our Eastern Provinces are not yet united in one great, generous effort to protect and spread the Kingdom of God in their own fair Dominion. The call of the Church in the West has not been heard.

Never has the importance of the West loomed up before the public mind as it has since the beginning of the war. To realize this you have only to remark its growing influence in our political life. It cannot be otherwise; the possibilities of the West are so great and so numerous. Immense virgin prairies are still waiting for the plough. After the war, during the period of reconstruction, necessarily so pregnant of great events, the producing powers of our agricultural West will be tremendous. This is, therefore, a trying period for the Church in the West. Beyond the waving wheat of the prairie we should contemplate the ripening harvest of souls.   Like a growing youth, the Church in Western Canada needs more than ever, help and support from the Mother Church of the East.   This assistance in the present stage of the Western Church is a pressing duty of conscience, not only for the individual Catholic, but particularly for the Church as a whole, in Eastern Canada.

This duty is a duty of the hour, a duty most serious, most imperative.   How can it be accomplished?   By the united action of the Eastern dioceses of Canada.

Each diocese is a constituted unity in itself, but not for itself alone.   Like each particular organism in the human system, it exists for the benefit of the whole.   The Catholicity of the Church implies this idea of solidarity whereby the strong help the weak and the rich come to the rescue of the poor.   Never, perhaps, has the Church suffered so much from the wasting of energies.   The torrent, if not directed, spends its energy on itself; turned into the mill race, every drop counts.

One of the great lessons the war has given to the world is the absolute necessity of centralized effort and the advisability of central organization rather than multiplying organizations.   We are living in an age of *efficiency* through *co-operation*.

Fas est ab hoste doceri.—The lesson coming from our separated brethren should strike home. One has to go West to see the feverish activities of the different denominations in that new field. Ask the mission organizers of the various non-Catholic bodies how much money comes from the East to support the struggling Protestant churches of the West; visit their immense printing establishments which are producing and distributing the literature you will find on the table of the lonely Western settler; study these organizations which are supplying field secretaries, teachers, social workers to our foreign Catholic settlements, then you will begin to understand this word of Pius X.: "The strength of the enemy lies in the apathy of the good." The mass of evidence, which can be had by the simple reading of the non-Catholic missionary reports, as to their activities in Western Canada, is nothing short of staggering. What examples! What lessons! Should they not turn our apathetic Catholics into enthusiastic apostles, stir them into watchfulness and action? And what could we not do *with more unity of action?*

Two conditions make united action possible—*uniform plan* and *authoritative leadership*. It would be rather preposterous on our part to attempt to formulate what we could call a plan of campaign for our Western apostles. We wish only to submit a few suggestions which may help to group our scattered energies and bring rescue to the Church, particularly in the unorganized districts of Western Canada.

To readjust our methods to conditions as we

find them *means efficiency with the least waste of energy*. Therefore, we claim that a "survey" of membership and conditions of the Catholic Church in unorganized districts is an absolute necessity. It is the only *logical basis* for true *knowledge of conditions* and for development. This "survey" will bring us into immediate contact with the fallen-away Catholics." As it is now, are we not too often *waiting* for the fallen-away to come to us? If the survey has proved essential in the solving of educational and social problems, why should it not commend itself in religious matters? Proselytizers—especially the English Biblical Society, with headquarters at Toronto and Winnipeg, have the survey of the West down to a science. Their map room in the Bible House of Winnipeg is a perfect religious topography of Western Canada. We are firm believers in what we would call the "Catholicization" of modern methods that have proved beneficial to any cause. "Without this survey and the grasp which it yields of the relative proportion of things, a vast waste of matter and energy alike is inevitable."

This Catholic survey of unorganized districts may appear to some as "a dream," a desk-policy of apostleship—as too modern, etc.* The only

---

*"The Universe" the great Catholic Weekly of England, had in its editorial notes the following remarks on this suggestion of ours:

A "DESK-POLICY" OF APOSTLESHIP

The Catholic Church in Canada possesses a Home Missionary

answer I can give are the facts and figures of the American Catholic Church Extension, whose work along similar lines proves their efficiency and high value.

The specific and ultimate object of the survey would be to keep Catholics who live out of the radius of parish life, in constant touch with the Church, its teaching, its sacraments and its authority. The mailing of Catholic literature pamphlets, devotional and controversial, and newspapers, the teaching of catechism by correspondence, as is practised in certain districts of Minnesota, the

---

problem of the extent of which we can scarcely form an idea. In making his appeal from the West to the East of the vast Dominion, Father Daly, C.S.S.R., who has just issued a pamphlet on the subject through the Church Extension Press, Toronto, brings out some salient truths on the subject of co-operation and organization which Catholics all the world over can well take to heart and apply to themselves. "Two conditions (he says) made united action possible—uniform plan and authoritative leadership. To readjust our methods to conditions as we find them means efficiency with the least waste of energy, and acting on this principle Father Daly advocates a 'survey' of membership and conditions of the Catholic Church in unorganized districts as the one means of getting at lapsed Catholics. 'Too often,' he observes, 'we are waiting for the fallen away to come to us.' This is true indeed. Protestant proselytizers in the west of Canada have the whole 'survey' scheme worked out on a scientific basis. Father Daly is more willing to learn from them. "I am a firm believer," he writes, "in what I would call the Catholicization of modern methods that have proved beneficial in any cause." The problem of unorganized districts and of a scattered Catholic population in our own case is, of course, minute compared with that of Canada; but it is there, and sufficiently in evidence to justify the Redemptorist Father's "desk-policy of apostleship." There is no reason, in short, why the interorganization of the members of the most perfect organization in the world should be committed to a kind of spiritual rule of thumb."

selection of teachers for foreign districts and of
boys for higher education, the establishment of a
central Catholic Bureau of information in each
Province, which could serve as a clearing house
and centre of Catholic activities, and other means
of apostleship, these would be the natural consequences of the survey. Who cannot see what a
help this would be to our scattered Catholics? A
great help to keep the faith among the scattered
home-steaders.

The service of an *auto-chapel* would bring
them also, at least once a year, the benefit of the
sacraments and the blessing of the priests' visit.
For, let us not forget it, one family now lost to the
Church means several families in the coming generation. This absence of contact with the Church
has been for our scattered English-speaking Catholics especially, one of the great causes of the loss of
faith.

And what about our mission to non-Catholics?
We have the truth; are we doing enough, not only
to keep it among our own, but to spread it among
others? Are we aggressive enough? And still I
hear the Master say: "And other sheep I have that
are not of this fold; them also *I must bring* and
they shall hear my voice and there shall be one
fold and shepherd (Jo. X, 16). *We must bring*
them back; they *shall hear our voice*. . . . On the
strength of that command and of that promise
should our policy not be more saintly aggressive?

What an immense field awaits the zeal of true apostles! Nowhere more than in the West has absolute disintegration set in among the different denominations. The universal desire for Church Union is, in our mind, the best proof of our statement. The most elementary principles of Christianity, of a supernatural religion, have lost their grasp on the mind of the average Protestant Westerner. Nominally, he belongs to a denomination, in reality he belongs to none. And what are we doing to give them the faith?

A uniform plan of action, once adopted, requires for execution, *an authoritative leadership,* if desired results are expected. In the Church of God the Bishops are our authoritative leaders— *Posuit Episcopos regere Ecclesiam Dei.* In the ordinary life of the Church this authority in matters spiritual is delegated to and operates through the parish priests. The parish is with the diocese, the established unit of religious organization. For the work in unorganized districts, which is here the special subject of our attention, could there not be in each Province or in each diocese, four or five "Free Lances?"* Let them be diocesan

---

*The following letter prompted by the reading of this very article was received by the President of the Church Extension, dated, March 14, 1919, at a point of Saskatchewan we know quite well; it is illustrative of conditions prevailing in many districts of our Great West:

Very Reverend and dear Father,—

I have just read your article in the Febr., 15 issue and I am

missionaries, priests chosen by the Bishops because of their special fitness for this great work. They would be to the Church what the R.N.W. Mounted Police have been to the Northwest Territories, or what the itinerant preachers are to certain denominations in sparsely settled districts. Their mission would be to visit, preach, baptize, say Mass in the distant districts not visited by a parish priest. They would be the advance-guard of the Church throughout the land. During the winter months they could continue their work by attending to districts within reach of a railway. The religious

---

so pleased with your suggestion for relieving the situation for scattered Catholics throughout the West that I must write my appreciation. I am sure that very few people in the East realize what a veritable necessity those *Free Lances* you spoke of are to so many Western people, or what a God-send those *auto-chapels* would be. Western homesteaders do not stray far from home for two very good reasons, lack of transportation facilities and lack of funds.

We live 12 miles from the church, that is my own family. The others live thirty-five and fifty miles away and up to this year we have had nothing but a waggon to travel in, and now those that live farthest away have still only a waggon. So you will understand that we have not made more than necessary trips or not many more. And I wonder if my brothers would make those, were it not for my mothers insistence. They are surrounded by such bad influences. It's not that it is a sectarian influence, but rather a total lack of religion altogether. The only things that matter greatly are the material things of this world. To confess yourself religious, especially Catholic, is to confess yourself old fashioned and to cause people to smile. You know that is harder to combat than bigoted opposition. Your plan to send out pamphlets would be appreciated by many—But above all we need the personal touch of a priest. We need it as our crops need rain, etc. . . .

Orders,—and they alone can more easily supply reserves and train subjects for this special work— the religious Orders surely will be able to enter into this field of missionary activity, at the same time protecting their subjects with the safeguards of the Rule as also of paternal vigilance and guidance. An itinerant "regional clergy" radiating from a centre where they are fortified by the advantages of common life, is one of the Bishop of Northampton's remedial suggestions among possible "new methods devised to meet new needs." This suggestion is to be found in his Lenten Pastoral of 1920.

The Church in the East, through the Catholic Church Extension Society, would gladly, if well informed on the matter, furnish the financial aid for the support of these "free lances"—and their apostolic activities. The Catholic Truth Society would gladly, contribute all the literature needed to spread the truth and to keep the fires of faith burning on our prairies. Grouping forces, co-ordination of efforts, is what we need most in Canada. In the rank and file of the Catholic laity treasures of enthusiasm, latent powers of energy go to waste because there is no leader to awaken and direct them. The policy of the *Catholic Church Extension* is to act on these long unspoken desires, to loosen the pent-up energies of the Catholic heart throughout the land.

The Specific Object of the Catholic Church Extension Society

Through its press, literature, auxiliary societies and various other activities, this apostolic society is ever trying to quicken among Catholics a profound sense of responsibility to the Church Universal. The welfare of our Western missions depends on how the Church in the East understands and shoulders its obligation.

By financial aid we do not only mean donations and contributions, here and there, from wealthy Catholics. What we have in view is the financial assistance of the Church in the East, as a whole, as a corporate body. Every Catholic in Canada must become more or less interested in "Home Missions" and be willing to do "his little bit." As the small fibrous roots are the feeders and strength of the tree, so also the small and continued donations of all Catholics in the East will be the support of our missions in the West. In the various Protestant denominations, for every dollar given to support of the local church another dollar goes to the "Home Mission Fund." At the last general Methodist Conference (Hamilton, 1918) that Church pledged *eight million dollars* ($8,000,-000.00) for their missions in the next five years. With the enormous sums these various religious bodies receive from the East they support the non-Catholic institutions of higher education to be found in all cities of Western Canada, they distribute free of charge tons of literature throughout the prairie, they defray the expenses of their social workers, field secretaries, etc. Among the Catholics of hundreds of parishes does not the prevailing policy seem to be: "Charity begins at home" —and we may add, often ends there. When one has paid his pew-rent and his dues, bought a few tickets for a sacred concert or bazaar, thrown on the collection plate each Sunday a few coppers or a small piece of silver, he thinks he has accomplished all his duty to the Church. The vision of too many Catholics does not go beyond the boundaries of their parish or their diocese. Circumscribed in their views, they remain illiberal in their sympathies.

Floyd Keeler, a neo-convert to the Catholic Faith, made recently this most instructive statement. "Perhaps the greatest problem which the convert is the most surprised to find existing in the Catholic Church, is the problem why the average American Catholic is so supremely selfsatisfied and seems to have so little thought for the propagation of the Faith which he professes. Coming from a body which has had for many years a well-organized system of missionary propaganda and which, in spite of its many and grave doctrinal difficulties, is fairly well permeated with missionary spirit, *it is a shock* to find that within the Fold so little attention is paid to what really ought to be the very breath of life to its people, the Extension of the Kingdom of God on earth, the carrying out of our "Lord's Last Will and Testament." To find Catholics whose ideals are bound up within their own parishes, who possess no sort of vision of the world beyond, still lying "in darkness and in the shadow of death" and no concern over its redemption, is a phenomenon which is hard to explain."

"It distresses us more than we can tell to find those who are nourished at the breasts of the Bride of Christ, callous to Her charms, unmindful of Her privileges, thoughtlessly and grudgingly rendering their minimum of service, for we realize how Christ is thus being 'wounded in the house of His friends' and His Bride made to lose Her comeliness in the sight of men. But the Catholic press and the Catholic pulpit, fired with the zeal of this new apostolate can, and we believe will solve the problem."—("America," March 13, 1920.)

Our parishes and dioceses will never suffer from an increased zeal in the broader interests of the Universal Church.* There can be no conflict

---

*As an illustration of what in a simple and unostentatious way can be done by any parish in the mission cause the editor of the Annals of the Propagation of the Faith (N.Y.) refers to an invitation extended to him to attend a Christmas sale. It took place in a parish of the Brooklyn diocese on Dec. 3, 1919, the feast of St. Francis Xavier, patron of the mission cause. Thanks mainly to the efforts of an energetic lady, but with the consent and patronage of the pastor, a Xavirian Mission Circle had been formed. Within eighteen months after its organization the newly found

of interests in the Church of God, if seen from the proper point of view,—the glory of God and the salvation of souls. "It is because we have need of men and means at home that I am convinced we ought to send both men and means abroad. In exact proportion as we freely give what we have freely received will our works at home prosper and the zeal and number of our priests be multiplied. This is the test and the measure of Catholic life among us. The missionary spirit is the condition of the growth, and, if Faith is to extend at home it must be by our aiding to carry it abroad" (Card. Manning). Was it not while he was building the Cathedral of Westminster, that Card. Vaughn founded the "Mission Society?"

This missionary spirit has also a bearing on the spiritual welfare of the flock in which it is fostered. For those who would object that giving money to our Western Church is "carrying coals to Newcastle," we would state that the West now needs

---

circle had paid off a $500.00 mortgage for a heavily burdened priest in the South, had adopted eight abandoned children of the Chinese Missions, had sent 1,000 Mass intentions, was supporting seven catechists in Africa, India, and China, was educating a Chinese seminarian, had given 150 volumes to the parochial library of a bigoted section in the South, and was able then to place upon exhibition a number of sacred vessels that were to be forwarded as gifts to poor priests. "And did all these activities not interfere with your parochial work? Mgr. Freri asked the pastor. "Not in the least"—was the answer—"My collections have never been larger." "EVEN PROTESTANTISM FINDS THAT HOME COLLECTIONS ARE IN DIRECT PROPORTION TO THE MISSION GIFTS."

more the help of the East than at any other time.
The organized parishes are indeed beginning to
be self-supporting; but the work we have outlined
in these pages, if it is to be done, has to be supported by the Catholics of Canada at large.

The spiritual aids will be the prayers, Masses,
sacrifices of all kind offered for our Home Missions.   Nothing strengthens faith and stimulates
genuine piety, as prayers and sacrifices for the
great cause of our missions.   They are so disinterested, they reveal true love for our Blessed Lord.

Only a chosen few are called to go into the
field at home and afar and reap the ripening harvest.   But all are commanded by the Master to pray
the Father for harvesters.   This sublime apostleship of prayer is the privilege and duty of every
Christian.   Is there anything more instructive and
more pathetic than the invitation of the Saviour to
co-operate with Him in this great work of the Re-
demption.   "And seeing the multitudes he had
compassion on them: because they were distressed
and lying like sheep that have no shepherd.   Then
He said to His disciples: the harvest indeed is
great but the labourers are few.   Pray ye therefore
the Lord of the harvest that he send labourers into
the harvest."   (Math. IX, 36, 37, 38.)

The Divine Master cannot but hear the prayer
asking Him to send "labourers to the ripening
harvest."   And could we give better proof of devotion to Church and Country?

Great is the seriousness of the present hour, tremendous the task that confronts us after the war. Never has any generation in history been so freighted with the responsibilities of the future as ours is, marching home from the battlefields of Europe. We are living in stirring and changeful times. Nowhere in the Dominion of Canada will the period of reconstruction have more far-reaching effects than in the West. The after-war problems will meet there with rapid and very often radical solutions. To understand this issue that faces our country, to grasp it in all its breadth and fulness, should we not broaden our vision, readjust it, we would say, to the new scale of changing conditions? Only then will we be able to marshal our forces and throw the weight of Catholic principles into the solving of the social, economic and religious problems of the hour. "The Church cannot remain an isolated factor in the nation. The Catholic Church possesses spiritual and moral resources which are at the command of the nation in every great crisis. The message to the nation to forget local boundaries and provincialism is a message likewise to the Catholic Church. Parochial, diocesan and provincial limits must be forgotten in the face of the greater tasks which burden our collective religious resources." (Card. Gibbons.) Let us give to the people that broad, Catholic vision of our present duty to our country and to our Church. The broader the outlook, the deeper the insight.

The measure of their vision will be the measure of their action. No leader can meet with success without a certain receptivity to work upon. This receptivity is formed by spreading ideas, by an educational propaganda.

It may take time before the vision struggles into consciousness and wins its way to the dominance of the mind. What we need is a systematized, continuous effort that will gradually crystalize that vision into a definite workable project. A flourish of trumpets and blaze of Catholic zeal, as we are accustomed to witness on the occasion of some special sermon and appeal by a missionary, will only prompt an act of passing generosity.

The special object of the *Catholic Church Extension Society* is to awaken the collective consciousness of the Catholic population and to give to Catholics that vision of their social responsibility and religious solidarity and to keep it, by its organization, in a healthy condition. It realizes that co-operation from the Church at large will exist and maintain itself only if preceded, accompanied and upheld by a strong and vigilant Catholic public opinion. In return public opinion, once created in the ranks of our Catholic laity, will make the *Extension Society* a live-wire, a dynamic force of the Church in Canada. Let us not forget, vision—and public opinion is the vision of the multitude—is the first and primary of constructive forces.

To have Catholic action we must first create a Catholic mind.

A publicity campaign, followed by a dominion-wide drive for funds, would be now in order. The spirit of giving and of giving for great causes is in the air. A campaign of that nature—we have seen it often during the war,—is in itself an education. It spreads information and arouses the sense of duty.

From the clearness, breadth and depth of that vision will spring the conquering spirit of united action. Forgetting then our lingual and racial differences that have created in the past among us so many unfortunate misunderstandings and have weakened our forces before the enemy, we will rise to the level of our faith, to the creative powers of true Catholicity.

The "Call of the West" has been heard. It comes to you with the *burning problems* of the *present . . . praesentia tangens . . .* and the *vision of brilliant promises* and heavy *responsibilities* of the future . . . *furtra prospiciens.*

WHAT IS YOUR ANSWER?

CHAPTER II.

BRIDGING THE CHASM*

MOST touching in its divine simplicity, most sublime in its inspired lessons was the invitation of the Master to His Apostles: "Behold I say to you lift up your eyes and see the countries, for they are white, already to harvest," (John IV, 35)—As He stood by the well of Jacob, facing the slopes of the hills of Samaria, He pointed out to them the crowds that were hastening to listen to His Message and believe in His divine mission. The fields around lay desolate and lifeless, for it was then winter. "Do you not say," asks Jesus, "there are yet four months and then the harvest cometh? Behold I say to you lift up your eyes and see the countries for they are white already to harvest." This human harvest, of which the Master speaks, is but the prelude of that immense harvest of souls ever ripening under the rays of God's divine grace in the great field of this world. The Church, like Christ, also invites us to contemplate that waving harvest and to pray the Lord to send labourers into the field.

This divine invitation, the Catholic Church Extension Society makes its own, to plead the cause of our Home Missions. Pointing to our Western

*This chapter formed the substance of a Sermon preached on "Extension Sunday" in St. Finnan's Cathedral, Alexandria, Ont.

Provinces, to that great Dominion beyond the Lakes, that missionary organization says to every Catholic in the land: "The harvest is great, but the labourers are few. Pray ye therefore the Lord of the harvest that he send labourers into the harvest."

The Catholic Church Extension Society has been founded in Canada, for the conservation and propagation of the Catholic Faith in our mission districts. Its very name, as we readily see, shows forth its object and explains its existence. Canada, as we all know, possesses vast areas, in her Western Provinces particularly, where the Church has not yet established the influence of her permanent organization. There, her children suffer from the prolonged absence of her teaching, of her sacraments, of her authority, and are struggling against the abiding presence of numerous, rich, aggressive, and unscrupulous proselytizers. Yet, on the vast stretches of prairie, where the lonely homesteader has just broken the virgin soil, amid the snows of the bleak North, by the rushing waters of the Fraser, the Mackenzie, the Peace, and the Saskatchewan Rivers, in the far distant valleys of the Rockies—the words of the Master are still a living reality. . . . "The fields are ready for the harvest and the workers are few." The Extension Society has been established in Canada to point out to our Catholic laity these fields where the harvest is waiting and to help to send labourers into them.

Its sublime mission is to *bridge the chasm* which separates the East from the West. It is the binding and living link between the organized Church and the mission field. This sublime object of the Society makes it most worthy of our commendation and of your loyal and generous support.

Principle and policy are the basic ideas of organized action. If the principles upon which an organization rests are true and elevating, if the policy it advocates and which governs its activities is practical, easy, and attractive, the organization itself is bound to meet in time with an unlimited success. The higher the principles, the more inviting the policy, the more living and telling will be the resultant action. Therefore, to place before our readers the principles and policy of the Catholic Extension Society will no doubt help them to understand better its claims and respond more generously to its appeal.

I.—*Principles*

The Kingdom of God comes upon earth through the Apostolate of the Church. "As the Father sent me, I also send you," said Christ to His Apostles, and to all who were to take their place in succeeding generations. For, these words of Christ created the Catholic Apostolate and maintain it. His words, indeed, are words of life.

The Apostolate of the Church is an absolute necessity, the very condition of Her existence and

progress. The Catholic Church Extension is one
of the most beautiful expressions of that Apostolate, for its object is, as we stated, the conservation
and propagation of the Faith in the Mission districts of Canada.

The principles upon which the activities of this
Society are based may be reduced to two: the *doctrinal* and the *historic*:

1. *Doctrinal Principle.*—All appeals for sympathy and help in the great cause of Catholic
Missions rest on one of the most fundamental doctrines of our Faith, the Catholicity of the Church.
"The Church Catholic," says the great theologian
Suarez, "means the Church Universal—*Ecclesiam
esse catholicam, idem est ac esse universalem*"
(Disput. de Ecclesia IX.,sect. VIII., No. 5). This
universality of Christ's Church implies the idea
of solidarity, whereby in her living and indivisible
unity She is always and everywhere the same. The
Church, like a perfect vital organism, is a divine
organic whole, solidly constituted, identical to itself, and in all its parts, throughout time and space.
The whole is reflected or rather found in each part,
and each part reflects and possesses the whole. The
Catholicity of the Church is but the expansion of
its Unity. It stands therefore as its permanent and
outward manifestation. Should we now wonder
why the Church of Christ is called Catholic? We
name things and persons by that characteristic
feature which conveys to our mind the most accur-

ate concept of them.   The very name of the Church
is, as you see, an ever living proof of her divinity.
And of that name, we may well say what is said
of the name of Jesus . . . *signum cui contra-
dicetur* . . . it will be forever "a sign of contradiction."

The moral aspect of this solidarity of the
Church is responsibility.   The Church at large
is responsible for each particular diocese and
parish, and each individual diocese and parish
is in return responsible for the Church universal.   This responsibility is to be shared by every
Catholic.   And as by its Catholicity the Church
overcomes the two great barriers to all human
power, time and space, so also should every Catholic manifest in the affairs of the Church universal
an interest equally as great as that he shares in his
own   particular   parish.   "Co-operation   among
Catholics," as Archibishop McNeil justly remarked, "is more than a means to a missionary end.
It is an essential part of Catholic life.   Boundaries
of jurisdiction are conveniences and means to an
end.   In the first century of the Christian era, it
was   centres   rather   than   circumferences   that
marked divisions of work and jurisdiction; but in
any case administrative divisions were never intended to be divisions of brotherhood.   The divisions of the Church into dioceses and parishes are
to further increase, and not to weaken or destroy
its Catholicity."

And what we say of these divisions of space, may also be said of those of time. As the glorious memories of the divine history of the Church belong to each individual Catholic, so also should the possibilities of her future destinies in our country and throughout the world, preoccupy his thoughts and affections in the present.

This is one of the most comprehensive and most pregnant aspects of the Church. It throws open the whole world to the zeal of every individual Catholic. Wherever the tents of Israel are, there he finds his home, be it in the wilds of Africa, or on the islands of Oceanica, under the scorching sun of the tropics or in the snows of the lonely North. But as we are more closely united with those among whom Divine Providence has cast our lot in this world, our home-missions have the first claim on our zeal and generosity. For, according to St. Thomas Acquinas, the more or less close relationship with our neighbor is the measure of the *intensity* of our love and devotedness.

We now understand what the Church Extensions' claim means for the missions of Canada. The intention of the Society, as we may readily see, is not to limit our zeal to any national issue, but rather, to develop more easily the missionary spirit and direct its first effort to the welfare of our own countrymen by the consideration of our own wants.

2. *Historic Principle.*—The lesson of facts is

very often more striking than that of doctrine. They are here the concrete expression, in the various nations, and through the course of centuries, of those fundamental principles we have just considered. It is indeed a law of Catholic History, that the more Catholic a nation is, the more apostolic, the more missionary it will prove itself to be. The missionary spirit is the test of Catholicity, the abiding proof of its solidarity.

The history of Catholic nations justifies this statement; their zeal for the propagation of the faith will explain their rise and downfall in the eyes of the Church. Ireland is a classical illustration of this point. Poor, persecuted, downtrodden, the land of the Gael still remains the seminary of the world's apostles. The foreign missions always appealed to the Irish people and "the limits of the earth have heard the voice" of its zealous missionaries. Does not France, notwithstanding the persecution of the Church by its government, still remain the great missionary country of the world? She sends more missionaries and gives more monetary aid to the "Propagation of the Faith" than any other Catholic nation. England's return to Catholicism is most promising, for her converts of yesterday are already in the field afar. The awakening of that same apostolic spirit in the Church of the United States is the most convincing sign of the great strides Catholicity is making in that land of Liberty.

This unwritten law which prevails throughout the history of Catholic nations and expresses so forcibly and so persistently the doctrinal principle of which we spoke, justifies the claims of the Catholic Extension and gives strength to its appeal.

Such are the two principles upon which rest the Extension Society—*dogma* and *history*. They strike the very bed-rock of our Faith. But if its *principles* are sublime and inspiring—its *policy* is simple and effective.

II.—Policy

The policy of an organization is the direction of its activities, the plan of campaign for the furtherance of its principles, the line of action in the realization of its ideal. *The Policy of the Church Extension is twofold*: *education and action.* To give to all the Catholics of our country, an accurate knowledge of conditions in our various mission fields, to develop in them the true missionary spirit, to make them think in terms of the Church Universal . . . this is its *educational policy.* To organize in every parish a branch of the Society and through it to enlist the sympathy and receive the spiritual and financial assistance of every member, to develop, co-ordinate and direct the missionary activities of all our dioceses in favor of our home missions; in other words, to promote efficiency through organization, centralization of efforts with the least waste of energy . . . this is its *policy of action.*

1. *Policy of Education.*—The acuteness of our sense of duty depends largely on the breadth and depth of our vision. This principle explains the importance of the Catholic Extension educational policy. Through its official organ, "The Catholic Register," by means of pamphlets, leaflets, and lectures and sermons, the Society is most intent on giving to the Catholics of Canada, first hand knowledge of conditions in our mission districts. We are perfectly convinced that when all our Catholics will have fully realized the truth of these conditions, they will immediately understand their responsibilities and fulfill generously their duty. But what is that "call of the West" which the Catholic Church Extension is sounding like a cry of alarm through the country? You all know, what I would call, "the Romance of the West."

A few decades ago Western Canada was but a bleak, lifeless plain, extending from the Great Lakes to the foothills of the Rockies, dotted here and there with the Indian wigwam, the roving herds of buffaloes, the solitary chapel of the Catholic missionary, and the lonely posts of the Hudson Bay fur-traders. Suddenly under the magic steel of the plough, that immense waste of land woke up from its age-long slumber. The desolate prairie became within a few years the greatest granary of the world. The Indian trail gave place to transcontinental highways, to those "long, long, and winding," steel trails that have led the youth of our Country and the exiles of Europe "into the lands of their dreams." These trans-Canada roads have conquered distances and linked the Atlantic to the Pacific. They may well be considered as the arteries of our Dominion; through them indeed flows rapid and warm the blood of our national life and in them one can hear, as it were, the pulsations of its great and noble heart. The transcontinental lines are responsible for the birth and phenomenal growth of our Prairie Provinces.

What are the conditions of the Church in these new and promising Provinces? It is not the time, nor is it the place to discuss errors or absence of policy that have crippled the Church's work and growth in that period of rapid transformation. We take facts as they are now. The Church in Western Canada to hold its ground, to extend its work and develop its institutions, has an absolute need of the help of the East. The barrier of immense distances to which are added, for long months, unfavorable climatic conditions; diversity of nationality, variety of racial ideals, differences of language, customs and traditions; absence of Catholic traditions and a prevailing atmosphere of unbelief and irreligion; such are, in a few words, the tremendous obstacles against which the Western Church in its infancy has to contend.

This vision of distress, the Extension wishes to place before every Catholic in Canada; this call for help, it wishes him to hear.

3

But particularly the *future* of the Church in these Provinces forms the subject of the Extension's preoccupations. We all realize the vast possibilities of our Western Provinces, and the important part they must of necessity play in the future affairs of our Dominion. The Church's influence *then* will be what we make it by our efforts *now,* and its progress will be in exact proportion to the amount of our foresight.

This responsibility of the *present* and the *future,* the Church Extension preaches to all in season and out of season. Like the beacon by the sea, it is ever turning its revolving lights over the immense uncharted ocean of our Western missions and hopes that with time, every Catholic in Canada will take his course on them. For, let us not forget it, if we do not take care of our mission districts, others will, and that to the detriment and loss of the Church.—*Fas est ab hoste doceri!* It is permissible, says the proverb, to receive a lesson from an enemy. Only those who have worked out West on the missions know to what extent unscrupulous and most aggressive proselytizers are always on the ground, ever at work among our people. They are digging broad and deep trenches around the settlements of our Catholic foreigners, particularly Ruthenians, draining to their profit the dormant energies of the new Canadian. The invasion is slow but sure, the leakage, great and continual. This lesson that comes from the tremendous activities of the various Protestant denominations should strike home more forcibly. The more stinging the lash, the more sudden the rebound.

This educational policy of the Church Extension appeals to the Catholic mind and tells it something it desires to know. It awakens that latent Catholicity which Baptism has given us and on which the narrow limitations of time and space have no claim. This education of our Catholic laity in the value and necessity of the missionary spirit, in the perfect knowledge and true appreciation of its character in the Church of God, is the end and result of the Extension policy. To make that spirit the inspiring, guiding and testing power of Catholic life, is the definite aim of its educational work, of its publicity campaign. When our laity will have absorbed the lesson, it will be ready for action. This knowledge will awaken our sense of responsibility and prompt our sympathetic support. This leads us to say a word on the Society's policy of action.

2. *Policy of Action.*—Vision resolves itself into action. When the mind sees deep and clear, the heart feels warm and generous, the will acts promptly and decisively. As the spark leaps bright and sharp from the silent battery, ignites the fuel and drives the piston, so will a broad vision give a generous impulse to action. You readily see the value of an educational policy, and its intimate connection with that of action.

Action to be efficient and lasting must be organized. Grouping of forces, co-ordination of efforts, are what we need most in the Church of Canada. In the rank and file of the laity, hidden treasures of enthusiasm, latent powers of energy go to waste, because there is no leader to awaken them, or if aroused, no organization to direct them. The policy of the Catholic Extension is to bring to vigorous activity these long slumbering desires, to give an effective vent to the pent up energies of the Catholic heart, to group all Catholic missionary work for the conservation and propagation of the Faith in our mission districts.

Have we not been working too much as separate units? Has not our zeal been limited by the boundaries of our parishes and dioceses? What activities have been absorbed by side-issues, while the great cause of the Church at large should have occupied our attention! We were deliberating . . . and the West was being lost to us! The time has come to rally around the Church in our mission fields and prove ourselves worthy of our name —"Christian" and our surname—"Catholic." The policy, therefore, of the Extension is to enlist the organized effort of every parish, of every diocese in a great missionary movement, and to throw the weight of the Catholic influence of the East into the immense field of our Western missions. It is not for the promotion of any project, for the benefit of any particular section of the Church in Canada, that the Extension Society exists.   True genuine Catholicity is the only inspiration of its activities.

This united action will manifest itself first and above all in *prayer*. The preservation of the Faith, and the conversion of souls are supernatural works depending primarily and in the final analysis on the grace of God.   Never has it been more necessary to emphasize this trait of the Catholic Aspostolate.   Confronted with elaborate schemes of finance and the co-operative action of various denominations, we may take lessons from them, but should never forget that there is something more fundamental; we mean, the grace of God. Our prayer—the prayer of every child, the prayer of every man and woman within the fold, the prayer of every nun and priest, should be the prayer of the Master to the Heavenly Father: "Send harvesters into the fields!"   How powerful should not that prayer be!   How strong a binding link between the East and the West!

But prayer, like faith, without works is dead. The Extension, therefore, not only solicits our prayers, but also our help to meet the needs of our home-missions—*Men and money,* financial aid and apostolic vocations, these are the needs of the hour. Money to build chapels, schools, orphanages, hospitals; money to help the Catholic press, the spreading of Catholic Literature; money to forward the great and vital cause of higher education. This organized financial assistance of the Church in the East, as a whole, as a corporate body, is the best expression of the reality and sincerity of Catholic solidarity. To boast of our beautiful churches and sumptuous cathedrals in the East and to leave our priests in the West without a decent chapel to say Mass denote either painful ignorance of actual facts or the fallacy of our Catholicity.

Great is the need of money, but greater still the need of men. The principal work of the Extension is to foster, develop and bring to fruition missionary vocations for the West. Burses are founded to assist young men in their studies, and in a few years, it is the hope of the Extension to be able to send to every diocese of the West zealous harvesters for the harvest that is awaiting them beyond the Lakes. Could we be invited to share a more noble task than to contribute to the education of the heralds of the Gospel, of the ambassadors of Christ to that Western Kingdom of ours?

Let us conclude.

These are the *principles* on which rests the Church Extension Society; this is the *policy* it pursues. The adoption of these principles and the furtherance of this policy will, we are confident, develop the true type of the Catholic Laity. The parish, its works, its pastor, will be the first to benefit by this missionary spirit of the laity. Long enough has the priest, the missionary, laboured alone in the harvest field and borne the heats of the day; long enough have but a few loyal and generous souls shouldered the burden of the missionary

work in Canada; long enough have our Catholics
limited their zealous efforts to the confines of their
parish or their diocese. The time has come for
every Catholic in Canada to answer the call of the
Master, to take his place in the harvest field, to
share the responsibilities of the present and prepare a glorious future for the Church in our great
and prosperous Dominion.

The appeal that comes to the Church of Canada from the Catholic Extension is straightforward. It needs no apology. It stands its ground
on its own merits. It is not—let us never forget
it—an appeal to our charity. It is a pressing call
to accomplish a sacred duty, a timely warning not
to neglect it. And indeed, active co-operation in
the work of Extension is, we repeat, an unfaltering
belief in the reality of our Catholicism. It knits
our soul to the very soul of the Church, our heart
to Her heart.

Strengthened by these highest motives of Catholic Solidarity and Christian Charity we should
give joyfully and generously. Let us levy a tax
on our income, no matter how small it may be, remembering the fiduciary character of our earthly
possessions. Let us give our time and our services
to this noble Cause. Let us give lovingly and willingly our children to the great harvest, if it be
God's will to call them to His service. But above
all let us pray that the Kingdom of Jesus Christ
may come in our beloved Country through the Extension of His divine Church.

CHAPTER III.

PRO ARIS ET FOCIS*

MILITANCY is the characteristic feature of God's Church on earth. New dangers, fresh struggles await Her at every turn of the road in Her onward march to eternity. Assailed from within by her own children, attacked from without by bitter enemies, she is ever working out through the frailties of human nature her sublime

---

*This chapter was the matter of a series of articles in the "North West Review," of Winnipeg. The Editor prefaced them with the following remarks, to give emphasis to the importance of this Problem:

"We wish to draw the attention of our readers to a series of authoritative articles now appearing in the Northwest Review on 'The Ruthenian Problem.'

"The writer is one of our foremost educationalists and knows his subject thoroughly. Furthermore his manuscript has passed through the hands of Bishop Budka and other members of the Hierarchy of the West who have given it their warm approval.

"It is, we think, very essential that the Catholics of this country should thoroughly understand the problem before them, so that when called upon to perform their duty in the matter they may be able to act promptly, wholeheartedly and with conviction.

"Our thanks are due to the author, 'Miles Christi' for having put before us such a clear presentation of the problem which sooner or later we shall be called upon to solve.

"The matter is one that to a very large extent concerns the laity and we think it should be thoroughly discussed in every council of Knights of Columbus throughout Canada. In districts where this society is not organized, any other existing Catholic societies might very appropriately co-ordinate in this good work.

"The question is also one of national as well as Catholic moment and so entitled to its due share of any 'forward movements' now anticipated."

destiny.   Not of this world, but passing through it, She has necessarily to suffer from the inherent weakness of her children.   It is the human side of the divine Church.   Those who would be scandalized at this ever renascent warfare against the Catholic Church, in all times and in all countries, should remember that this hall-mark of true Christianity is the fulfillment of Christ's promise and the realization of his prophecy.

In this great firing line of the Church militant every Catholic has his place.   His marked duty is to make the divine triumph over the human in his individual life and through it—no matter how limited his circle of influence may be—in the great life of the Church and in society at large.   He should make his own the various problems confronting the Church in his country and help, within the sphere of his activities, to offer a happy solution.

Two great problems now face the Church in Canada, and tax to the utmost the wisdom of its leaders: The race problem and the Ruthenian problem.   In many centres the former has weakened the principle of authority and paralyzed our efforts of co-operation; the latter means a tremendous leakage through which the Church, particularly in Western Canada, is losing every day an important and vital factor.

The race problem has always existed and will always exist in the Church of God.   This problem is imbedded in human nature. It plunges its roots into the very depths of the human heart. Language is the tap-root which gives life and vigor to its various manifestations. Language is indeed the best expression and highest manifestation of the race. The race problem therefore is generally complicated with the language problem.

The Catholic Church has always respected the racial feelings and the language of nations, for they are based on natural law, and natural law is nothing else but the expression of the fundamental relations constituted by God. Yet history can tell what the Church had to suffer from racial and language differences. We all agree on principles, but often differ on policies. The angle of vision varies; facts are misrepresented; ideals misinterpreted; feeling and not judgment is appealed to, in these racial conflicts. But it is not our intention to deal with this great problem. Only let us ever remember the words of Benedict XV. in his letter *"Comisso Divinitus"* to the Catholics of Canada. He sees in our divisions a source of weakness for the Church, a subject of scandal for our separated brethren and a cause for him of sadness and anxiety. Let us therefore hope that the wishes of the Common Father of Catholicity will soon be realized and that the Church in Canada will see the clouds of misunderstanding lift and a brighter day break on the horizon.

The problem to which I would draw again the

attention of our Catholics throughout the land is one that has been frequently of late placed before the Catholic public. But as its aspects are ever changing and its importance growing, I would wish to throw light on some new factors at play in this momentous issue.

.   .   .   .   .

Immigration has brought to the Church of Canada many serious and knotty problems. Among these stands first and foremost the Ruthenian question. Only those who have followed the various developments of this perplexing problem and are fully aware of the unceasing activities of the various Protestant denominations among Catholic foreigners, grasp their meaning and understand their importance to the Church. The average Catholic, we are sorry to say, is not awakened to the reality of this live issue and fails therefore to meet his responsibilities.

Over 250,000 Catholic Ruthenians, of the Greek rite, have settled in Canada within the past decade or so. They are scattered throughout the length and breadth of our immense Dominion. You will find them in the very heart of our large industrial centres, from Sydney to Vancouver, and in compact groups on our Western prairies. The vast majority of these Ruthenians belong to the Catholic Church and are our brethren in the Faith. To protect them against unscrupulous proselytizers, to help them to keep the faith in the trying period of their acclimatization to our Canadian national life, in a word, to make the Church of Canada assume the proper responsibility which Catholic solidarity imposes on all her children in regard to this new factor of Catholicity in our country, . . . this is the Ruthenian problem as it presents itself to us with its various aspects and critical issues. Problems of the moral and religious order are of a very complex nature. Principles remain but circumstances change with the fancies of imagination, the impulse of passion, the whims of the will. This explains how, in the great and everlasting war between right and wrong, truth and error, the line of battle is ever shifting, the methods of attack ever changing. Various therefore have been the phases of the problem under discussion. But, we presume, they may all be related to two periods: the period of settlement and the period of assimilation.

The Period of Settlement

When a few years ago our shores were heavily invaded by the rising tide of an intense immigration from the British Isles and Continental Europe, the Church had to face conditions heretofore unknown. Without doubt, the most complex in its elements, the most serious in its consequences, was the Ruthenian issue. It was a case of providing for the spiritual wants of over a quarter of a million souls. The dearth of priests, the difference of rite, the difficulty of language, and the great number of Ruthenians, created for the Church an almost insurmountable barrier which nothing short of a miracle could otherthrow. This sudden and large influx of Catholics belonging to the Greek rite, into a Country where the Latin Church alone prevailed, constitutes a fact that has never been seen before in the history of the Church. Thousands and thousands of these Greek Catholics were scattered through the prairies; roaming flocks without shepherds, a prey to ravening wolves. Heresy, schism, atheism, socialism and anarchy openly joined hands to rob these poor people of the only treasure they had brought with them from the old-land,—their Catholic Faith. Presbyterian ministers were seen to celebrate among them "bogus masses"; schismatic emissaries tried to bribe them with "Moscovite money"; fake bishops were imposing sacrilegious hands on out-laws and perverts; traitors from among their ranks, like Judas, bartered away their faith for a few pieces of silver; a subsidized press,—"The Canadian Farmer" and "The Ranok"—was ever at work, playing on their patriotism and exploiting their racial feelings, to cover with ridicule their faith and pious traditions. The public school became in the hands of the enemy the most powerful weapon. Government itself, through its various officials, often went out of its way to thwart the efforts of our missionaries.

It is not without poignant emotion that we have followed, at close range, this struggle for the mastery of the Ruthenian soul. We hardly know which we should admire the more, the faithfulness of the simple-minded Ruthenian, or the devotedness of the few missionaries who, for the last fifteen years, have lived, worked and died among them. We all remember that cry of distress, that demand for help which came from Archbishop Langevin in favor of his Ruthenian children. It broke upon the land as a clarion call and its voice was heard in the first Plenary Council of Quebec. The Oblates of Mary Immaculate—the pioneer missionaries of the West, the Basilians, the Redemptorists, and a few French-Canadian secular priests, were the first to answer the call. They divided among themselves that immense field of labour. God alone knows what sacrifices, what heart-burnings, what hours of discouragement and loneliness, were theirs in that strenuous period of settlement when the wilderness began to blossom, when homesteads were seen to spring up on the bare soil. We have a faint idea of these difficulties when we read the *"Memoir: 'Tentative de Schisme et d'heresie au milieu des Ruthènes de l'Ouest Canadien,"* of Father Delaere, C.SS.R., (1908), and Father Sabourin's pamphlet, *"Les Ruthenes Catholiques"* (1909).

Let us hope that the Church in Canada will keep sacred the memory of these harvesters of the first hour.   The Catholics owe them a debt of gratitude.   We sincerely hope that the history of their heroic efforts will not be lost and that the first to appreciate them will be the coming Ruthenian generation.   Father Delaere, C.SS.R.—who has laboured among the Ruthenians in Western Canada for the last twenty years will one day give us, we sincerely hope, the history of the settlement and struggles of his adopted people.

Little by little the Ruthenian Church in Canada is emerging from its first chaotic state.   The visit of Mgr. Septeski to Canada, the appointment of the Very Reverend N. Budka as Bishop of all the Ruthenians in Canada, marked a turning-point in their history.   Authority is, in the Church of God, the only great vital centre from which proceed true order and permanent development.   The war, it is true, complicated the Ruthenian issue. We all know what difficulties the Ruthenian Bishop had to face during this trying period, under what dark clouds of ungrounded suspicion he lived.   But the most painful feature of this long and cruel ordeal was the absence of sympathy and the lack of co-operation in those from whom, as a Catholic Bishop, he had a right to expect them.

The Period of Assimilation

The period of settlement has passed, and already a young "CANADIAN" generation has sprung up sturdy, thrifty, progressive from the transplanted Ruthenian stock. The numerous children of that prolific race are gradually passing from the home into the schools and from the schools into the community life of the country. This Slavic race is striking deep roots in Canadian soil, particularly in our Western Provinces. The loss of faith has been heavy, we believe, especially in our large cities. Naturally, allowance must be made for the drift-wood which always follows the tide of immigration. In our rural centres, be it said to the praise of that simple-minded people, and to the confusion of the enemies of their faith, the great majority have kept their allegiance to the Church of their baptism. But, where the "bogus mass," the false priests and "Moscovite money" have failed, the neutralizing process of a so-called "Canadianization" may succeed. The flank envelopment has often a greater success than the frontal attack. This leads us to dwell on another phase of the Ruthenian problem.

In the history of the human race there is nothing more complicated than ethnic assimilation. It is a slow, delicate and, in many cases, very dangerous process. In the laboratory of the world many explosions are due to the ignorance of what we would call "human chemistry." "One cannot play with human chemicals any more than with real ones. We know by experience that at times they are *fulginous* and ready to break into open flames." But there are two elements which have to be treated with the greatest care: **Religion and Race.**   They are the two *foci* of the elipse in which moves history; the two shores between which oscillates the tossing tide of humanity. Lord Morley calls them "the two incendiary forces of history, ever shooting jets of flame from undying embers."   This explains why the soil of history is so volcanic, so filled with burning lava which time itself has not cooled.

The racial element in ethnical assimilation is gradually modified by the imperative adjustment of the immigrant to his new conditions of life. For the observer and student of history there is nothing more instructive and, at times, more pathetic than that borderland which lies between what has been and what is to be in the life of the immigrant. This violent breaking away from the past and gradual assimilation with the present has its dangers.   Unknown and occult factors are at work with the blood of several generations, pulsating in the veins of the new Canadian.   Whilst beckoning hands stretch out to receive him on our shores and initiate him into our national life, other hands, the hands of the dead, stretch out through several generations to lay claim on him.   Like everything in nature this change or rather this transformation should be imperceptible.   Mutual toleration is the factor of a healthy assimilation. This has given to the United States a greater solvent power than has been shown by any other

nation, ancient or modern.   Coercive assimilation arouses national feelings, alien elements, and
racial self-assertion.   The worst enemy of Canada
is the political power which, to please a blatant,
ultra-loyal faction, pursues the policy of crushing
into uniformity the heterogeneous elements invited
to the country and allured to our shores with the
bait of liberty.   This patriotism may be well
called the last refuge of scoundrels; it is nothing
but Prussianism wrapped up in the very folds of
the Union-Jack.   Therefore, when in the great
work of Canadianization this law of social psycho ·
logy is not observed, we not only prevent assimilation, but we deprive the nation of the fertilizing
contact and invigorating contrast of various
ethnical elements and ferment future conflict.

The religious element belongs to a higher
plane.   Although independent in its nature of
any particular racial feature, yet it co-exists
with the love of country, giving to our patriotism
something of its sanctity and durability.   But the
point at issue here is: Can the religious element
prevent racial assimilation?   In the eyes of many
Canadians the Ruthenian's religion is looked upon as one of the greatest obstacles to his Canadianization.   Under the cover of that specious plea,
many agents are at work in our Ruthenian settlements.   With the preconceived idea that their religion with its ritual, language and traditions, is
the greatest obstacle to their nationalization and

to its inherent benefits, these agents are multiplying their efforts to wean new Canadians from the faith of their fathers. The last report of the Methodist Missionary Society—1918, openly states the designs of this Church in the matter. *"Many of these Ruthenian people are ignorant and degraded; and under the sinister leadership of their priests are resolved to resist all Canadianizing influences. . . . For the Christian Church to act at once is the need of the present hour, if the foreign peoples are to be made Christian citizens of the great West."*. This statement is symptomatic of the curious Christianity that now prevails among the various non-Catholic denominations. With them Christianity is nothing more than social welfare inspired by a vague philantropy. Differences of creed are being cast to the winds, and *Social Service is the basic idea of their forward movement,* around which they are trying to rally their dwindling forces. It is then but consequent to have the burden of their message and the policy of their apostolate bear on Citizenship. The inevitable and perfidious neutrality of state officialdom unconsciously seconds their efforts in this direction. But the most efficient co-operators in this nefarious work are the fallen-away Ruthenians. They have a smattering of education which makes them the more dangerous among their own.

This organized opinion and co-ordinated action of the "churches" against the CHURCH should give to all Catholics food for thought. To be indifferent would be criminal. We can say with Augustine Birrell: "It is obviously not a wise policy to be totally indifferent to what other people are thinking about—simply because our own thoughts are running in another direction."

. . . . .

This diagnosis of the Ruthenian problem should suggest practical lines for individual and group action. It would be preposterous on our part were we to assume an attitude of destructive criticism without having a remedy to propose. But what we have in mind is to suggest means whereby the Church as a whole, and the laity in particular, will come to the help of a few heroic, struggling missionaries and to the rescue of their Ruthenian flock.

The Ruthenian people in Canada are now going through their assimilation period. In another generation or so they will be, at least they should be, all full-fledged Canadian citizens. This "land of opportunity" that has adopted them has a right to see them all become good citizens, as ready to shoulder their share of the common burden as they were to receive the benefits of our liberties.

In our large industrial centres their transformation is rapid. The stranger is swallowed up in the vortical suction of the city and is soon carried away in the maelstrom of its strenuous life. He rapidly loses his identity; only the strong individ-

ual will survive, bearing the features of his race.
In our rural settlements where the foreigner has
established colonies, the assimilation is slow and
gradual.   The change affects the community and,
through it, the individual. But in all cases this
transformation is a necessity, and necessity should
be a deciding factor.

If this process of assimilation, we contend, is
not surrounded with Catholic influence, if it is
not carried on by Catholic agents—and is left only
to those who see in the faith of the Ruthenian, a
"relic of the Middle-Ages," an obstacle to Canadian citizenship—the danger to the faith of our
Ruthenian people is greater than in the days of
open attack. This method of neutral proselytism
is more insidious, and in the long run, more telling.
We know perfectly well that if the Canadian
Ruthenian is "to give to Caesar what belongs to
Caesar" he must first "give to God what belongs to
God."

It is therefore our bounden duty to help our
Ruthenian brethren to swing into the main stream
of our national existence; and there is no reason
why our religious duties and patriotic endeavors
should work at cross purposes.   In fact, if in the
present crisis, the two are not merged into one,
there will be a distinct loss to the Catholic Church
in Canada. Have we not waited long enough for
the immigrants to come to us? We contented ourselves with giving them as often as possible a priest

of their language; and have left to others, to neutral and, most often, openly anti-Catholic agencies the duty of initiating them to Canadian life. The American Bishops have understood this necessity, and with what marvellous foresight and wonderful organization have they thrown into the work of reconstruction the whole weight of the Catholic Church! Their joint letter—the most timely and most luminous pronouncement on the labour problem,—their general meeting in Washington, the constitutions of the Catholic National Board with its various departments, all go to prove that they grasped the signs of the times and have readjusted the sails of the Ship of Peter in America to the new winds that are sweeping over the world. We should never forget indeed that the Church of God is not of this world but is in this world. To strip ourselves of crippling "formalism" and to bring the Church nearer the realities of the times, is, in Byron's words, making "realities real." Is it not indeed time to broaden our apostolate and give more scope to the laity? If the non-Catholic denominations are able to find young men and women who consent to live among our foreigners as teachers, social workers, field secretaries, lay missionaries and catechists, surely we should be able to find the same among our own to protect the faithful against apostasy. We must remember that the Ruthenians who have come to this country belong, generally speaking, to that class for whom even existence was a problem in their native land. They are the very ones who have been protected in their faith by language, tradition, customs and all that goes to make up the mental atmosphere of the uneducated mass. When that atmosphere disappears these poor people are exposed to all pernicious influences. We are therefore responsible to the Church to build around them the protective wall of Catholic life. The initiation to their Canadian life should not be at the price of their Catholic life.

This is the situation. What can be done? Naturally, to quote Lord Morley: "A settlement of foolscap sheet, independent of facts, of local circumstances and feeling, and passion, and finance, and other appurtenances of human nature" . . . will lead nowhere. To do effective work along the lines suggested in this chapter we must take facts and circumstances as they are, and work into them the idea, and then work the idea into the people. The LANGUAGE, the SCHOOL, the COMMUNITY LIFE are the THREE GREAT FACTORS that the enemies of the Ruthenian's faith unscrupulously exploit in their nefarious work. We must meet the enemy on this common ground and beat him with his own weapons.

Language.—The right of a man to his language is an incontestable right; the free use of it is a primary human liberty. The Church has always respected this right as one of the most elementary laws of nature. In the evangelization of nations She has always accommodated Herself to the ways and language of the people. In this, She is faithful to the illuminating lesson the Master gave to Her on Her birthday, Pentecost Sunday, when the Apostles were heard each speaking his own language. "They began to speak with divers tongues according as the Holy Ghost gave them to speak . . . *Every man heard them speak in his own tongue.*" Since that day the true Apostle of Christ has respected the language of the people he evangelized.

The theory of compelling a nation to learn a certain language as if it were the only vehicle of the "Great Message of Christ" or of waiting until the people know the missionary's own language . . . is not Catholic. The Church of Christ is not a nationalistic Church. No one has to deny his race nor to give up his language to become or to remain Her faithful child.

But, facts are facts and one must face them and take from them one's bearings. They stand as the tossing buoy on the drifting waters of our ordinary life. To ignore them often spells disaster. Now, the fact of paramount importance is that the English language is fast gaining ground among the Ruthenians. The recent school laws (we do not discuss here their wisdom)*, the anti-foreign feel-

---

*Judge Buffington, of Pennsylvania, gave a lecture lately on "Americanization." From it we cull the following paragraph on the foreign language question:—

ing that has held the country in its grip during the war, the violent campaign of a certain element, the general drift of the various annual conventions, the studied plan of action of Provincial Governments, the eagerness of the Ruthenian rising generation to know English†, and above all the unbounded zeal of non-Catholic denominations who make the learning of English the trump card of their game, these are facts, and have to be reckoned with. The sooner our Ruthenians are made to grasp these conditions, the better will they be equipped for the struggle of Canadian life and for the preservation of their Catholic faith. Is it not time, therefore, for some English-speaking priests to go out among the Ruthenians and share the work with those valiant missionaries who, the great majority at least, are strangers to our country, and who have learned the language, em-

---

"The solution is not in the abolition of foreign languages in this country. I have heard loyal patriots who found English twisting their tongues, and Bolshevism has come from the lips of those of New England culture like Foster. This country has not only been remiss in failing to teach the foreigner but in teaching the native. I believe in the English tongue and in the amalgamation resulting from common speech, but we do not accomplish our aims by destroying other languages."

†In a recent report of the Department of Education of the Province of Saskatchewan, of 177 schools in Ruthenian settlements only 28 have engaged teachers holding provisional certificates or permits; all the others are fully normal-trained and perfectly qualified. In many school districts salaries range between $1,000 and $1,500. The Ruthenians are among those who pay the best salaries to teachers.

braced the rite and for the last twenty years have been doing our work for us? Their presence is a stimulating lesson and an abiding reproach. A dozen or so of young English-speaking priests would be a great boon to the Ruthenian mission, particularly in the West with its present mentality.

The *School* is the great melting pot. One has to read "The New Canadian," by Dr. Anderson, to understand the full meaning of this statement in its relation to the Ruthenian problem. The schools among the Ruthenians in the Western Provinces are practically all public schools. The number of Catholic teachers is exceedingly small and yet, were they available, the Ruthenian trustees would be at liberty and glad to give them the preference. Only those who know the influence the teacher wields in a Ruthenian settlement will fully appreciate the presence of a Catholic teacher. Were a good Catholic teacher to give to this cause a year or two of her teaching life she would be doing a great missionary work. If the Baptists, Presbyterians and Methodists can get girls and young men to go, surely we could also, were we to organize and try it. This is the reason why the foundation, in Yorkton, of the English speaking Brothers of Toronto, is one of the wisest moves in the right direction. The idea is to prepare teachers for the Ruthenian settlements by giving them the benefit of a higher education under Catholic influences. The Governments of the various Western

Provinces made several attempts to equip the Ruthenian schools with Ruthenian teachers. With a few exceptions, these embryo teachers proved to be a failure and from a Catholic view-point a real calamity. We remember personally how in a certain normal school the special Ruthenian class was nothing but a hot-bed of infidelity and anarchy. The students were collaborating with the worst subversive elements in the country. Therefore, our practical suggestion would be to encourage the recent foundation of the Christian Brothers by contributing liberally to its support and to the extension of the work of which it will become a natural centre. Could there not be a bureau in the East for the recruiting of teachers? A campaign of education to this effect, in the Catholic press, would be in season.

Community work is without doubt a deciding factor in our civic life. Considered from a Christian angle it is nothing else but the practice of charity. When animated by mere philanthropy it may play havoc with souls, particularly among our foreign element. The Church in the United States has realized its importance and has outlined a social service programme for Catholic agencies. They have field-secretaries and instructors—often Knights of Columbus—throughout the country, carrying on this welfare work. I would refer the reader to the monthly Bulletin of the National Catholic Welfare Council for an idea of the extensive work of their Catholic social activities.   It is simply wonderful.   As times change our activities also have to be modified.   New questions call for new treatment.   The initiation of the Ruthenian people to Canadian life should be our work.   Being Catholics they are our wards in this new country and it is our sacred duty to see that they receive true ideals of Canadian citizenship without losing the higher ideal of their Catholic life.   At times Canadian liberty has proved to be to some extent too strong a tonic.   It is through a sound, intelligent, local government exercised in the school district and our municipal life that the new Canadians can learn best to play their part in the greater life of Provincial and Federal politics. If any one desires more details on this subject we refer him to the National Catholic Welfare Council's Reconstruction pamphlets No. 5 and 7.

Who has not followed with pride the launching of the great educational programme of the Knights of Columbus, particularly their nation-wide scheme of supplementary schools for the explanation of the "American Constitution" to foreigners? It is an open challenge to radicalism.   To educate a citizen in the chart that governs his country, in the right use of his franchise, is an act of real patriotism and real Catholicism.   Picture to yourself the results of the Ruthenian vote on an issue in which the Church is involved.   Eventually time will bring such issues.

We would say to our laity what the editor of

the 'Columbiad' wrote in the October number: "The vista of the glory of service that opens before the mind musing on the power for good within our grip is sublime. To each the image rises. An army, a host of faces keen with knowledge, calm with contentment, eager with honest ambition looks up. Men, women, boys, girls—humanity gazes at the beholder. The eye does not glimpse the last face, far out beyond the faint horizon of the panorama. . . . The vista is unending."

Yes, the apostolate among the Ruthenians is, we claim, a necessity of the hour; its possibilities are beyond realization. Procrastination in this matter is nothing short of treason and will prove a disaster to the Ruthenians, and to the Church. Turning to the Knights of Columbus in Canada and pointing to the feverish and unceasing activities of other agents among this our people I say: *Go and do likewise.*

.   .   .   .   .

Our conclusion is obvious. The Ruthenian Question stands to-day as a religious problem to solve and a national duty to fulfill. Church and Country present a united and pressing claim for our co-operation. This appeal to the two strongest feelings of the human heart should awaken patriotic sympathies and quicken Catholic conscience into action. The issue is serious and far reaching in its consequences. Only organized opinion with united and determined action can successfully meet it.

CHAPTER IV.

WHY? WHAT? WHO?

The Necessity of a Field-Secretary for the Organization of our Missionary Activities

NO one can read the Encyclical letter which His Holiness has recently addressed to the Catholic Church on the Propagation of the Faith throughout the world, without being deeply moved by the yearnings of the apostolic heart of our Common Father, and vividly impressed by the lessons that come from his inspired and timely message to each and every one of us.

Without doubt our own dear country is witnessing that movement which, inspired by the Holy Ghost, is being felt throughout the Catholic world in favour of home and foreign missions. The growing interest of our people in the Catholic Church Extension Society; the enthusiasm with which the great and noble work of Father Fraser, for Chinese Missions, was greeted everywhere; the recent foundation and marvellous development of the community of the "Missionary Sisters of the Immaculate Conception" in Montreal, for service among the lepers of China; the wonderful response which the call of Africa met with among the college and convent youths of the Province of Quebec; the increasing number of vocations to the mis-

sionary orders, both for men and women,—to
mention only a few outstanding and significant
facts,—are evident signs of the *"stirring of the
waters"* in the Church in Canada.

To help to promote and develop fully this
providential movement in the Church of God, we
beg to submit a few suggestions which may be of
some use in the great cause of *Home* and *Foreign
Missions.*

I.—*Why?*

The continued progress and abiding success of
a movement depend on its organization. For, to
realize its proposed aim and accepted plan of action, organization alone can enlist and keep secure
the sympathies of patrons and members, co-ordinate the various forces, and call into play, when necessary, new and fresh energies. The greater the
number to be reached by the society or societies
which embody this movement, the more efficient
should be the organizing power.

Experience and reason prove that an organization destined to affect the masses and hold its
grip on them, will not live and thrive only on an
occasional appeal or a printed message. These
are indeed of great value, particularly the insistently repeated message in print. We are great
believers in the force of a persistent, regular and
frequent circularization. But, in our humble estimation, there is something more essential in the

matter under consideration, and that is the human contact and continued influence of a "field-organizer." An extensive organization without this factor will not be efficient, will not last. As Floyd Keeler wrote in "America" (July 10, 1920): "It is the personal equation between the organizer and the various units of the Society that counts. . . . The masses are accustomed to think in concrete terms. . . . Long distance appeals and those made to total strangers do not produce permanent results." This influence of the field-organizer is so great that we may safely state that the life of a society fluctuates with the various impulses it receives from him. He is the very heart which gives health and vigor to its organism.

Here lies the secret of the mission-organizations in the Protestant Churches, to which, of late, we have referred so frequently in our Catholic papers, under the heading of: *"Fas est ab hoste doceri."* . . . Every denomination has its field-organizers entirely consecrated to mission activities among its people. Financial results tell to what extent they are effective in their work.

We have also among our own missionary societies, examples that illustrate the point we wish to emphasize. Since when has the Society of the Propagation of the Faith, in the dioceses of New York and Boston, leaped into prominence, and headed by generous contributions the list of the whole world? How did that change come

about? Where is the secret of this success? The
establishment of permanent diocesan organizers is
the answer. What they have done, why could we
not do? *"Quod isti—cur non et nos?"*

Never, we claim, will the missionary poten-
tialities that lie dormant in Canadian Catholicism,
be actuated to bear its message of spiritual light,
heat and power to the Church at large, until we
establish in the field at various points, secretaries
or organizers, whose life-work will be to call into
play, to systematize the mission forces of the
Church in Canada. If on the contrary, as in the
past, we content ourselves with an occasional appeal for missions, a collection now and then, a
spasmodic effort here and there, a subscription to
a Catholic paper or missionary magazine, the work
for Home and Foreign missions will remain ex-
terior to the corporate life of the Church, will not
be woven into its very fibre to permeate its activities. As shadows on the wall, they will suggest
rather than reveal the possibilities of our missionary effort. The great and pressing call of the
White Shepherd of the Vatican will go unheard.
If there is a response that comes from Canada, it
will not be from the Church at large.

II.—*What?*

The *"raison d'être,"* the definite function of a
field-secretary is organization. This work implies
the double duty to spread, by an intelligent and

well thought-out propaganda, the knowledge of the Home and Foreign Missions and of the responsibility it entails, and to found and maintain efficient the various societies established to promote and help their great work.

1. *Vision*. The effective presentation of the case of Catholic Missions, both to the clergy and to the laity, is the field-secretary's first and important duty. Nothing indeed can be hoped for, nothing can be accomplished until the Catholic people fully grasp and intensely feel what their help and co-operation—however little it may be— mean to the Church, to the salvation of souls, to the honour of our Blessed Lord, to the glory of God. *Fac ut videant!* The clear, broad and deep vision of these great possibilities in the mission fields will alone overcome selfishness and apathy, awaken interest, stimulate energy.

The field-secretary is the official expert in mission-matters. He will be able to accumulate strong evidence, sum up striking statistics and draw burning comparisons for the effective presentation of his case. An enthusiastic advocate, he will plead with thrilling appeals, the great cause placed in his hands.

During his absence from the field of action, the vision he pointed to, will be kept bright by the recurrence, at stated intervals, of the printed message. Missionary literature receives its life, vigour and impulse from the field-organizer and continues his work in his absence.

2. *Action.* To realize that vision and incarnate it in work for the Home and Foreign Missions, the Field-secretary will take the diocese as a unit of his organization. In each diocese, with the permission, authority, and co-operation of the Ordinary, he will establish the Societies recommended by our Holy Father in his Apostolic Letter, and others that have been created to meet the specific needs of the country or to favour certain particular missionary work. Therefore:—

(a) *Among the Clergy* will be founded *"The Missionary Union of the Clergy,* which our Holy Father desires to see established in every diocese. For loving sons and faithful priests of the Church of God the desire of the Sovereign Pontiff is a command. This, we think, could be easily done by the field-organizer when he visits each parish for the purpose of organizing missionary parochial units, as we shall see later.

The beautiful programme of action which is so easily combined with the ordinary work of the priest in the parish, the facility of his moral and material co-operation in this great work of missions, the spiritual favours and wonderful privileges which the "Union" grants to its members, together with the explicit desire of the Holy See, these are so many motives and incentives, which should induce all the members of the clergy to enter the ranks of the "Missionary Union" and assure to the Church their co-operation in the great mission work, both at Home and in the Field-Afar.

(b) *Among the laity* of each parish will be founded:

The *"Propagation of the Faith"*—for Foreign Missions;

The *"Church Extension"*—for Home Missions.

The permanent success of these societies, once established by the field-organizer, will wholly depend on the selection and appointment of trustworthy *promoters,* who will distribute the missionary literature, and collect from their respective circles of 10 or 20 members the monthly fee, stipulated for each society. This monthly collection comes as a reminder and is more effective, both morally and financially, than an annual collection taken up in the Church, as is now the prevailing custom in several dioceses. The monthly call of the promoter is a fresh awakening of the missionary spirit in the home, and stands as the continued call of the Master of the harvest. It keeps the interest alive and awakens anew the sympathy for the missions.

(c) *Among the Childen* of our Separate Schools and Sunday-Schools, can be established, with great profit, The *"Holy Childhood Society."* It is wonderful what interest the kind and sympathetic hearts of children will take in missionary work. The results obtained by the distribution of mite boxes are marvellous. To quote an example given to us by the Protestant Episcopal Church of the United States, we would say that through their Sunday-School classes, they raise annually the sum of $200,000.00.

But above all, the great asset to be considered in this educational work, is the broad Catholic spirit we create and maintain in the soul of the child. This is far more important than his actual financial contribution, and at the same time it prepares him to be, in later years, a generous contributor. Without any doubt, the Protestants can teach us here a lesson of organization.

(d) In *Colleges, Boarding-Schools, Convents and Universities* why should we not have branches of the *"Catholic Students Mission Crusade?"* This organization is doing wonderful work in the United States, and will prove soon to be a potent factor in the Missionary activities of the Church across the boundary. 250 delegates from various institutions of higher learning, throughout the country, gathered in Washington, last August (1920), for the second annual Convention. Among the delegates, we are proud to note, were a few Canadians.

(e) The *"follow up"* work is what counts in the long run, in a movement of this kind. If we do not wish to see all this beautiful zeal for missions burn away in a passing blaze, we must have a *Central Bureau,* which will keep in touch with the promoters, and act as the centre of Missionary activities, in the diocese. There all lines will converge, gathering information, bringing results; from there, as from the power-station, will go out to the workers in the field, enthusiasm and energy. "Unity," says F. Kinsman, "cannot be created by agitated fragments of a circumference; it must issue from a central force and be sustained by a centripetal instinct." The Central Bureau, or Clearing House could be confided to a trustworthy person, who would willingly give his spare hours to this great Catholic work, until it would grow to the point of necessitating a permanent and salaried secretary.

It is useless, we believe, to state that a *crusade of prayers* would be the sustaining force of this movement. We all know that the salvation of souls is above all a supernatural process. We may sow, another may water the seed,—but it is for God to give the growth,—*Deus autem incrementum dat.*

The *development and fostering* of *"missionary vocations"* would be the natural sequel to this movement at large, in the Church of Canada. How many young men and women could not the field-secretary find here and there, and direct to the mission fields where the harvest is plentiful and the harvesters few.

III.—Who?

The function of a field-secretary or organizer is a delicate one, we fully understand. But we are firmly convinced that priests can be found, who, with tact, intelligence and enthusiasm for the great Cause of Missions, and backed with the authority and sympathy of the Ordinary, are bound to make this work a success. There is a wave of the missionary spirit passing over the Church of God. The clergy and the people are eager to help missions at Home and Abroad. But they desire a concrete, workable plan to pin their activities to; they are waiting for something definite to act upon, and a responsible representative of the cause to work with.

Until the development of the organization would call for a diocesan organizer, *one priest* could act for a *Province* or *Region* of the Country. The ordinary objection which our proposal here would meet with, would be the lack of personnel. There is, we know, a shortage of priests everywhere. But would not the Church, as a whole, in Canada and throughout the world, receive more benefit from the life of a priest entirely dedicated to this work of Missions, than if it were given to a specific parish or diocese. Even were a parish or small country mission to be deprived for the time being of a resident pastor, should not that sacrifice be made, generously and cheerfully, for the sake of a greater cause. It is assuredly a shortsighted policy to sacrifice hundreds of thousands of souls for the care of a few, to prefer the welfare of a parish to that of the Church at large. This reasoning and its disastrous consequences are sure-ly not Catholic.

We emphasise the necessity for the organizer to *consecrate his life solely to this proposed work.* At this price alone will he make it a success. With-out doubt, it is the work of a man, the work of a life.

God grant that we may see the day when all the latent Missionary forces of the Church of Canada will be awakened and united in one great gigantic effort of apostolate! These forces form an invisible army of reserves on which the Church is to draw, to fill, as it were, the depleted ranks of Her Missionary units throughout the world. The lack of organization is the weakness of our strength. Let the leaders come forward, and we ourselves shall be astonished at the latent powers of Faith in the Church of Canada.

CHAPTER V.

PLOUGHING THE SANDS

*The Church-Union Movement: its Causes and
Various Manifestations. The Protestant
and Catholic View-Point.*

CHURCH-UNION is to-day the outstanding
feature of the Protestant world. The possibilities and promises, the necessity and advantages
of this movement are widely discussed in the press
and magazine, in the pulpit and on the platform,
in Church conferences and synods. Denominational barriers are being swept away; creed lines
lowered; inevitably great changes are impending.
This universal unrest is assuredly symptomatic of
a chaotic Christendom outside of the true Church.
The peace and self-confidence of the Catholic
Church pursuing the even tenor of Her life is indeed in striking contrast.

No serious-minded Christian can be disinterested in this supreme effort of the various Christian
denominations for unity. We are not allowed to
doubt the good intentions that animate and direct
the promoters of this inter-church movement. For,
as Lord Morley said, "in the heat of the battle it
often happens that men manifest towards the *heretic* feeling which should be exclusively reserved
for the *heresy.*" Yet we believe that the explanation of *our* attitude, so much misunderstood and

misinterpreted, cannot but help to hasten the day of the true and everlasting union, when in accord with the great desire of the Master, there will be but "One Fold and One Pastor." Gladstone said: "Any man who advances one step the cause of Christian unity in his life may well lie down to die content that he had a life well lived."

We said advisedly *"our"* attitude, for it is a vastly interesting point to note with Hilaire Belloc: "The Catholic understands his opponent, whereas that opponent does not understand him. A similar contrast existed once before in the History of Western mankind, to wit, in the latter days of the Roman Empire. The Catholic understood the Pagan; the Pagan did not understand the Catholic."

Church-union was always more or less an ideal in the various non-Catholic denominations. Periodically efforts were made to realize this ideal; but they always failed in the presence of the bitter antagonism that existed between the leading factions. The Church-union movement manifested itself, timidly at first, in the interchange of pulpits, the united services and inter-communion of several denominations. This exchange in the ministerial field now prevails among the Nonconformists and has also affected to a large extent the Anglican communion. But the multiplied divisions and multiplying sub-divisions among the conflicting creeds, a wasteful overlapping and disastrous competition in the mission field, the enlightening experience of the great war, have forced an issue upon the Churches.

In Scotland the "Old Kirk" is trying to bridge the chasm that has separated it from the "Free Church" in the past years. In England, under the leadership of Mr. Shakespeare, the Nonconformists are fusing their differences and presenting a united front to the Established Church. Only last year, (1919) in Kingswall Hall, did not the Bishop of London make most remarkable overtures to the Wesleyans and propose to them a scheme of union! By the introduction of Evangelical methods and particularly by the association with Nonconformists on doctrinal grounds, or in services in which doctrines are involved, the Anglican Church has been engaged—to speak with Newman—"in diluting its high orthodoxy."

Last August, 1920, Geneva was the meeting place of "The World Christian Congress." The Congress adopted a resolution to form a "League of Churches" whose object is to put an end to proselytizing between Christian churches and promote mutual understanding between them for Christian missions among non-Christian peoples; secondly, to promote an association and collaboration of Churches to establish Christian principles; thirdly, to help the Churches to become acquainted with one another; fourthly, to bring together smaller Christian communities, and unite all Churches on questions of faith and order.

But it was reserved for America, the land of daring schemes and audacious plans, to formulate the most chimerical project of all.

The Episcopalian Church has promoted *"The World Congress on Faith and Order."* Bishop Weller, of Fond-du-Lac, Wisc., is directing this gigantic movement. A committee of bishops has already called on the various heads of Christian Churches, and we all know of their visit to the Vatican and of the refusal of the Holy See to participate in the Pan-Christian Congress.

Sponsored by the Presbyterian Church of America, "The United Churches of Christ" were formed some months ago, with a complete organic union of the Protestant Churches of America in view. This is . . . "an advance of the present existing organization of the Federal Council of the Churches of Christ in America, as it opens the way for consolidation of administration agencies and the carrying forward of the general work of the Churches through the council of the United Church."

But the most ambitious scheme is that of the *"Inter Church World Movement."* It has been called into existence (1918) for the purpose of developing a plan whereby the Evangelical Churches of North America may co-operate in carrying out their educational, missionary and benevolent programme at home and abroad. To discover and group the facts concerning the world's needs; to build a programme of inspiration and education based on these facts; to develop spiritual power adequate for the task; to secure enough lives and money to meet the needs: such is the tremendous task the "Inter Church World Movement" has set itself.   At a meeting in Atlantic City it was voted to raise the stupendous sum of $1,300,-000,000 to meet the requirements of this Pan-Protestant project.   Two thousand men and women are now (Feb. 1920,) busy at the head-office, in New York, preparing the world-wide survey and financial campaign.*

The Protestant Churches in Canada are also falling in line in this universal movement for unity. *"The United National Campaign"* which marked 1919 with thirteen national conventions, represented the co-operative feature of various churches in a general *"Forward Movement."*   The war, we all know, has impeded the projected union between the Methodist, Presbyterian and Congregationalist denominations.   There is hardly any doubt that this union will be effected in the near future.   But as usual, while the East was deliberating, the forward and aggressive West was acting.   Church-Union is an accomplished fact in many centres, particularly in the Province of Saskatchewan.

---

*The withdrawal of the Northern Presbyterian and Northern Baptists and the failure of the financial drive have imperilled the existence of this ambitious project.   Is it not a case of repeating with the Psalmist: "Unless the Lord build the house, they labour in vain that build it?"—Ps. 126.

Last October the "Union Church of Western Canada" held a convention in Regina and reported progress.   Conditions in the West, especially in the rural districts, naturally favour this movement. The strong denominational feeling is becoming more and more a thing of the past.   The identity of churches is being absorbed in "social service" work, and sectarian peculiarities considered "obsolete impertinences."

These are the various manifestations of the "Church-Union Movement."   Although loose thinking and indefiniteness of purpose characterize most of these various moves, a close analysis reveals two different underlying principles which support and explain them.   As an Anglican clergyman stated: "There are two courses open, uniting on points of agreement and allowing the differences to settle themselves, or facing differences with a view of settling them."   The first course promotes a *"co-operative union"* in social and Christian work.   This union does not interfere with matters of belief, but aims solely at the co-operation and co-ordination of all services which the Churches can render in the missionary, educational and social fields.   It means a League or Federation of Churches, with a view to "greater efficiency."

The other course goes deeper into the problem under discussion, for it has as object an *"organic union."*   This union means the fusing of all denominational creeds and forms of worship, or, at least, the acceptance by all of a certain doctrinal minimum as a basis of the *entente cordiale*. The Anglicans in the Conference of Lambeth, 1888, formulated the famous "Quadrilateral" whereby the Scriptures as Rule of Faith, the Apostles' and Nicene Creeds, the two sacraments of Baptism and of Eucharist, and the Episcopacy or apostolic succession, are "as the irreducible minimum on which they would open negotiations for reunion."*

II.

The Protestant Inter-Church Movement is a fact; we know its causes, its various manifestations, its ultimate aim. To what extent this universal movement reflects the general, deep and conscientious convictions of the masses, it would be hard to say. The prevalent indifference and profound ignorance as regards the specific tenets of each denomination would lead us to believe that this movement does not spring from the very soul-depths of the masses. Yet the fact is there, and assuredly of importance in the religious realm. What is the meaning of this fact? What is its message? For, every universal fact of that kind reveals and interprets an ideal.

---

*In the last Lambeth Conference—1920— the Church of England has again reduced this minimum by implicitly recognizing the Nonconformist ministry and abandoning its claim to reunion through the absorption of all sects in the Anglican communion. It has so shifted from its former position that it has openly expressed in the Bishops' manifesto the desire to place itself on some "no man's land" where all the dissident Churches may safely meet and unite.

Naturally the view point of the Protestant will be different from that of the Catholic. The explanation of the attitude of both, as we stated, cannot but help to hasten the coming of true union in Christendom. The non-Catholic mind sees in this Inter-Church Movement the ultimate triumph of Protestantism, the vindication of the leading principles of the Reformation. The Anglican Archbishop DuVernet wrote in the "Montreal Star," May 10th, 1919: "Reviewing the movement towards Christian Union in Canada, a very natural evolutionary order is at once detected, which gives us the assurance that a spiritual cosmic urge is at work behind this united action of the Anglican, Presbyterian, Methodist and Congregationalist Churches of Canada, *the great evolutionary movement towards the comprehensive Church of the Future.*"

We all know of the sensation created in Anglican circles by the extreme views of the Bishop of Carlisle. In a recent article on the "Nineteenth Century and After"—entitled "Monopoly of Religion," he protests against the claims of right and the privilege of monopoly in Religion, either in doctrine or in form of government. He says that the Free Churches have been right in resisting unto death the doctrines of religious monopoly."

Robert H. Gardner, in the "The Churchman," (*Episcopal*), acknowledges that "The unanimous recognition of the plans (Interchurch World

Movement) is only a beginning; the hope of all that it will lead to a more perfect union, and the evident anxiety to leave the Catholic (?) churches free to maintain their principle without compromise or surrender, have converted him to the belief that God the Holy Ghost is guiding this movement, and, therefore, that it is truly Catholic (?)."

If such are the views of the Anglican Church, which, among other denominations, has always been considered as most conservative, what may we not expect from the other Churches? And indeed, the reading of addresses made at their different Conferences and General Assemblies, the resolutions passed, and the very atmosphere of these meetings tend to uphold the Church-Union Movement as the realization of unity in Christendom. "The Christian Century" (organ of the Disciples of Christ) says: "It marks out the best path yet that has been described for the attainment of unity. It outlines the goal and bravely takes the first step towards its realization." The New York "Christian Advocate" (*Methodist*) thinks: "It will mark a definite step toward that fusing of Protestant forces whose absence hitherto, is responsible in large part for the failure of Christianity to make powerful headway among men." As the Presbyterians were the originators of the movement, "The Continent" takes a justifiable pride, in quoting from a contemporary, that:

"They are perfectly ready to contemplate a Christian unity that involves the passing away of this particular organism called the Presbyterian Church, finely wrought though it be," and exhorts: "Presbyterians, this sort of reputation is a lot to live up to. But we must not fall from it."

The principles of evolution—principles which we find underlying modern thought—are freely called upon to explain this movement and justify its consequences. Our millennial-minded doctors and preachers are celebrating already the apotheosis of the Universal Church of the future.

And what does the Catholic Church think of Church-Union? What is its point of view on this "Movement" which has now such hold on the Protestant denominations? As the Catholic Church is in itself the largest Christian body, it is but natural to presume that all Christians will be interested in knowing Her views on this vital subject. For is She not that Church which Gladstone himself calls, "the most famous of Christian communions, and the one within which the largest numbers of Christian souls find their spiritual food!" (Gladstone to Acton, Nov., 1869.)

The Catholic Church sees in this movement of Church-Union the complete disintegration of Protestantism and the open condemnation of its fundamental principles. Those who are not of the "Fold" will perhaps resent, but not be astonished at this sweeping statement. We would only ask

them to follow our argument and then judge for
themselves.

*Union—and therefore unity—will not and can-
not be the result of the present Inter-Church
Movement.* This statement involves a question of
fact and of right. *In facto.*—Let us examine first
the question of fact. Union, as now promoted, is
either *"co-operative"* or *"organic."* *Co-operative
union ignores differences of creed or form of worship; organic union suppresses them or merges
them into a neutral mixture.*

Co-operative Union,—as a basis of religious
unity affecting the religion of the individual, can
be at once dismissed. For, what *religious* action,
—*i.e.,* action prompted and guided by a principle,
a religious doctrine,—is possible without that
principle, that doctrine? Moral action,—and
Religion is at the same time the foundation and
the highest expression of the moral order,—presupposes immutable and recognized principles.
"The mental attitude defined on paper as 'undenominational,' Miss M. Fletcher says rightly, has
no existence in the human mind. Below all sustained enthusiasms lie strong convictions."—
Therefore to ignore the directing principles of
their various denominations in a common religious
action, and yet to pretend to keep their denominational identity, involves, on the part of the Churches, an absolute impossibility. Because doctrine is
the very foundation, the *"raison d'être"* of intelli-

gent Christian action.   Diversity of opinion is
bound to bring, in religious matters, diversity of
action; for, to be consequent one must act according to his belief.   Baptism, for instance, is necessary or not necessary for salvation.   On this doctrinal point will necessarily hinge a diversity of
action in the mission field alloted to this or to that
denomination.   The position is quite different
when common action is confined to merely social
work.   But "social service," stripped of all its
Christian principles and reduced to pure philanthropy, is not Christianity; it is mere naturalism
or neo-paganism.

The great majority of those for whom Christianity is yet a *living reality* understand the nefarious consequences of *"co-operative-union."*   To
protect themselves against this scheme of a perfidious neutrality, they advocate an *"organic
union."*   This even is to the fore in the Philadel-
phia plan of the "Inter-Church World Movement."   "The plan of federal union will have this
result, that after it shall have been in operation
for a term of years, the importance of *divisive*
names and creeds and methods will pass more and
more into the dim background of the past and acquire, even in the particular denomination itself,
a merely historical value, and the churches then
will be ready for, and will demand, a more complete union; so that what was the 'United Churches
of Christ in America' can become the 'United

Church of Christ in America,' and a real ecclesiastical power, holding and administering ecclesiastical property and funds of such united church."

The promoters of *"organic union"* do not ignore the differences between creeds, but they are trying to reduce them. This union strikes at the very bed rock of Divine Revelation. For, the suppression of differences, or their limitation to a certain doctrinal minimum, implies a compromise, and a compromise, in matters of truth, is unacceptable. Truth is eternal and therefore does not change. If the Westminister and Augsburg Confessions were true yesterday, why should they not be also true to-day? If the 39 Articles were the rule of Faith for the Anglican Church in the past, why should they be to-day but "definitions of theological opinions of the time of the Reformation," as Anglican Bishop Farthing, of Montreal, recently stated.—"You change . . . therefore you are not true," we may say, with Bossuet, to those Churches.

In jure.—This universal readiness to compromise should not astonish us when we know that the very fundamental principle of the Reformation is *"private judgment"* in matters of Faith. The divine message of Revelation is to be interpreted as each one sees best. This principle makes, *"de jure,"* every Protestant independent in his religious belief, and opens the door to the most conflicting interpretations of the Divine Message. "The High

Church clergyman to-day," writes A. Birrell, "is no theologian, he is an opportunist." Dogma degenerates into religious emotionalism. Doctrine becomes nothing but a *"scheme of theological impressions."* To tolerate every doctrine is, for a Church, to teach none. Doctrinal chaos, such as we now see outside of the Catholic Church, is the inevitable result of compromise. Winston Churchill's famous novel, "Inside of the Cup," is nothing but the diagnosis of this disintegration which Protestant Churches are now witnessing.

The history of Protestantism is but the history of its changes of religious belief. For "between authority and impressionism in matters of Revelation, there is no alternative." As Christianity is not the product of the human mind, but a Revelation from God, authority,—a divinely constituted infallible and living authority—is a necessity, and the only possible bond of unity.

This disintegrating principle of "private judgment" in matters of Divine Revelation has been at work since the inception of Protestantism. By the very force of its dissolving power the primary elements of a supernatural religion have fast disappeared from the various creeds. One by one the different Churches have drifted away from their Christian moorings and taken to the high seas of Rationalism. Assailed by the storms of unbelief they are breaking on the rocks of religious indifference. Empty churches are the natural outcome of empty creeds. "The dominant tendencies are indeed increasingly identified with those currents of thought which are making way from the definiteness of the ancient Faith, toward Unitarian vagueness."   If Bishop Kinsman, Anglican Bishop of Delaware, a recent convert to the Catholic Faith, gave this statement as one of the reasons for leaving the Anglican Creed, with how much more truth could it not be made of the kaleidoscopic tenets of other denominations?

This process of dissolution of doctrinal grounds is bound to continue. The fluid condition of the various churches testifies to the uncertainty of their actual position and forces them to seek the lowest doctrinal level. "Their standard is determined by the minimum, rather than by the maximum view tolerated, since their official position must be gauged, not by the most they allow, but by the least they insist on." (F. Kinsman.)   The remnants of Christianity that were still to be found in their teachings are now looked upon as "obsolete dogmas" and, as such, obstacles to unity. The very fundamental mysteries of the Incarnation and the Redemption are fast growing dim in the minds and hearts of men.*

---

*Canon E. W. Barnes, of Westminster Abbey, in a sermon to the members of the British Association, at their meeting at Cardiff, Aug. 29, 1920, declared that, to harmonize Christian Doctrine with modern science, particularly with the theory of evolution, he found it necessary to abandon the doctrine of the Fall of Man and arguments deduced from it by theologians, from St. Paul onward.

The Protestant Churches will never come back to their former position. In this Church-union movement they are burning their bridges behind them. The gospel of pure "humanitarianism," which is the absolute negation of a supernatural religion, will eventually be the last result of this present unity.

Destructive criticism, to be profitable, should be followed by constructive suggestions.

"That they may be all one!" This ideal of the Master, this supreme wish of His last hours, remains the ideal, the wish of His Church. But its realization cannot be at the expense of truth. Cardinal Gasparri outlined to the promoters of the "World Congress on Faith and Order" the view and position of the Catholic Church in this most important issue. "The Holy See has decided not to participate in the Pan-Christian Congress which it is proposed to hold shortly, *as the Catholic Church considering her dogmatic character, cannot join on an equal footing with the other Churches.* The feeling at the Vatican is that all other Christian denominations have seceded from the Church of Rome, which descends directly from Christ. Rome cannot go to them; *it is for them to return to her bosom.** The Pope is ready to receive the representatives of the dissenting churches

*Father Leslie Walker, S.J., in a recent work on "The Problem of Reunion," suggests we should enquire rather *how we came to differ than what we differ about.*

with open arms, since the Roman Church has always longed for the *unification of all Religious Christians*.   Pope Leo XIII. was deeply interested in this question and wrote two famous encyclicals on the subject of the *unification of the Christian Churches."*

The divine Founder of Christendom did not leave to several Churches the conservation and propagation of His doctrine.   He founded only *one* Church and gave "unity" itself, as the supreme test of its divinity.   Therefore the Church, that has remained "one" through time and space, and has conquered those two great enemies of unity, bears the birth-mark of its divine origin.   The Catholic Church alone makes that specific claim. History is there to substantiate it.   Matthew Arnold himself could not help acknowledging this universal fact.   "Catholicism is that form of Christianity which is the oldest, the largest, and most popular.   It has been the great popular religion of Christendom.   Who has seen the poor in other churches as they are seen in Catholic Churches? Catholicism envelopes human life, and Catholics in general feel themselves to have drawn not only their religion from their Church, but they feel themselves to have drawn from her, too, their art, poetry and culture.   *And if there is a thing specially alien to religion, it is division.   If there is a thing specially native to religion it is peace and union.   Hence the original attraction towards unity*

*in Rome, and hence the great charm when that
unity is once attained."* The sharp contrast between the actual restlessness and uncertainty of
the dissident Churches, and the calm assurance and
self-possession of the Catholic Church, is not that
an abiding proof of the security of the Catholic
position?

Father Palmieri, O.S.A., Ph.D., D.D., who has
made the problem of Christian Unity a life-study,
made, in a recent article, these pertinent remarks:
"The reunion of Christianity in the Catholic sense
is not a Babel-like confusion of different sects
which oppose creed to creed, which proclaim
their absolute indifference in the doctrinal field,
which take the individual reason as a judge of
Christian revelation or Christian discipline. It
would be an absurdity to suppose for a moment
that Catholicism or Catholic Theology would propose this hybrid confusion of concepts and human
caprices under the name of unity. For Catholicism and Catholic Theology, the reunion of Christianity is the return of dissident Churches and of
the non-Catholic sects to Christian unity, to the
one Church of Jesus Christ, which not only teaches
this unity theoretically but also puts it into practice, in its doctrine, in its government, in its dogmatic and moral teaching, in its principles of authority. By logical sequence the Church of Jesus is
one. This unity is not broken by political barriers,
ᵛ ethnic divisions, by opposing national aspira-

tions. To tend therefore toward Christian unity signifies to tend toward the only Church of Jesus Christ, and to effect this unity is the same as to adhere to it."

Father Palmieri concludes his study with these words: "An impartial study of many years' duration has fully convinced us that the union of the dissident churches can be brought about only under the leadership of the Catholic Church. Outside of Rome there is a principle of dissolution which breaks up and disintegrates the most solid organisms and which will cause the breaking up even of the Orthodox Churches. It is therefore in the supreme interest of Christianity that the Catholic Church addresses its appeals for union to the dissident Churches, and it will never cease to exercise this, its noble mission. Its efforts have been crowned with success several times, and I am convinced that that day will come in which by means of prayer and action the aspiration of Christ's Vicar for union will be realized."

Our non-Catholic reader may say that the position we take tends to strengthen that exclusiveness, that narrowness, that aloofness with which he has always charged the Church of Rome. But we would ask our dissenting brethren, can it be otherwise? Truth is indivisible and unchangeable. Were the unity of the Church Universal to exist only in the Church of the future we would have to conclude that there was a time when the Church of Christ did not exist on earth. This would be absurd and would destroy Christianity in its very foundation. The true Church of Christ has a right to claim the monopoly of Christianity. The Church which, through a so-called spirit of broadmindedness, accepts the conflicting claims of the various dissident bodies, and is ready to merge its entity with other denominations, immediately, *de facto,* invalidates its claim to be "The Church of Christ." For, its position involves a contradiction and is in itself a self-condemnation.

Yet, the Catholic Church cannot feel indifferent toward this general and supreme effort of the various fragments of Christendom towards unity. Confidently she waits for the hour when all will return to her as to the only centre and source of permanent unity. Yet, we would say with the Bishop of Northampton, "If we may not compromise the very object of this remarkable movement towards unity by accepting the pressing invitations of our separated brethren to make common cause with them, neither can we rest content to be mere spectators of their perplexities like those who watch from the shore the efforts of distressed seamen to make their port." Let us hope that Divine Providence, always gentle and strong in its dealings with human liberty, will hasten the day when there will be but "One Fold and One Pastor." In the meantime the efforts made to constitute unity of Christianity outside of its true centre will prove as futile as *ploughing the sands of the desert.*

CHAPTER VI.

"THEM ALSO I MUST BRING"

(Jo. X, 16)

The Apostolate to Non-Catholics—Its Obligation.
What have we done? What can we do?

THE spiritual influence of a Christian is commensurate with his appreciation of responsibility. The breadth and depth of vision give to this moral feeling its field of action. The circle of our influence ceases with the limits of our spiritual outlook. The boundless and clear visions of all the Great Apostles in the Church of God give us the key to the generosity and artfulness of their zeal. Just as the narrowness of our views explains the restrictiveness of our charity and the limitations of its activities. This is particularly noticeable in our dealings with the spiritual needs of those outside the Fold. The claims of our non-Catholic brethren to our charity do not seem to affect us, because our spiritual outlook has not the proportions of that of the Master. With Him we do not stand on those heights from which we could see beyond our own green pastures, "Other sheep that are not of His Fold and which we must also bring." This explains how the claim—*"Oportet"* . . . *"We must bring"*—awakens in us no sense of responsibility and meets with no answer in the ordinary activities of our life. Every one seems more or less contented with the lines of denominational demarcation as he finds them around him in the community. Not to discuss religion, not to busy oneself with the other man's belief, to be very frequently rather reticent about our own, is a policy generally accepted in the West. This habit of evasiveness is not Christian and often leads to the sacrifice of Catholic principles. Far from us be the idea of advocating rash obtrusiveness, of untimely aggressive and inconsiderate zeal. But between this excess and that of a *"laissez faire"* policy there is a golden mean. What is then wrong, our method or our zeal?

A right understanding and a deep conviction of our duties in the matter under consideration are of the greatest value for the Church in Western Canada. May we preface our chapter by asking the reader to keep before his mind the illuminating distinction of St. Augustine between the Body and Soul of the Church. Many souls outside of the visible Body of the Church are nevertheless within the beneficial influence of her invisible pale. This is a commonplace of theology, we all know, but evidently, very often forgotten.

Are we in conscience bound to spread the true faith among our non-Catholic brethren? Most undoubtedly we are. The examples and precepts of the Master, the canons of the Church, the love of God and our neighbour, are among the pressing motives which should appeal to a true Catholic and make him zealous within the sphere of his influence.

"Thy Kingdom Come!" That prayer of the Lord, which has become our morning and evening prayer, is vain, if in the ordinary course of life we do not try to extend the boundaries of that spiritual kingdom in the very souls of those with whom we come in daily contact. Is not the light of our life to shine out so that it may serve as a beacon to those outside the Fold? But nothing is more striking than the words of the Good Shepherd: "And other sheep I have that are not of this Fold; them also I must bring and they shall hear My voice" (Jo. X., 16). Who could explain the profound yearnings of the Divine Master's heart and the deep feeling of obligation that are summed up in these words: "Them also I must bring." The Divine Shepherd finds Himself responsible for the sheep that are not of His own Fold and His only ambition is to bring them in.

This recommendation of Our Lord, His Church understood when in her Canon-law She makes it a duty for all bishops and priests to look upon the non-Catholics residing within the boundaries of their jurisdiction as recommended to them by the Lord and placed in their charge. (Canon 1350, No. 1.)

The Plenary Council of Quebec, the authoritative voice of the Church in Canada, is most emphatic in its recommendation of our separated brethren to the zeal of all Catholics. (No. 331)

The obligation of conscience to come to the help of our non-Catholic neighbour is moreover founded on the precepts of Christian charity. If Christ will condemn to Hell those who did not give Him to eat and to drink in the person of the needy, what will He not say to those who neglect the spiritual works of mercy. The activities of Christian zeal, to one who rightly understands the spirit of the gospel and the economy of the re-demption, have the same binding force as alms-giving, and fulfill in the spiritual world the part charity has to play in the scheme of Christian economics.

The obligation of alms-giving is complement-ary to the right of property. For, as St. Thomas says, "It is one thing to have a right to possess money and another to have a right to use money as one pleases." (II. *a*, II. *ae,* Q. XXXII., art. 5, ad 2.) This duty when conscientiously performed re-establishes that economic and social equilibrium which strict justice alone is not able to create. For, the inequitable distribution of wealth greatly de-pends on the inequality of power of production. This inequality of natural gifts in man remains an unchangeable fact which faith alone in a Divine Providence can explain, an ever renascent problem which Christian charity only can solve.

This mystery of Christian solidarity reveals it-

self also in the spiritual world. We may say of
each Catholic what St. Ambrose said of the priest-
hood: *"Nemo Catholicus sibi,"*—no one is a Catholic for himself alone. By a mysterious law of
Divine Providence the conservation and propagation of the faith are, after Divine Grace, largely
dependent on the influence of man on man. We
are all verily "Our brothers' keepers." We are
commissioned by Christ not only to keep the faith
but also to hand it down to others, not only to keep
its fire burning in our hearts but to spread it, and to
fan it into a conflagration. The gift of faith implies the charitable obligation of weaving our
belief into our every day life and, through that life
and its influence, into the lives of others. The
plenitude of some make up for the penury of
others. If St. John, to urge the precept of alms-
giving, said: "He that hath the substance of this
world and shall see his brother in need, and shall
shut up his bowels from him: how doth the charity
of God abide in him?" (I. Jo. III, 17), with how
much more truth cannot the condemnation of the
Beloved Apostle be applied to one who, rich in
Faith—"that substance of things unseen," makes
no effort to help his brother who is deprived of
it? Therefore charity, through its spiritual works
of mercy, re-establishes the equilibrium in the
spiritual realm and stands out as a vital factor in
the economy of our religion. To understand rightly this principle and to reduce it to action, is to be

a true and ardent apostle. Then, and then only, are we able to say in truth, with the martyr, St. Pacien, "Christian is my name, but Catholic is my surname."

How pressing is this obligation to be an apostle, to be truly Catholic, among our non-Catholic brethren? Why should we particularly turn the energies of our zeal to the conversion of non-Catholics? What special claim have they to our prayers?

The supernatural element of Faith, often the fruit of a valid baptism, which still lingers in the souls of many non-Catholics; the fact that numbers of them, because they are in good faith, belong thereby to the "Soul of the Church;" the rising tide of indifference and unbelief which is now burying under its water the last remnants of Christianity to be found among the conflicting creeds: these are the predominant motives which, according to the principles of St. Thomas Aquinas, should attract the preference of our zeal. For the order of the charity, says the Holy Doctor,* depends on the *relations* of those we love, to God and to ourselves, and on the *urgency* of their spiritual needs. By this doctrine, among those outside of the Church, those professing Christianity have the first

---

*Since the principle of charity is God and the person who loves, it must needs be that the affection of love increases in proportion to the nearness to one another of these principles. For wherever we find a principle order depends on relation to that principle. (Summa. II, II Qu. 26 art. 7.)

claim to our apostleship. Therefore missions to non-Catholics, *caeteris paribus,* take precedence over foreign missions.

We all recognize the reality of this obligation and understand, vaguely perhaps, the burden of its responsibility. We all indeed, at times, say with the Divine Master: "There are other sheep that are not of this Fold; them also I must bring." —But, what have we done to bring them?

Outside of a few casual cases of conversion prompted often by marriage, and of some spasmodic efforts during a mission, are we not bound to admit that our policy in our relation with non-Catholics has been one of aloofness and waiting. This attitude of aloofness may be traced to many causes. The certainty of his faith gives to the Catholic an assurance which he carries with him into his every day life. A sense of superiority is its natural result. It gives him that self-confidence in religious matters which our separated brethren are so prone to call "Roman Pride."

There exists in the Catholic soul that feeling we might name "The timidity of faith." This sensitiveness is but the instinct of preservation. We have been impressed from our youth that faith is the greatest heirloom of our Christian heritage. To protect it against any influence that would endanger it, is always considered a sacred duty. This is particularly remarked among the masses, whose chances of education finished with the grammar schools, and in countries or localities where Catholics are the minority.

The natural result of this attitude and feeling is an estrangement from those of another faith, a bashful reluctance to meet them and to co-operate with them in social or civic matters, an unconscious tendency to see motives that do not exist and, at times, to refrain from the most elementary acts of charity and courtesy. "It often happens that we manifest towards the heretic the feeling which should be exclusively reserved for heresy." (Lord Morley.) That this is precisely the frame of mind of the ordinary non-Catholic in his dealings with us, is by no way an excuse for our own unkindness. Retaliation is not Christ-like. Does not our aloofness confirm our separated brethren in their false ideas, wrong impressions and bitter prejudices. We must not forget that centuries of strife and untold antagonism of misunderstandings and ignorance, stand as a granite wall between their souls and ours. The teachings and influence of their home, of their school, and of their church lie in their minds, strata upon strata, as the silent and lasting mementoes of the great religious upheaval of the Reformation. Only the influence of a genuine, frank, Catholic life, seen and felt in daily intercourse will gradually wear the barrier away. It is a long and slow process, we know, but one worth trying. Like the ever returning tide it eats its way into the most solid rock of prejudice and bigotry.

That this aloofness carries with it for the unguarded soul and untrained mind a great protection, is made evident by the too many examples of lukewarm Catholics, who by their continued association with those outside of the Fold have lost the right appreciation of their faith and are open to compromise. Principles in their lives often yield to a policy of so called broadmindedness and alleged charity. But those we have in mind, are the leaders, among the clergy and the laity. They are grounded in their belief, know its principles and should be prepared to throw off that aloofness which shades the light of their faith and prevents it from being seen by those who are bound to them, in the everyday life, by national, social, commercial, and often by family ties.

This *quasi* universal attitude of aloofness has developed among us what we might call "The policy of waiting." The festive board of Christ's faith is ready, but the guests from another fold are wanting. Have we gone "by the highways and byways" and forced ourselves upon their attention by our pressing invitations . . . *"compelle intrare?"* No, we stand at the door of the Banquet Hall, receiving politely and with joy, it is true, those who ask to come in; and there, for the most part, ends our apostolate. This naturally leads us to say frankly what we think could be done. For we believe that our methods of apostolate call for revision, need readjustment. The way to become like

St. Paul, "All things to all men, that we may save them all," (I. Cor. I., 22) changes with the times.

In the great drama of life the stage-settings are ever shifting and the *dramatis personae,* changing. The success of the actor is to fit in as the play goes on. This he does by adopting ways and methods most appropriate to his surroundings. The problems we face are always the same, but to be efficient our methods of handling them must evolve and adjust themselves to the temper of the age. What should be then the characteristic features of our apostleship among non-Catholics? The neglect of readjustment of our methods in dealing with our separated brethren is the avowed cause of the tremendous waste of energy and the explanation of meagre results. "An enormous amount of energy," said Father Benson,—and he had the experience,—"has been expended uselessly in the past, assaulting positions that are no longer held, and by lack of appreciation of present conditions." In this age of loose thinking and of rapid dissemination of ideas, *aggressiveness,* supported by active propaganda, characterizes every world-wide movement in government, industry, science and religion. Every doctrine, every theory comes into the open and makes a strong bid for our hearing, for our following. Why should not the true doctrine of Christ assume this new shining armour of sane aggressiveness, come more into the open, and throw down the gauntlet to unbelief and indifference everywhere rampant and openly defiant? For, if conviction is the father of devotion, if our belief in the mastery of ideas is genuine, we cannot help but be aggressive. Needless to say we are not asking for vulgar aggressiveness, we are not asking for cheap sneers and attacks on the ignorance and the illogical position of others. By aggressiveness, we mean coming out in defence of truth which it is our privilege and responsibility to possess. Never have times been more inviting for an aggressive Catholicism. The great war has been for Protestantism the acid test. The result is for the Anglican and Evangelical Churches a complete failure,* and, as the soldiers said "a wash-out." They have lost their grip on the masses who are rapidly slipping into a religious chaos. The universal disintegration of creeds, strangely combined with a secret thirst for truth and unity now sweeps the English-speaking world. Are not these portentous events that manifest, as "The stirring of the waters," the movement of the Holy Spirit.

Our policy of aggressiveness, if it be true and resolute, will find expression in an intelligent, active and persevering propaganda. Propaganda is the dissemination of ideas, with the view of giving them a strong foothold in the mind. The gradual development of the message it carries and the re-

---

*Cfr. "Army and Religion."—Book written by Protestant Army Chaplains. It is a candid record of the failure of the Churches, Anglican and Evangelical, at the front, during the great war.

currence of its lessons at stated intervals are the principal factors of this great force. To be efficient and successful our propaganda among our non-Catholic brethren will assume two distinct forms: The open and the silent form.

The *silent propaganda* is the spreading of Catholic ideas through the contact of our every day life with those who are not of our own Faith. Willingly or unwillingly we are bound to leave an impression of our belief in the business and social circles into which our life is cast. Our silence and abstention alone often militate against the Church. Let then the purity and spirituality of our lives, the honesty of our commercial relations, the sanctity of our home, bear witness to the sacredness of our religion and to the seriousness of its teachings.

A true Catholic life is in itself a living antithesis of the prevalent neo-pagan ideals, and stands as the best proof of our Faith's sincerity and of the depth of its conviction. "If life is the test of thought rather than thought the test of life," wrote Van Dyke, "we should be able to get light on the real worth of a man's ideals by looking at the shape they would give to human existence if they were faithfully applied." For, as Cromwell said, "The mind is the man."

The participation in civic, social and national activities will afford the occasion of meeting our non-Catholic neighbours. This personal and repeated contact, particularly with the leaders of the community, on occasions when the best brains can concentrate together without clash of principle, is, in our humble estimation, of the greatest value. The participation of the Knights of Columbus in war activities and reconstruction work is a striking illustration of this point. Nothing has more helped the Church in the American Republic, in breaking down the barrier of anti-Catholic prejudice, than the stand its Catholic laity took during and after the Great War. Have we not in Western Canada been rather remiss in our participation in public activities? If we have not had our share in public life, it has often been, we must confess, our own fault.

The strength of the silent propaganda lies in its *persistency* and *consistency*. A silent continuous and intelligent activity, and not a mere passivity, on the part of Catholics, is what characterizes this tremendous force. Like the tide, it creeps from pebble to pebble, from rock to rock, submerging every thing under its conquering waters.

The logic of Catholic life lends its consistency to this silent force. Our life is indeed the best proof of our principles. No one on the contrary does more harm to the Church than a Catholic whose life is not in harmony with his belief. The non-Catholic points to his life, with a sneer, and says: "See, he is no better than others!" This reasoning, we know is false, but for the unthinking masses, very often conclusive.

This silent drive is the necessary background of the *open propaganda* of which we would now say a few words.

The sincerely aggressive Catholicism of the laity cannot confine its activities to the home and narrow circle of friends, no more than that of the clergy can find its limit in the pulpit and the confessional. Let us go into the open. The sun of liberty is blazing bright for us all, under the blue skies of Canada. To witness at times, our cringing spirit, our childlike timidity, our cowardice, one would think that we were still under the penal laws and legal disabilities known by our fathers and forefathers. "What is there to check our dash forward?" we would ask with Father Vaughan. "Absolutely nothing, but ourselves, nothing but what we term prudence." Prudence! thin veneer, hardly able to conceal our apathy and unwarranted timidity.

Has not the time come to throw off this false timidity and "To go out into the highways and hedges and compel our separated brethren to come in, that the Master's house may be filled." (Luke Ch. 14). Long enough have we waited for them to come to us. An intelligent Methodist was recently asked the question: "What do you think is the greatest obstacle to the spread of the Catholic Faith?" And he answered: "Ignorance,—because Protestants do not understand what Catholic teaching is, and if your people have the courage of their convictions and claim that they know the truth, why do they not come out like the Socialists, Radicalists, Salvation Army, and other bodies who have come out, and explain to the public what they believe and why."

Did not Cardinal Newman in the conclusion of his lecture: "The Position of Catholics," make similar statements? "Protestantism," he says, "is fierce because it does not know you; ignorance is its strength; error is its life. Therefore bring yourselves before it, press yourselves upon it, force yourselves into notice against its will. . . . Oblige men to know you. . . . Politicians and Philosophers would be against you, but not the people, if it knew you."

Yes, we willingly endorse what the English Dominican, Father Hugh Pope, advocated in his article, "The Modern Apostolate," in the August issue, 1919, "The Ecclesiastical Review," and in several other English newspapers and magazines. Has not indeed the time come when we should revolutionize all our methods, when we should apply to Home Missions something of the methods which now we have fancied pertained solely to the Foreign Missions. Some we know will criticize this forward policy as bold, open to ridicule, an innovation, an undignified intrusion, a Billy-Sunday method, etc.—"On analysis what does all this opposition come to, but that we are afraid." "Afraid!" our critics will exclaim, "of what? I should like to know?" Is not the answer: "Yes, afraid of what the people will say" (Father Pope, O.P.). Anchored in the past they will continue to spend their energies in giving what we would call "spiritual delicacies" to the few good souls around them, while at their very doors crowds are dying of spiritual hunger for want of bread. And in all tranquillity of conscience they will raise their eyes to Heaven and thank the Lord that they are not like them. If indeed we wait until the non-Catholics come to our churches and to our rectories and ask to be received into the Church, we shall wait until Doomsday. After all, what we here advocate, is nothing new. Is it not the modern interpretation, suited to our times, of the *"Omnia Omnibus"*—"All things to all men," of St. Paul?

Along what definite lines should this aggressiveness be developed? Zeal, we know, is very ingenious in its ways and means, and has in their use the freedom of the spirit of God. Yet, there are certain methods, certain activities, which have proved successful and could be adopted to suit the circumstances of each community. Missions to non-Catholics and lectures in public halls, if well and intelligently advertised, will always draw an audience. Nothing appeals more to the mind of the inquirer than a lucid and simple exposition of the Faith. Controversy beclouds the issue. Were there any particular doubt in mind, the Question-box affords an opportunity to elucidate it. The distribution of literature will confirm the message of the spoken word and continue to carry on its work, helping the seed to germinate in God's own time. Inquiry classes and information bureaus are of a great help to those who are reluctant yet to meet a priest, or to be known as wavering in their faith.

The great error in connection with this matter is to expect immediate results from such work. Truth and Divine Grace work slowly. To measure the success of a lecture or a mission to non-Catholics by the number of immediate converts is completely unfair and against reason. The main and direct object of these lectures is to combat the three obstacles in the way of conversion, indifference, ignorance, and prejudice, and to prepare the soil for the Great Sower. The important point we should not forget is that, as in all propaganda, the *"systematic follow-up work"* counts. The persistency and recurrence of the message give it its strength and influence.

In all we have said and suggested it must not be supposed that we forget Faith to be a gift of God . . . *Donum Dei*. The salvation and sanctification of a soul are essentially a supernatural process. We can no more trace the ways of God than we can forecast the ways of the wind. Therefore the greater our activities are, the greater should be the supernatural force behind them. Prayer, constant and fervent prayer, for the conversion of our separated brethren should be ever on our lips and in our hearts. Yet, strange thing! We hardly ever hear of public prayers and masses said for this great work. If our desires were more real, should they not find expression here and there in some public form of prayer.

We should close this chapter with the instructive and inviting example that comes to us from our Catholic brethren in Protestant England. A wonderful Catholic campaign is now on through Scotland and England. Various societies have grouped the active Catholic laity into various units, with the one great object in view, to give back to England the faith she has been robbed of centuries ago.

The "Catholic Truth Society" stands in the background as the heavy artillery that has been firing at long range at positions the enemies are gradually leaving. For the last thirty years it has been breaking the way to victory. "The Catholic Evidence Guild" and "Social Guild," like the light cavalry are reconnoitering the lines and positions. The "Motor Chapel" and "The Bexhill Library" —that Catholic Post-Library, with its 16,000 volumes—are what we call the flying corps of this great Catholic army. And while the various militant units are pushing forward their lines, the members of "Our Lady of Ransom's League" are praying on the mountain with up-lifted hands for the conversion of their Country.

The Catholics of the United States are following suit. The Paulist Fathers with their missions to non-Catholics, their press and "Catholic Missionary Union," devoted to the conversion of America, have undoubtedly done splendid work. The Catholic laity have also been most active under the auspices of the Knights of Columbus. MM. Goldstein and Peter Collins, Dr. Walsh and Mrs. Avery are lecturing through the country and have met with great success. This awakening of the missionary spirit is one of the most healthy signs of the Catholicity of the Church across the border. It is with reason that the Holy See looks to America for the future wants of the Mission Field.

These examples of an apostolic awakening that come to us from countries where religious conditions are very much the same as those that prevail in Western Canada, are most illuminating. They sound to us like the Master's voice: *"Why stand idle all day . . . go you also into my vineyard."*

CHAPTER VII.

PROS AND CONS

Obstacles that impede. . . . Circumstances that help the work of the Church in Western Canada.

THE opening of the North West Territories to immigration, and their creation into distinct Provinces of the Dominion stand as land marks of portentous meaning in the History of Canada. The settlement and development of these immense fertile prairies of the West were bound to react on the economic powers and political outlook of our Country. By the sheer weight of their economic value these new Provinces have leaped into prominence and forced themselves upon the attention of the Country at large. The Western issues are now so weighty that only the greatest prudence and wisest statesmanship will maintain the equilibrium between the conflicting forces of the East and the West of our broad Dominion. Canada now stands at the parting of the ways in its home and foreign policy. Every true and patriotic Canadian is proud of the progressiveness of these new Provinces beyond our great Lakes and anxious to see them bring their contributions to the Commonwealth by sharing in the direction of its government. Their presence around the family table is not that of strangers or intruders, but of young, stalwart and rightly ambitious sons.

Yet, as Religion is the necessary factor of true prosperity, the religious outlook in these young Provinces is what naturally appeals to the Catholic mind. What are then the prospects for the Church in Western Canada? A rapid survey of conditions will enable us to take our bearings and impress upon our minds the value of our co-operation at this juncture of our History. The Church in the West is in its making and we cannot over-emphasize the responsibility of every Catholic in the matter. The knowledge of existing conditions will be to us what the topography of the country under survey is to the engineer. It helps to adjust the vision, to give the sense of proportion and to suggest the easiest grades.

To know well an obstacle is often the best means to overcome it, just as in modern warfare to locate the enemies' batteries is to silence them. In our Chapter, "The Call of the West," we have explained the obstacles with which Catholics have to contend on the prairie and in small towns. We pointed out those obstacles, *geographical* (distance and climate), *ethnical* (race and language), *religious* (absence of catholic traditions and surroundings), and marked how they were as wide crevices through which vitality is being lost to the Church in Western Canada. It is our intention here to dwell only on difficulties of a general character, inherent to the state of this new country and effecting the Church in its corporate existence.

The materialistic spirit, in all its forms, characterizes the West. The youth of our Eastern Provinces and foreigners from every shore flocked to this Eldorado by the thousands and hundreds of thousands with the one particular aim in view, to better their material condition. Their success has been so great that we may well say that the very atmosphere of the West is surcharged with commercialism. The "crop" is the everrecurring factor and eternal topic of Western life. No better picture reflects this attitude than that which is offered to the traveller as his train goes rolling on through the even prairie. Ever emerging on the horizon and dotting the landscape of the bald plain the *grain elevator* stands indeed as the most conspicuous land mark of our Western towns. The elevators are in our prairie landscapes what the church spires are in the Quebec villages, along the shores of the St. Lawrence. Here and there they stand as symbols; they interpret an ideal. Naturally a population so immersed in material pursuits and frequently, not to say always, separated by the very force of circumstances from the vitalizing contact of spiritual influence, rapidly loses grasp of the supernatural and becomes refractory to the doctrines and practices of the Church. Nothing is more adverse to the influence of Christianity than material prosperity combined with the absolute ignorance of its divine teachings. The wealthy and prosperous farmer out West is inclined to look down on the Church and consider Her "out of date."*

This materialistic atmosphere and the absence of catholic traditions and associations act also as a corrosive on the faith of Catholics, particularly of our young people. Like a strong acid it eats away the teachings of good Christian parents and the impressions of a Catholic home. Only those who have seen at close range these sad soul transformations can believe in their painful reality and explain their frequency.

The *activities of non-Catholic bodies among the foreign element* are another obstacle to the work of the Church. Like the locusts of Egypt a cloud of proselytizers have alighted on those parts of the Provinces where the new Canadian is in the making. We have seen in another chapter (*Pro aris et focis*—or, the Ruthenian Problem) how under the cover of Canadianization, the foreigner is being weaned away from the Faith of his Fathers and what menace this is for the Church.

This systematic effort of the various denominations is being supported by the combined action of their clergy and laity in the East. Men and money are flowing into the West to Christianize (*sic!*)

---

*"Catholics to a certain extent will remain an alien body. We differ from those around us in a profound fashion, not in matters of direct doctrine, for which the modern world has largely ceased to care, but in the effects of that doctrine. The Catholic's whole conception of man and of the fundamentals of human life is a different thing from that held by those about us."—H. Belloc.

our Catholic foreigners.   The final result of this proselytizing effort is not a permanent increased membership for these churches, but rather indifference and irreligion among our foreign element. Facts and figures prove it.   And to re-establish these souls in the Faith of their Baptism is no easy task, we all know.   It is far easier to tear down than to rebuild.

This united action of the different Churches stands out in sharp contrast with the *lack of co-operation* among Catholics throughout Canada. The absence of co-operation of the East with the West affects very seriously the welfare of the Church in the new Provinces. We all willingly and gratefully acknowledge the contributions in men and money that have come from the East through the channels of the Religious Orders, of the Catholic Church Extension and from other sources. But absorbed by parochial and diocesan interests the Catholic Church in Eastern Canada has not as yet fully realized the seriousness of our Western problems.   With its co-operation only can the weight of the Church as a whole be brought to bear in their solution.

This policy of unity of action is also most urgent for the Catholics of the Western Provinces. We are a minority in each Province; concerted action can alone press our legitimate claims and bring to us success in these activities which necessarily overlap the boundaries of dioceses and provinces, as is the case with the Catholic Press and Higher Education. Diocesan isolation, if we are not careful, can become the weakness of our strength, in these critical stages of rapid development. Yet, there are no Provinces in the Dominion where the Church faces so many identical problems under identical conditions as in the Western Provinces. Should not this alone suggest to our leaders a unity of plan and realize among our Western Catholics concerted action?

.   .   .   .   .

As there is a silver lining to the darkest cloud, there is a bright side for the Church in conditions out West.

The striking feature of the Canadian West is the *newness of the country*. Youth is stamped everywhere clear and bold; the dash and buoyancy of the people reflect it faithfully. Optimism is the predominant note in that land of immensities and great possibilities. Untrammelled by set traditions and cast-iron customs, every one is there to start a new life. The past does not seem to exist for the Westerner; the future is his sole concern.

This newness of the country and the optimistic mood which it creates can be called into the service of the Church. They form an atmosphere of tolerance which proves most helpful for the preaching of Her doctrine and the maintenance of Her institutions.

The youthfulness of the country has left its mark on the *character of the Westerner*. There is something of the vastness of the prairie in his mind. He is generally broad, and boasts of it most willingly. This trait is very noticeable in his passion to revaluate theories, to redefine notions brought from the East. The great success with which he has met in various co-operative schemes has also developed in him a high sense of self-reliance. The only danger is that he carries that same self-assurance into domains where he often over-reaches himself. This fact is very noticeable in the various annual Conventions. Unconsciously, in matters beyond his grasp, he is at the mercy of a few leaders. Resolutions are passed, legislation is suggested, without realization of their consequences.

The rapid *disintegration of Protestantism* is another factor with which the Church can count. Church union is in many places an accomplished fact. This alone is a convincing proof of the want of grasp, of definiteness that exists in religious matters. We would refer our reader to the Chapter "Ploughing the Sands." To what extent this rather negative disposition will hasten the spreading of the true Faith, is difficult to state. Will it, as is evident in England, promote a movement of return to the Church or accentuate, as in the United States, indifference and unbelief, the future alone can tell. But, is it not our duty in the meantime to make use of every tide and wind to bring the ship to port?   The tide, as it is now running, shall bring to the Church many a shipwrecked soul. This is our firm belief.

This rapid survey of Western conditions in their relation with the Church, without being a searching examination, outlines, as it were, the actual religious topography of our new Provinces. Our sole ambition is to help to wipe away, in our work, useless curves, make easier the grades and map out the straightest and most direct route to success.   With the knowledge of conditions, less energy will be lost and more time will be gained. Time and energy are the necessary factors of true and permanent progress.

PART II
EDUCATIONAL PROBLEMS

"To-day's boy is to-morrow's man."

CHAPTER VIII.

WHY SEPARATE?*

A Moral Reason—A Social Reason—A Political Reason—A National Reason—A British Reason—A Historical Reason—A Religious Reason—For "Separate Schools."

THE West is without a doubt the classical land of the "School problem in Canada." The Prairie Provinces will remember the struggles that have marked their birth in the Dominion. The words, *"separate schools,"* rang loud and angry over the cradle of these youngest partners in our Confederation. The conflict has not subsided with

*This chapter formed a series of articles in the North West Review of Winnipeg. The following editorial comment accompanied our concluding article.

"This week we publish the last of the series of articles by Father Daly, C.SS.R., dealing with the separate school question.

"We consider his contribution on this ever topical and historic problem one of the best reasoned and for the average man the most concise and useful yet published. It might well be issued in pamphlet form and kept for reference in every Catholic home in Western Canada, because the subject is one likely to be controversial for an indefinite period. Sometimes one finds Catholics who are not as well acquainted with the fact as they should be that the question of Catholic education can never be compromised. A solid and reasoned knowledge of this fact is in some respects as essential as if it were an article of faith, especially in Western Canada, which, as Father Daly points out, is the classic land of the school problem.

"Doubtless attempts will be made in the future to bring elementary education through the pretext of Canadianization, under the "invisible head" of this country. Or as in the United States segre-

years. Although the rights of the minority, at least in Saskatchewan and Alberta, are partially recognized by law, there are yet some who seem to have a mission to reopen the conflict by ever dragging the problem into the open arena of our political life. Under the specious pretext of national welfare they would foist upon the Canadian Public opinions and measures opposed to our existing system and to the broad spirit of liberty that in-

---

gated attempts may be made to abolish parochial schools altogether.

"Where there are so many probabilities and so much at stake it might be well for the average Catholic to be in a position to give a good account of himself by showing a thorough understanding of the question.

"If the present civilization succeeds, it will do so by adopting the methods of some, if not all, of our big corporations of to-day, and thus make of nations, huge Trust socialisms where the individual will hunger no more for freedom because of his having never tasted it. The one great desideratum to this end is the absolute control of education—an end that will never be reached so long as the Catholic Church continues to save Christian civilization through its religious schools.

"Would that our fellow citizens of other faiths knew the ruin that they court by relinquishing to a material power control over the minds and hearts of their children.

"In every country the public school is bringing young minds under the spell of worldliness. The result is selfishness, jingoism, narrow nationalism—an unthinking, a gullible generation to become the easy prey of exploiters and the docile slaves of commerce.

"No man who has drunk into his heart and mind in youth the truths of religious education can readily become the willing dupe of a materialistic state.

"Commerce to-day is the God of nations. It makes wars, compels peace and tramples upon morality and justice. Surely then Catholics should study in a particular way the only safeguard left them against such a fate—the sound philosophy of a religious education."

spires and maintains it. But we all know that in this persistent and methodical opposition to our separate schools the fundamental issue is a religious one. Life, after all, is a spiritual value. The school is the great loom on which the rising youth weaves its thread into the great and amazing tapestry of the nation. Who has the mastery of the school, has in the making that mysterious tapestry of human life.

This problem is but an aspect of the eternal struggle between the Christian and the Pagan ideal. The pagan ideal of civilization is the absorption of the individual by the State, the confiscation of liberty by the political monopoly of the nation.

The Christian ideal is the State at the service and for the protection of the individual and of the family. "To Caesar what belongs to Caesar; to God what belongs to God." Before the ever recrudescent forces of neo-paganisim it is most useful, we contend, to reassert in plain, terse language the principles, the reasons that explain and justify our persistent attitude on the school problem. They will be our answer to the question which is ever thrown at Catholics in Western Canada: *"Why separate?"* We have placed the discussion of this problem on the higher plain of the unchangeable and unchanging principles of truth and justice, for, we are firm believers in the pacific penetration of ideas and in their conquering power.

In truth alone, the Master stated, is true and abiding liberty: "You will know truth, and truth will make you free."   Every true Canadian readily grasps the transcendent importance of the problem under examination and should bring to its discussion open-mindedness and sincerity.

I.—A Moral Reason

It is the right and duty of the parent to educate his child.   This right is founded on nature.   The child is the offspring of the parents, the continuation as it were of their own life.   They are therefore the natural educators of their children.   When they commit them to the care of others for instruction it is their right to have them educated as they wish.   As by the supreme and sacred right of conscience man is free to give to his life its moral direction, so also does the same principle apply to the education of a child for whose conscience, as for whose life, the parent is responsible.   The moral right of the parent, which is one with that of the child in that period of life, is fundamental. It constitutes the bed-rock on which rest all other rights in matters of education.   To deny that principle, to deflect it from its proper meaning, to recognize it only partially, is to blast the very foundation of human nature.   No reason of common good, of citizenship, can overthrow this right; on the contrary, it presupposes it; for, the State can only interfere to protect and help this right.   It can never suppress it, and only supplement it when the parents are deficient and fall short of this sacred duty they owe their offspring.

II.—A Social Reason

Society is made up of various units, lending to one another support by the mutual participation in the activities of life. The family—the first in order of time and dignity—is beyond doubt the principal and central unit. The other social factors presuppose it and exist for its protection. Is it not the source from which springs the very life of the individual and wherein society replenishes its forces? The placing of the individual as the specific social unit of our modern democracy is a pernicious error. This fallacy has destroyed Society by upsetting the essential order of its units and has robbed the individual of his most elementary rights.

The substitution of the State for the family is most detrimental in any sphere of life. In matters of education it is nothing short of a disaster. The "State School Teacher" is an anomaly. It is the subversion of true social order for it constitutes "an unwarranted interference of the State in a function preeminently social. Education is a social function and cannot be converted into a governmental charge without violence to it." What Treitsche said of the Judiciary Power in a country may well be applied to education. "We find the first and fundamental principle of jurisprudence to be that no one should be withdrawn from the jurisdiction of his natural judge." The natural school of the child is the family; the common school should be nothing but an extension of the home. The mission of the school is to supplement the home and not to supplant it. The child and the parent therefore are entitled to have the same atmosphere pervade both school and home. Everything that is relevant to education belongs to the family. A policy that favours intrusion of an undue influence of the State in the school and destroys home authority and parental influence is unnatural and therefore anti-social. The State is not the natural teacher of the child.

This fusion of the political and social orders—which in reality means the suppression of the latter to the profit of the former—is the fatal error of the day and producive of great evils. An Educational Department is the open door through which any Government may force its particular views on the growing generation. The monopoly of State education is nothing else but the conscription of the minds, an "intellectual militarism," which eventually leads to the absorption of the individual and the family and to greater disasters than war. Under the cover of citizenship it will legalize a country into servitude. The school ambitions of Prussia prepared the catastrophe the world has just witnessed. Always and everywhere the same cause will produce the same effects.

III.—*A Political Reason*

Authority and liberty are the two poles on which revolves Society. The perfect equilibrium of these two contending forces, one centripetal, the other centrifugal, make for its safety and welfare. The encroachment of one upon the other displaces the social axis and throws a nation out of its natural orbit. Political Society then oscillates between autocracy and anarchy. The infringement of this supreme law of moral gravitation has strewn the paths of history with the ruins of kingdoms and empires. The violation of a natural law bears always with itself its own punishment. For, society is not the conventional creation of man; it is governed by laws that man does not make, but, which his reason and experience discover and to which he must submit.

This perfect equilibrium of authority and liberty is perfectly expressed in Lincoln's famous definition: "A sane democracy is one of the people, by the people and for the people." The reason of this law of the political order is that liberty is previous to authority, for authority only exists to protect liberty against tyranny and to safeguard it against its own excesses. He is best governed who is least governed. LePlay, the celebrated French economist, made this just and pertinent remark: "The truly free nations are those who, without compromising this prosperity, extend the benefices

of private life at the expense of public life."
(Réforme Sociale II, page 92.)

Therefore the ideal State exists when all civil
or social rights—which stand for the *public enjoyment* of all natural rights—are fully protected by
political rights. These political liberties moreover
claim not only the negative protection or non-inter-
ference of authority, but also its positive financial
help. For political liberty exists for the protection of civil liberty, and not *vice versa*. The collective forces of a society are for the benefit of the
individual and not the individual for them. A
State is an institution for the protection of rights
inherent to a free people.

The negation of this principle leads to the
State paternalism which stands for the interference
of State in matters which by right belong to the
individual and the family. Never has State interference and State protection been more exagger-
ated than they are nowadays. The passing and
pressing emergencies of the great war have accen-
tuated these tendencies. The nations have kept the
habit of being governed by orders-in-council, by
arbitrary censorship and dictatorial methods. "The
Executive has usurped the functions that rightly
belong to the legislative assembly, with a virtual
dictatorship as the inevitable result." The consequence of State Paternalism is the death of individual liberty either through socialism or autocracy. Man becomes the chattel of a bureau-
cratic government.

Of all civil liberties there is none more sacred, more fundamental than that of education. The freedom of education means the right of a parent to give to his offspring an education in harmony with his concept of life, with the dictates of his conscience. As education is nothing but a preparation for life, its theory goes hand in hand with the theory of life. To this liberty of the parent should correspond in society a political right. To deprive a free citizen of this right is to penalize him and oblige him—as is the case in Manitoba— to buy twice over a right of conscience. This condition wherever it exists is a flagrant abuse of political authority and consequently a social disorder.

Some may object to our argumentation and answer that in a modern democracy the majority rules, and the majority in the West are against "separate schools." The political right of the majority cannot cancel a moral right of the minority. It is a case here of repeating the statement of Burke: "The tyranny of a democracy is the most dangerous of all tyrannies because it allows no appeal against itself." This autocracy of numbers is often more dangerous and more brutal than that of a caste, of a czar, or of a king. Russia is giving us an illustration of this autocracy of number. Did not Germany use the same argument to crush Belgium and to try to dominate the World? Our sons have fought and died in this war against Prussianism and yet some of our Canadians—not worthy of the name—would willingly vote drastic measures of governmental repression which would make the Kaiser smile and the Czar Nicholas turn in his grave. The velvet glove may cover the mail-fist, but the blow is the same.

Others may claim that the State has a right to "Uniformity in the education of its citizens." This is the pretension of those who now are advocating so strongly and so widely the "federalization of our schools." We will not discuss the value of this plea for uniformity. It would open a very interesting pedagogical debate and we are inclined to believe that the "anti-uniformists" would carry away the honors. We do not pretend that the State has no rights in matters of education. But its interference should be consistent with the prior and more fundamental rights of the individual and the family and not become a usurpation or abrogation of them. Otherwise it would be the wrong way of doing the right thing.

IV.—A National Reason

The Constitution of a country has as its specific object the maintenance of the perfect equilibrium between authority and liberty. "It is the charter of a people's liberties, the shield of the individual against the possible tyranny of government, the effective check upon the ambition of every government to extend the sphere of its delegated powers. Unlike the law, its primary purpose is to restrain the Government, not the citizen. . . ." (P. Blakely, S.J.) America, Sept. 18, 1920.

The greatest liberty for the individual, combined with the greatest good of the commonwealth, has always been the ideal aimed at by the Fathers of a democratic country. To tamper with the Constitution on vital issues, to conceive it as an experiment, to ignore its spirit,—that obvious intention of its framers—is always eventually fatal to the peace and welfare of the nation. No one lays hands with impunity on that Ark of the Covenant. The essential changes in the Constitution of a country act as a time-fuse. An explosion necessarily follows, although it may take years and generations for a faulty legislation to disclose its real consequences. This is particularly true in matters of education. Laws of the educational departments may change to become more efficient in their administration but should never touch the fundamental rights guaranteed by the Constitution.

In Canada the protection of the minority rights is a principle embodied in our Constitution, in the Imperial Statute of the British North America Act. Even where the letter of the Provincial Law has established the "public school,"—as is the case in the Maritime Provinces—the spirit of the law is generally observed, and by a compromise and tacit agreement the rights of the minority are to a great extent recognized.

In the West, Manitoba stands out in Canadian History as the battlefield of educational rights. Although the British North America Act, 1867,— that intangible charter of Canadian liberties— stipulates, section 93, that in the carving out of new Provinces in the vast domains of the North West Territories the existing educational rights guaranteed to the minority should be respected, yet, the Manitoba Legislative Assembly has broken away from the letter and spirit of the Constitution and constituted a grievance which demands rectification.

The Federal Parliament partially recognized the principle of Separate Schools in the formation of the Provinces of Saskatchewan and of Alberta, by introducing, in section 17 of the Autonomy Bills of 1905, the section 93 of the B.N.A. Act, and by reasserting the existing rights granted by the N.W.T. School Ordinances of 1901. We say "partially," for it is not the right of collecting separate taxes and teaching Religion during the last half hour of the school-day that constitutes a really Catholic school.

The "Separate schools" in Saskatchewan and Alberta stand on the solid granite of our Constitution. The highest tribunals of the land and the Empire have implicitly recognized the principle of the minority-schools in many of their decisions. Moreover, let us not forget it! the separate school system in Canada is *"protestant"* in its origin. It was to protect the protestant minority of Lower Canada that this system, Catholic in Ontario, Protestant in Quebec, was adopted on September 18th, 1841. In the West the minority school-law was also enacted to protect the protestant minority of the Territories. Our Non-Catholic opponents should not forget this origin of our separate schools. What their fathers appreciated then for their children, we appreciate now for ours. The principle remains unchanged.

Some may be surprised at our contention to make an argument in favour of separate schools out of the very point on which rests the scaffolding of those who oppose them. They claim that the minority school principle is the greatest enemy of Canadian Unity. What we need, they say, is to standardize our schools, and bring all Canadian children under one system. No genuine "Canadianization" is possible without this unity of education. The advocates of these ideas are now at work promoting through the country the "nationalization of schools." The Conference of Winnipeg, 1919, was the first tangible result of this movement. A National Bureau of Education— a non-government institution, at least for the time being; a survey of school text-books throughout the Provinces, a study of matters affecting the status of the teaching profession—such are the duties that this National Council of Education has assumed at its first gathering.

This movement towards Federal control of schools involves the denial and the eventual suppression of the minority-principle in our system of Education. This nationalization of Education, we claim, is erroneous in its principle, anti-constitutional in its operation, and dangerous in its consequences. Uniformity in education, as a source of efficiency, is one of the fallacies of our materialistic age. Schools to be successful have not to be submitted to the same laws of a commercial or industrial combine. Ethnical and moral values do not follow the laws of the mart and the stock exchange. If in our extensive Dominion even a unity of tariff, readily acceptable to the East and to the West, is Utopian, how much more so would be the unity of the school system? Education, to be effective, must take the colour of the environments to meet the needs of the community. The levelling process would be most detrimental, for uniformity in education is the seed of decay.

And it is on the plea of making better Canadians that the promoters of "national schools" are drifting from the very basic principle of our educational system, from the law and spirit of our Constitution. Our form of Government, as we all know, is dual. Matters of education are relevant to the Province. The more the Province will abdicate its claims, and submit to the growing influence of the Federal powers, the greater will be the danger of losing the political equilibrium of Confederation. Unstable equilibrium, once disturbed, is hardly ever re-established. The centrifugal forces of the Province protect our liberties against the possible excesses of the centripetal forces of the Federal Government. Any movement that tends to break the harmony of these forces is, we claim, anti-Canadian. The Premier of Quebec speaking to the Deputy Ministers of Education and Superintendents of Public Instruction, at an interprovincial Conference sounded this note of warning: "The absolute control by each Province of its educational system is the keystone of our Confederation; and the whole structure of Canada would crumble away if any attempt were made at suppressing that which holds its several parts together." (Nov. 4, 1921.) Quebec is blamed for being the great obstacle to the realization of the dreams of our nationalizers. Quebec, we maintain, is the most sane Province of the Dominion, and the greatest help to the maintenance of Confederation. This is now an admitted fact by every serious and broad minded Canadian. Its conservatism acts, we would say, as the governor on the complicated machine of Canadian political life. It regulates its speed and keeps it within the limits of safety. Moreover, we ask, how could a system which would deny the principles and rights of over forty per cent. of the population be rightly and justly named "national"? No one has the right to assume the monoply of "nationalism."

"The self-appointed or State-appointed nation-alizer, we would say with Father Millar, S.J., ignorant of our real history or its true meaning, is fast becoming a menace to the sanity of our laws and to the supreme wisdom of a traditional national policy."*

And what will be the consequences of this level-ling uniformity that crushes parental right and fuses the powers of Provinces into a Federal unit? The Prussian ideal is the answer. We all know what that means and where it leads. Its principles are the solvents of what remains of Christianity—unconscious to many, it is true—in the political life of our country. The armies that our boys fought on the fields of Flanders were formed and trained in the national schools of Germany.

V.—*A British Reason*

The great misfortune of many who clamour against our separate schools is their total ignorance of our history and of the spirit that the liberty-loving Fathers of the Confederation have breathed into our laws. To them "national reasons" may not appeal. This is very often the case of the average Westerner. The West is in its making and has no past behind it. This fact alone can explain how easy the Western mind is open to in-fluences opposed to the spirit of our Canadian in-stitutions. It has no traditions, and traditions are

*America, Aug. 21, 1920.

the hidden roots that plunge down into the soil of history, into the hearts of past generations, and give to a people, its real national life. Therefore, a "British reason," a reason founded on British traditions, on the British way of doing things in the Colonies, may make a stronger appeal to our Western mentality.

Freedom and fair play for every citizen within the Empire, the recognition of racial and religious rights, have been the strength and success of the British Government in its Colonial policy. (We underline "colonial policy" for, we cannot say the same of England's policy with Ireland—) We would quote here what a well known Western public man wrote some years ago when, under the pen-name of "Daylight" he discussed the "Separate School problem" in the columns of "The Regina Leader," January 3rd, 1916.

"In conclusion there are one or two general remarks I should like to make. It has always appeared to me that there is among our English-speaking people of Canada a section of the community that holds extreme views on all matters pertaining to nationality and religion. This section holds and advocates the idea, that there must be no compromise in dealing with matters pertaining to race and religion. In a word, they would set about at once to "Prussianize" our complex population. They forget, or entirely ignore, the fact that this is not the British plan. If the British Empire is the glorious Empire it is to-day is it not because of the fact that long ago the British statesman and the British citizen have learned the lesson of tolerance? To-day, Great Britain with its forty-five millions of people rules over hundreds of millions of people of diverse nationalities and religious faiths, and throughout the whole scheme of government and constitution runs the idea of reasonable and just tolerance and compromise. Were this not so the British Empire would quickly fall to pieces. Why then should we not have more of this spirit in Canada, and particularly in Western Canada? Some people are mightily concerned about our foreign-born population. They imagine that the process of assimilation can and should be accomplished in a day. Nothing is further from the truth. The process is necessarily a slow one. It is bound to take two or three, and in some cases, more generations. In the meantime we should strive to make these people feel that they are welcome to our broad open plains and to our citizenship. As to the final outcome no one need have any doubt."

The principle that has created the British Empire is the only principle that will keep it on the map of the world. This is history, philosophy, and common sense.

And when we see England recognizing the Catholic elementary schools and subsidizing to a certain extent our secondary schools, when Scotland has just brought the Catholic schools of several cities into its system, is it not painful, to say the least, to hear our ultra-loyalists ever up in arms against our separate schools? To them we feel like saying, "Go back to England and Scotland, from whence you or your forefathers came and learn from the Home Country the lesson of tolerance, of sane political government."

VI.—*A Historical Reason*

In the discussion of many problems we are liable, particularly in the West, to limit our vision to conditions as they present themselves to the observer. This is more noticeable in the educational field. This frame of mind may be traced to various causes. But there is one cause which, we believe, is more responsible than others.

Unconsciously our age is *"evolutionist."* "The intellectual movement of 'evolution,'" said Glenn Frank," was not the private plaything of biologists in sequestered laboratories, but a force that altered men's conceptions in every field of affairs." ("Century," Sept., 1920.) The theory of evolution has such a grasp on the modern mind that its concepts of government, of economics, of education are looked upon as the last and improved effort of man in his eternal struggle to express an unknown and always receding ideal. This has accustomed the mind to look upon the past but as a rudiment, an outline, a preparation of the future.

Without entering into the discussion of the objective evidence of the theory of evolution we may say that as far as education is concerned its premises are false. The human soul remains substantially the same and the process of its education has not varied very much with centuries. Those therefore who look upon our modern Educational system as the apex, the summing up of all past phases, are greatly mistaken. "The lessons of past history," writes Dr. Walsh, "are extremely precious not only because they show us where others made mistakes but also because they show us the successes of the past. The better we know these, the deeper our admiration for them, the better the outlook for ourselves and our accomplishment."

The State-school is an institution comparatively of very recent date and has no right to be heralded as the final expression of an educational system in a democracy. The history of education shows a lineage of men who can be more than favorably compared with the sons of our common schools. The mass of the people have indeed more instruction but, at times, we doubt if they are better educated. Results are the best judges of educational values. History and experience prove that success in education depends more on the sense of responsibility in the parents and of duty in the children, than on palatial school-houses and elaborate programme of studies. This sense of duty and the feeling of responsibility are not a necessary consequence of state schools. On the contrary they are more liable to be found in independent institutions. For, as we have seen, when the State substitutes itself for the family, the first consequence is the unchallenged yield of parental rights.

Those who would make an excursion into history and compare our modern educational systems with those of the past will find illuminating points of comparison and instructive conclusions. We would advise them to take Dr. Walsh, M.D., Ph.D., Litt.D., as guide. His books: "Education, how Old the New"—"The Thirteenth Century"—will prove most interesting reading.

Already a reactionary policy is being enacted in several countries where for years the State-School was the only one to share in the public treasury. In Holland, the Parliament of June, 1920, by a vote of 72 against 3, passed a new school-law which recognizes and subsidizes all separate primary, high and normal schools. In Italy, the Minister of Education, Benedetto Croce, in a speech on the "reorganization of education," stated publicly that the neutral school was theoretically absurd and practically impossible. In Spain,* by a Bill of May, 1919, the State universities have passed out of the hands of the Government.

*Cfr. Article by Father Vaughan, S.J., on this subject—America, Feb. 21, 1920.

France, Portugal, Argentine Republic are fighting for the same freedom. In Poland's new charter of liberties, granted by the Treaty of Versailles, the rights of the minority in school matters are guaranteed. Our Canadian representatives signed this document. We were granting then to the new Republic a sacred right which we still refuse to our own at home, in the Province of Manitoba!

VII.—*A Religious Reason*

The creation of the state-school, necessarily undenominational in character, has made the "separate school" an absolute necessity. If religion has any meaning in life this reason of our separation should be most convincing.

In education one cannot separate the utilitarian side,—the fitting of the child for the struggle of life,—from its main purpose,—the development of moral character. The moral aspect alone gives to human life its true character, its real value. As there is no morality without religion, the system of education that would debar this essential feature falls short of its full meaning. With this principle in view any fair-minded man will understand how true Christian parents demand a school where their children will receive religious education. They are in conscience bound to exact for their offspring such education, and, where the State refuses them their own money to support their "separate schools" they willingly penalize themselves to give them this benefit. The child's eternal welfare is not to be sacrificed to a school system that has not even accomplished the purpose for which it was established. For, as we shall see, a neutral school is a practical impossibility.

Those who fail to understand the pressing force of this viewpoint have in our opinion lost the sense and sacredness of religion. They are astonished at the bitterness that characterizes at times the conflict. Are not religious and racial issues so intimately united with the very conception of life that they hold to the most intimate fibres of the human heart? For a Catholic, Religion is life itself in its most sacred aspect.

But, our opponents will argue, in a country like Canada, where "organized" religion—to speak their language—is so denominational, religion in school is an impossibility. Is it because other denominations cannot agree as to their religious tenets that we, who count over one-third of the total population and who stand united in our faith, are to surrender what we consider most essential in education and—lest we forget it—most protective to the best interests of our Country?

What does the State give us to replace the "separate school"? A neutral, undenominational, irreligious school. This neutrality we claim, is erroneous in theory and impossible in practice. The theory of the neutral school is erroneous because it is against the teaching of sound psychology and true pedagogy.

The soul of the child cannot be, as it were, divided into watertight compartments so as to segregate religious influence from its daily training. As Cardinal O'Connell stated, "We Catholics believe that as character is by far the most important product of education, the training of the will, the moulding of the heart, the grounding of the intellect in clear notions of right and wrong, obligation and duty, should not be left to haphazard or squeezed as an afterthought into an hour on Sunday. The moral and spiritual growth of the child ought normally to keep pace with his mental growth and the Church is convinced that taking human nature as it is, the result cannot be obtained effectively without including a judicious mixture of religious training with the daily routine of the school."

In fact a neutral school is an impossibility. We will simply ask our readers a few questions and rely on their fairmindedness to formulate the answers. Can the teaching of history be neutral? The Catholic Church and the Reformation are historical facts: how are they to be judged? How are ethics to be treated, without reference to God, to Jesus Christ, to an eternal sanction? Can a teacher divest himself of his mental attitude in the teaching of these subjects and answering the questions of the pupils?

Were the teaching really neutral, the very atmosphere of the school-room is what counts. This

atmosphere is indefinable and yet everywhere felt.
It is made of trifles, but of trifles that count at that
receptive age of childhood. As a subtle perfume
it impregnates the soul of the child with ideas and
impressions which it will carry through life.
Therefore the atmosphere of the class-room, we
claim, should be as near as possible, that of the
home. The parents have a right to see that it
should be so. Is this possible in a neutral school?
Its very negative character impregnates the class-
rooms with an irreligious feeling which the impressionable mind of the child cannot but notice.
How is the child to grow up with the feeling of
Religion's importance in life if the ban is placed
upon Religion the moment he passes the threshold
of the school-room? "What we most dread," said
Bishop McQuaid, "is not the direct teaching of the
State-school, it is the indirect teaching which is
most insidious and most dangerous. It is the moral
atmosphere, the tone of thought permeating these
schools that give cause for alarm. It is the indifferentism with regard to all religious belief we
most of all fear. This is the dominant heresy that,
imbibed in youth, can scarcely ever be eradicated.
It is one that already has in our large towns and
cities decimated Protestant Churches."

Even the provision of optional religious instruction at the dying hour of the class-day cannot
redeem the neutral school. In fact the Survey of
School conditions in Saskatchewan conducted by

Dr. Foght, in 1918, revealed there a state of things which in our mind is an eye-opener in the matter under examination.   Out of over 4,000 schools not more than 212 reported as availing themselves of the law on religious instruction.   We leave to the reader to draw the conclusion these recent statistics suggest.

To conclude this already too lengthy argument, facts are vindicating in every country the saneness of the Catholic view-point on religious instruction and atmosphere in the school.   The alarming increase of religious indifference, the rising tide of anarchy, the universal feeling of unrest, have prompted the unequivocal admissions of leaders of thought as to the moral failure of the neutral school.

Mr. William Jennings Bryan, in an address before the constitutional convention of Nebraska, a few years ago, brought this striking indictment against the State educational system of the United States.   "The greatest menace to the public school system of to-day is, in my judgment, its Godlessness.   We have allowed the moral influence to be crowded out.   When I say moral, I mean morality based upon religion.   We cannot build a system of morality on any other than a religious basis.   We have gone too far in allowing religion to be eliminated from our schools.   I would not have religion taught by public school teachers, but all sects and creeds should have equal opportunity to furnish at their own expense to students whose parents desire it, such instruction not to interfere with the hours of school. Our people will be better citizens and stronger for their work if along with the trained mind there is also an awakened moral sense."

In a recent report of the Interchurch Movement, based on a survey of American Education, prevailing conditions that now threaten the safety of State and Church are openly imputed to the neglect of religious training of childhood and youth in the schools. This deficiency in religious education on the part of the Evangelical sects is called by the authors of the report "Protestantism's weakest spot." Emphatic endorsement is given to the "denominational school" and full credit is not denied to the emphasis placed upon religious teaching in schools by the Catholic Church.

"It would be absolute madness," said Cardinal Bourne, at an Educational meeting in Edinburgh, "on the part of any civil authority at the present day to spurn and reject the educational assistance and educational power the Catholic Church was willing and ready to place at their disposal."

In our own country, the urgent necessity of introducing religion in our public school is now for every serious-minded Canadian an agonizing problem. How many attempts have been made to solve it? Was it not the principal topic discussed at the Educational Conference of Winnipeg (1919)?

The neutral school, we conclude, has been weighed and found wanting. The hand-writing is on the wall of every country where the experiment has been made and tells the same tale. *Facts* and *principles* give reason to our "Separate Schools."

.　　　.　　　.　　　.　　　.

Why "Separate Schools?"—Because it is our *right* and our *duty* to have them.—This is our simple and straightforward answer to the ever renascent objection of those who are not of our opinion. That *right* rests on the solid rock of Justice, of History and of Religion; that *duty* we owe to our children, to ourselves, to our Church, and to our country.

CHAPTER IX.

A WINDOW IN THE WEST*

*A Crusade for Better Schools in Saskatchewan—
Its Lessons: an Invitation and a Warning.*

"A WINDOW in the West!"—This was the suggestive title given to a course of pedagogical studies instituted in a Folk High-School of Denmark. The object of this course was to promote the study of these English and American educational ideals which Denmark may assimilate with profit. They looked to the West for light!

May we be allowed also to open here, in this Educational Conference. . . . "A Window in the West." Through that window will come to you the bright vision of the educational activities of our Western Provinces, and, with that vision, I hope, the sunny and breezy atmosphere of new and progressive ideas. I will limit my present remarks to a brief sketch of what was known in Saskatchewan as the *"Better School Movement."* This educational movement has an interesting history and carries with it a very profitable lesson. As the object of this Conference is to forward the cause of education in this part of our great Dominion, we thought it would be both interesting and instruc-

*This chapter is the substance of a lecture given in Antigonish, N.S., at the Educational Conference, Aug. 11, 1919.

tive to hear that history and learn that lesson that comes to us from beyond the Great Lakes.

The West, we know too well, has many things yet to learn from the East; but good old Mother East should at times forget "what has been"—and consider more "what is to be." In many points her growing western daughters can give her helpful suggestions. Moreover this exchange of ideas in an immense Dominion like ours is, we claim, absolutely necessary to keep the mental equilibrium between East and West. There are let us not forget it, many other problems beside the tariff problem which are widening the breach, deepening the chasm between these two sections of our Country. True patriotism demands co-opera-tion, and not antagonism, between these two main sectors of that immense firing line, which is flung between the Atlantic and the Pacific.

1. *History.*—The history of the "Better School Movement" in Saskatchewan is not very old, but, like the vegetation on the western prairies had a rapid and healthy growth. It crowded into a few years a whole epoch of the educational life of the Province. On June 22, 1915, the Hon. W. Scott, then Premier and Minister of Education, made his epochal speech which launched the idea of a reform movement. The object of this movement was the re-adjustment of the school system, of its curriculum and administration, to conditions exist-ing throughout the Province. The people of Sas-

katchewan were invited to constitute themselves a grand committee of the whole on education, to study facts and to suggest means.   This invitation of the keen-sighted Premier was accepted by the people without any distinction of race, creed or language.   The leader of the Opposition indorsed the idea and pledged the support of his party. This non-partisan movement crystallized itself in the "Saskatchewan Public Education League" which was formed at the general meeting of delegates from all over the Province, held in Regina, in Sept., 1916.   The league became a forum for the expression of public opinion.   The newspapers of the Province gave wide publicity to the new movement and threw open their columns to a public discussion.   Teachers' associations, inspectors' conventions, church synods, grain growers' meetings, labour unions, medical councils, trustees' conventions particularly, made school improvements a fruitful topic at all their meetings of the year.   Educational problems and reforms were in the air: never have we better understood the educational value of a publicity campaign; never have we seen it crowned with such a success. The climax of this campaign was a public holiday, June 30th, 1916; meetings were held in all the school districts of the Province, speeches were made, resolutions passed.   Public opinion had been moulded and was ready for a "Survey" and Legislation.

By order in Council, June 7th, 1917, Premier Martin, successor to Hon. W. Scott, whom ill-health had forced to retire—made definite provision for an educational Survey. "This survey is in no sense of the word an investigation; for investigations are necessarily based on assumption of some sort of misfeasance or malfeasance. It is instead a sympathetic inquiry into the schools of the people as the schools actually exist. Suggestions for enlargement and re-direction are made throughout."

These are the very terms of Dr. Foght's report to the Government. This specialist in rural school practice, of the Bureau of Education, Washington, was engaged in this survey from August to November, 1917. His report was dated Jan. 20, 1918. At the session of that year it was submitted to Parliament and served as the basis of new legislation. Its reading will prove most interesting to friends of education, and most suggestive in the outlining of new policies of administration and in the remodelling of the curriculum.

II. *Lesson.*—This Saskatchewan Crusade for better schools carries with it a pointed lesson. In our humble estimation and from our view-point this lesson is a call for action; at the same time it sounds a warning.

1. *An Invitation.*—There is nothing, we believe, nothing more inviting than the readiness of our Western Provinces in dealing with prob-

lems.   Here we have a beautiful example of that boldness of western youth, so confident in its resources, so optimistic in its views.

Like the West, let us diagnose our educational problems; a survey of prevailing conditions will show facts and figures.   Let us see and admit the truth; camouflage is a poor policy in matters of such importance.

This diagnosis will naturally suggest remedies. Although there are certain standards in education, which are as stable as human nature itself, nevertheless, we must not forget that the human mind is a living thing—ever re-adjusting itself to environments that various factors have created.   This re-adjustment of our methods in teaching and of our policies in administration, we know, is a very delicate process.   But it has to be done and done rightly if education is not to be a misnomer.

This re-adjustment will demand the co-operation of the educational expert and the masses.   The expert has his ear to the ground, his hand on the pulse to grasp the trend of human thought.   He walks ahead to blaze the way.   To find or, at least, to train specialists to direct the forward march is the easiest part of the problem.   The greatest difficulty in all great movements is to overcome the profound and widespread indifference of the masses.   Yet through this co-operation of the people will come the only valuable and permanent reforms.   Without it our experts will court failure.

Two initial tasks impose themselves if we wish to enlist in this great educational movement the sympathies of the people: 1. To arouse interest in local communities. 2. To organize individual and group action.

A wide publicity campaign (in the papers, by means of lectures, distribution of literature, in season and out of season) is the only means of arousing the people from their apathy. It takes time to see the ideas of leaders and experts filter down into the lower strata of society. Yet we should always have faith in the mastery of ideas, in the ultimate triumph of truth and right.

The organization of units for a concerted action is a work of time and patience. Like the incoming tide it creeps in. This will suppose, to be efficient, a recognized leader and an established and well thought-out plan. This should be the definite result of this conference.

2. *Warning.*—But all is not gold in the El Dorado of the West. Many schemes and laws have its lustre; but they have the brassy sound of the neo-pagan state-monopoly ideal. This thought of the supremacy of State in matters of education permeates Dr. Foght's report from cover to cover. In general, legislation is looked upon in our new Provinces as the universal panacea for all evils. The West is the land of experimental legislation. In this we should not imitate our younger sisters. Let us beware of fads! Let us never forget that

legislation, to be just and beneficial, should but help the individual and the family in the forwarding of their true interest and in the protection of their inalienable rights.

This extent of State Monopoly is noticeable in two of the most important recommendations of Dr. Foght's report. They are the enlargement of school districts, so that the limits of the district will coincide with those of the municipality, and the consolidation of rural schools. Reasons of better administration and great efficiency, no doubt, militate in favour of this change. Particularly "Consolidation" is on a working basis in many Provinces. But the great danger we see in this change is the placing of primary schools further away from the influence of the parents. The school ceases, to a great extent, to be "the extension of the home." The control of the parents is less direct. The doors are wide open to State interference.

These are the lessons we may take from the "Better School Movement" in Saskatchewan. Let us accept the invitation and heed the warning.

.   .   .   .   .

One parting word.—Let the people of Nova Scotia be up and doing! The West is draining the East to its advantage. Your sons and daughters are doing the thinking for those new Provinces and creating another Dominion beyond our Lakes. If conditions are not changed, the Provinces "down by the sea" will lose their influence and cease to play their part around the family table of our vast Dominion. "Light comes from the East"—our Maritime people will proudly claim. "Yes! . . . and it travels westward!" . . . answers the Westerner.

CHAPTER X.

UNICUIQUE   SUUM*

Principle on which should be Based the Division of Company-Taxes between Public and Separate Schools.

WHEN a point of law is ever before the courts it is an evident sign that the legislation governing that issue has been either defective in its basic principle or deficient in its proper application.   Such has been the case of the "Company-School-taxes" in the Provinces of Saskatchewan and Alberta.   Every court in the land has had to deal with this problem, and if legislation is not changed and placed upon a more just and solid basis, it will ever be a source of trouble for the community.

Before dealing with the merit of this school question, we beg to state that the time for co-operation in educational matters has come.   The day of wrangling and narrow conceptions has passed, we hope.   If there is a sacred liberty ever protected by the British flag it is surely that of education.— The recognition and protection of ethical and

---

*This memoir was presented to the Premier of Saskatchewan at a time when this problem was widely discussed in the Press.   As the legislation, then enacted, did not bring a satisfactory solution we thought that the argument as presented would be of service for a future date.

religious ideals are the most potent factors of the British Empire. He is a true lover of British ideals who places himself upon that higher level to judge the rights of minorities and the duties of majorities. If our Province of Saskatchewan has not known the sterile struggles of a sister Province it is because this principle has been respected and protected by our legislation. In suggesting a remedy to our laws governing Company-school-taxes, I appeal to that broad and fair minded spirit which seems to characterize our banner Province of the West. The solution we propose would give more satisfaction to the interested parties and relieve the problem of its acrimony.

.   .   .   .   .

In the Provinces of Saskatchewan and Alberta the separate schools are an integral part of the public primary educational system. They are not parochial nor private schools, but public separate schools. Their existence is not a favour conceded to the Protestant or Catholic minority, but rather, the acknowledgement of a natural and constitutional right. Therefore the separate schools come under the common law. With the purely public schools, our separate public schools share equal obligations and equal rights. The same official inspection, the same qualifications for teachers, the same curriculum of studies, the same school text-books are required in both cases by the Department of Education. Equal right to public money is recognized in the indiscriminate distribution of Government-grants.   So both schools stand side by side with equal duties and equal rights. If this point of law had been kept in view no painful issue would ever be raised; co-operation, and not antagonism, would be the aim of the community at large in the great and sublime work of education.   Hard and bitter things have been said in the press, on the platform and even in the pulpit: but they do not change a right.   Might itself cannot stamp out RIGHT.

Public service is the principle of taxation.   In return for the benefit which a business corporation derives from dealings with the public, distributive justice demands that part of the profits made, return to the community under the form of taxes. This feature of a business corporation makes it, I would say, *soulless*.   One goes into business not to make a profession of faith, but to make money. He deals with every one indifferently.   The dollar of a Christian or of a heathen has the same value as the dollar of a Jew.   Were a company to discriminate with the public on lines of creed the public would be justified in retaliating.

Public utility, in matters of Company-taxes, is the basic principle of assessment; it should also be the reason of their equitable distribution.   As the money of the public goes to Companies, irrespective of creed, so also should the taxes of these Com-

panies come back to the community, irrespective
of creed.   As Companies are assessed in school
matters for the *benefit of the children* of the community, the proceeds of the assessment should be
therefore divided—*not according to the faith of
the shareholders of the company, but according to
the number of children in each school district.*
And as the majority rules, the school district in
the majority should strike the rate of taxation for
both districts.

.   .   .   .   .

The division of Company-taxes according to
the faith of the shareholders is *neither just, nor
practical.*   It is not *just* for the reason we have
brought forward.   The principle involved in the
present law is *just when the individual is concerned,* especially when the individual is the father
of a family.   As such, one has a right to support
the school which his conscience obliges him to
support.   This natural right, our present law
recognizes.   *But in the case of a company the
principle of public utility and not the test of faith
should be invoked, we believe.*

This present law governing Company-taxes is
not *practical.*   The onus is on the Separate School-
Board to enlist each year the sympathies of the
companies.   Before how many Boards of Directors
is the matter brought up?   The local manager is
the one who deals with the problem, and he often
is a stranger to the laws of the Province, with no

sympathy for separate schools. Facts, stubborn facts, are there to prove our contention. In no city of the Province of Saskatchewan is the Separate School Board getting its part of Company-taxes. This is one of the reasons why our rate is often so high when compared with the Public School rate, and why our Boards are crippled in their finances.

. . . . .

This simple reasoning should appeal to every fair-minded man. This change of legislation we advocate in the matter of Company-taxes, is not a favour we beg—but the mere recognition of a principle of distributive justice we ask.

NOTE. 1. The argument as presented herein is still stronger when applied to Companies of public utilities such as tramways, express companies, etc., for their nature and profits depend absolutely on the public.

NOTE. 2. SCHOOL LAW OF QUEBEC PROVINCE IN THE MATTER. No. 2892.

"When immovable property of such corporations and companies is within a territory, placed under the administration of two corporations of school commissioners of different religious beliefs, established in virtue of Article 2590, the corporation which comprises the greatest number of rate-payers entered on the valuation roll, shall be bound to levy the taxes affecting such property and to divide the same proportionately to the number of children from five to sixteen years of age residing in each municipality." —62 V. c. 28, s. 399.

CHAPTER XI.

DREAM OR REALITY*

Higher Education in Western Canada—Duty of the Hour—University Training Condition of Genuine Leadership—For Catholics Higher Education means Higher Catholic Education—The Concerted Action of all Catholics in Western Canada can make a Western Catholic University a Reality.

NEVER has the world manifested a keener and more general interest in higher education. The facilities which Governments offer to place within the reach of the mass of the people; the benefits of university education; the enormous sums left by wealthy individuals for the endowment of chairs and the foundation of scholarships; the eagerness with which these offers are grasped by men of all classes; the extraordinary success of the Overseas University in the American Army, which had a student body of 10,000—these are, without doubt, manifest signs of public opinion on the matter of higher education. The world-struggle, we all feel, has shifted to another battlefield, and the future in every realm of human activity rests on the mastery of ideas. In that intellectual

*This chapter appeared as a series of articles, in the North West Review of Winnipeg,—under the signature of "Miles Christi."

conflict, the primary school rooms are the trenches on the first line of defence; the college and university lecture halls stand out as the strategic heights from which the heavy artillery of ideas smashes the way to victory. Hold the college and university heights to-day, and the hinterland of industry, commerce, science, art and politics will be yours to-morrow.

Catholics throughout our Dominion begin to realize that higher education is the price of leadership. "Of the many points of contact between the Church and the modern world, education is the point where Catholicism has most to gain by energetic thought and action, and most to lose by an atmosphere of indifference." We are waking up from our deep lethargy and beginning to understand that we shall not have our share in the shaping of the destinies of our own Country until our leaders, particularly among the laity, impose themselves upon the nation by their number and their value. The magnificent campaign of the "Antigonish Casket" in favour of higher education and the exchange of views this point at issue brought from various correspondents, the successful drive in favour of Loyola College of Montreal, the growing influence of the Catholic student bodies in the various universities, the creation of Laval, in Montreal, as a distinct unit from Quebec; the tremendous success this newly born organization met with in its drive for $5,000,000; all these facts indicate concentration of forces in the direction of higher education. The national Catholic conscience is awakened into action. "One of the most pressing needs of the Church at the present time, is to have a well-connected body of university-trained Catholics." This statement of Father Plater, S.J., is true also for Canada and more particularly for Western Canada. And indeed, this pressing need of higher education has come home of late to our western Catholics as is evidenced by the great efforts made to establish colleges in the various Provinces. As this move is of the greatest importance for the welfare of the Church in that promising part of our country, we thought to be of some service to the Western Church in drawing the attention of Catholics to this important issue and bringing to a focus certain indefinite, hazy views on the subject.

Higher Education—Duty of the Hour for Western Catholics.

"When a reflective man of middle life walks along the embowered paths of Oxford and Cambridge or through their quadrangles whose walls have echoed to the footsteps of so many brainy men of England, he realizes what these institutions have been and still are to Great Britain and the Empire." From the lecture halls of these seats of learning have gone, generation after generation, the men who framed and directed the course of

studies of other universities, the legislators and
statesmen that have shaped the destinies of the
British Empire. "There is not a feature or a point
in the national character which has made England
great among the nations of the world, that is not
strongly developed and plainly traceable in our
universities.   For eight hundred or a thousand
years they have been intimately associated with
everything that has concerned the highest interest
of the country."   (W. E. Gladstone.)   This
example of the power of Oxford and Cambridge
is so typical that one immediately grasps its
meaning and appreciates its full value.   On that
immense background of the Empire they stand out
indeed in bold relief as the embodiment of higher
education, as the great portals that open on the
highway of true leadership.   Is not the affiliation,
that subtle intellectual bond which units our universities of Canada to those two great seats of
learning, a permanent and living proof of this
fact?

A university is the vital centre of a nation's
life.   Around it, by a gradual process of elimina-
tion and a natural force of gravitation, centre the
master minds; from it, as from a fountain-head,
flow with true leadership in every branch of human
society, progress, wealth and prosperity.   On the
force of this *centripetal* and *centrifugal* movement
of a university depends its value in the community.
"The increase in number and efficiency of uni-

versities," said Bishop Spalding, "is the healthy proof of the vitality and energy of a nation."

In the educational system of a country the university stands out as the apex, the culminating and crowning point of its intellectual life. For, as the college course develops the studious and acquisitive powers of the mind, the university course has in view its creative and formative powers. "Glorious to most are the days of life in a great school," says Morley, "but it is at college that aspiring talents enter into their own inheritance." "It is the function of education in the highest sense, to teach man that there are latent in him possibilities beyond what he has dreamed of, and to develop in him capacities of which without contact with the highest learning, he had never become aware." (Haldane.) We may well call the university "the brains of a nation." It equips the student with standards and tests of objective truth. . . . It makes him dig down to the bed-rock on which truth in its various manifestations rests. . . . Universities are indeed the nurseries of the higher life, the living sources from which knowledge and culture flow in abundant streams. They do the thinking for the teeming masses who have neither the leisure nor the opportunity to think for themselves and who live on that mental atmosphere we call "public opinion." From the heights of our universities, ideas and principles gradually filter down into the lower strata of the nation. The novel, the Sunday supplement, the stage, the cinema screen—these post-graduate courses of the working man—are popularizing to-day the theories and ideals that were yesterday honoured in our secular institutions of higher education. It may take time, perhaps centuries, for this process of intellectual filtration; but ideas, like the stream, are bound to follow the incline of the water-shed.

If the change that takes place in the mind and conscience of the individual is a slow and subtle process, what should we not expect when there is question of a nation? Yes, the process is slow but it is sure. The permeation of evolutionism into every domain of human thought is a recent and most striking illustration of it. This fact stands out conspicuously on the pages of history. "Lord Acton's view of history," said Shane Leslie, "was that ideas, not men or events, made the differences between one era and the next." The mind is always the storm centre of revolutions, the breeding ground of the most conflicting theories. The great storms that sweep over humanity always gather on the high summits of religion and philosophy, blackening the mental horizon; sooner or later, they break out on the lower plains of the economic social and political world, spreading everywhere revolution and destruction. The blasphemous Proudhon gave utterance to a great truth when he wrote: "It is surprising how at the bottom of every political problem we always find some theology involved." We lay stress upon this aspect of universities, for, in our mind, from a catholic view-point, it is of the greatest importance in the discussion of the present issue.

The university is not only the focus of the intellectual life of a country; by its research work, by its applied science it becomes also the very fountain head of all national progress and prosperity. The natural resources lie dormant, the soil—that perennial source of wealth, is stagnant, the export-trade of manufactured goods and agricultural products is at its lowest ebb, until touched by the magic wand of the university expert. It is he who discovers, develops and shows how to make use of with profit, the hidden wealth of the land. The research bureaus instituted by the Government of Canada and the United States, co-operating with the various universities, are now considered as the most important factors of national prosperity. The Reclamation Service of the U.S. by irrigation, drainage and the pulling of stumps will reclaim nearly 300 million acres for colonization. To bring the economic value of a university nearer home to us, who does not know the beneficial influences of Saskatoon University on the agricultural pursuits of Saskatchewan? This relation of the university and the material prosperity of a country is so marked that the Mosely Educational Commission sent by England to the United States, most strongly emphasized that living connection and necessary correlation between the universities and the industrial and manufacturing prosperity of the United States.

A university is therefore not a mere luxury, but rather a necessary asset in a nation's life. "The development of the true spirit of the University among a people is a good measure of the development of its soul, and consequently of its civilization" (Haldane). "No country," we will conclude with "Catholic" in the Antigonish Casket, "ever attained to any degree of political influence, nor have any people ever risen from a lower to a higher level of intellectual and social culture, without the light and inspiration that flow from a genuine university." This vision was before the eyes of Cecil Rhodes who founded scholarships throughout the British Empire. These scholarships glean every year in the wide fields of the Empire the brightest minds and throw them as a beautiful sheaf at the foot of the great English Alma Mater, Oxford. Millions and millions have been left for the same purpose to the American Universities.

The university may well then be called the Alma Mater—the nursing mother, of the leaders of a nation. From its halls "emerge those who have that power of command which is born of penetrating insight. Such a power generally carries in its train the gift of organization, and organization is one of the foundations of national strength." (Lord Haldane.) The belief that the self-made men were the real successful men is a thing of the past. A careful investigation has proved that ninety per cent of the men who stood at the head of large financial, political, philanthropic, economic, industrial and commercial institutions of the world were graduates of universities.* The self-made man as a leader is the exception and has necessarily his limitations which he is the first to feel and acknowledge. Munsterberg in his book "The Americans" has a page which is very much to the point. "The most important factor of the aristocratic differentiation of America is higher Education and culture and this becomes more important every day. The social importance ascribed to a college graduate is all the time growing. It was kept back for a long time by unfortunate prejudices. Because other than intellectual forces had made the nation strong, and everywhere in the foreground of public activity there were vigorous and influential men who had not continued their education beyond the public grammar school, so the masses instinctively believed that insight, real energy and enterprise were better developed in the school of life than in the world of books. The college student was thought a weakling, in a way, who might have fine theories, but who would never help to solve the great national problems—a sort of academic "mug-

---

*"Less than one per cent. of American men are college graduates Yet this one per cent. of college graduates has furnished: 55% of our Presidents, 36% of our Members of Congress, 47% of the Speakers of the House, 54% of our Vice-Presidents, 62% of our Secretaries of State, 50% of the Secretaries of the Treasury, 67% of the Attorney Generals, 69% of the Justices of the Supreme Court."—Dr. Jones, of the University of Missouri.

wump," but not a leader. The banking house, factory, farm, the mine, law office and the political position were thought better places for the young (American) man than the college lecture halls. . . . This has profoundly changed now, and changes more, with every year. . . . The change has taken place in regard to what is expected of the college student; distrust has vanished and people realize that the *intellectual discipline* which he has had until his twenty-second year in the artificial and ideal world is after all the best training, less by its subject-matter than by its methods, is the best possible preparation for practical activity. . . . The leading positions are almost entirely in the hands of men of academic training and the mistrust of the theorizing college spirit has given place to a situation in which university presidents and professors have much to say on all practical questions of public life, and the college graduates are the real supporters of every movement toward reform and civilization." (Munsterberg—"The Americans" 600-602.)

The true *leaders* in society are like the snow-capped heights of a mountain range: they are the first that the new light of a breaking dawn, of a coming period, is wont to strike with its rays, to be then reflected on the silent and sleeping valleys.

The men who hold to-day the pen or draughting pencil in the university are the men who will handle the levers of the world's intricate machinery. There they grapple with the various problems of the scientifical, economic and political world and their views, later on, will gradually influence the whole mental attitude of the masses, who, in their daily life, are confronted with these same problems.

This leadership of *thought* and *action* is no more the privilege of a few; in our democratic country every one can aspire to it. The days when primary education was for the masses, secondary or college education for the middle classes and university training for "the quality," have passed away and gradually the benefits of higher education are being extended to all. The *equality of opportunity,* not that of wealth and position, is *the test of true democracy.* This condition has created the aristocracy of brains and character before which the aristocracy of wealth, of blood and lineage fade into insignificance.

The predominance of the "vocational feature" over the "cultural" in the scope of our modern universities, the vast "extension work"* carried on in the various fields, the multiplicity of "free scholarships" open o the competition of the brainy

---

*Lord Haldane addressing the Co-operative Educational Association (May, 1920) made this statement: "The universities of England must be made able, as national institutions, with a larger range of activitiy than at present, to undertake extra-mural work on a scale so great that it will be of general application throughout the land, and they must be put in a position to be fitted to bring this about."

and ambitious boy, are other proofs of this democratic trait of our modern higher education.

.   .   .   .   .

Since higher education is the stepping stone to
leadership, the question most vital to Catholics in
this particular and most momentous period of our
history is: "What share have we in the college and
university life of the country?" "The progress of
the Church in any country is attributable to the
indwelling Spirit which guides the Church.—
Next, to the piety, zeal and education of its *priest-
hood,*—and lastly, though in no mean degree, to
the devotion, activity and education of the *laity*.
Where these three features combine, then the
Church is writing the brightest pages of Her history." (Archbishop Glennon.)

I will not repeat here what "Catholic" in the
Antigonish Casket, and Henry Somerville in
his pamphlet, "Higher education and Catholic
Leadership in Canada"—have been writing on for
the past year or so. With them we conclude that
outside of the Province of Quebec, the Catholics of
the Dominion have not the influence they should
wield. Naturally there are many reasons to explain this fact. But we will say with the Editor of
the North West Review, "facts cannot be ignored
with impunity, the sooner they are admitted and
faced with courage the more readily shall difficulties be overcome. And the necessity for an awakening to the demand for higher education is very
real."

In the firing line of the world's gigantic struggle we shall never hold the strategic points to which our number gives us a right in our Canadian Democracy, unless our leaders are strong in number, and in power. Catholic leadership will give us the occasion to present, explain and promote "our solution" to various problems confronting the world. During this period of universal upheaval and momentous crisis, when all the ingredients, we would say of the social and economic fabric are in a state of flux,—like bronze in fusion,—Catholic leaders should be to the front to supply the casts of Christian civilization. If in the public press, the legislative assemblies, the labor meetings, public gatherings, where mind meets mind, ideal clashes with ideal, knowledge with knowledge, where facts are being examined and weighed, where ideas are thrown into the melting pot of public debate, if then and there, there is no one to stand for Catholic views in the various matters under discussion, can we be astonished that we are absolutely ignored, and our views not considered? "We believe that an attitude of merely destructive criticism, of aloofness, scepticism, pessimism, is a deplorable mistake. It is not by standing aloof from the movements of our day, but by going fearlessly into them with the message of truth entrusted to our charge, shall we best fulfil our high mission towards our fellow countrymen. We must seize these opportunities in the spirit of high confidence

and dauntless zeal which befits those who have
the Truth, know they have the Truth, and are
assured that the Truth is great and shall prevail."
(Universe—June 13, 1919.)

Never has a greater opportunity challenged
the Church and her leaders than at this great turning of the tide in the history of the world. Canada
itself is on the threshold of the most eventful and
decisive period of her national life. "The war has
brought our country into the broad stream of inter-
nationalism . . . and a new *national consciousness* is being born and is sweeping over the land."
In the future, as in the past, our Dominion will
remain divided by race and creed. But let us not
forget that the various religious and ethnical
groups will have only the influence that gives true
leadership. The value and the measure of higher
education among Catholics will therefore give the
value and the measure of their participation in the
remodelling of their great country.

If such is the case of Catholics throughout Canada, what would we not say of Catholics in our
Western Provinces. In this reconstruction of our
Dominion the prairie Provinces are without doubt
to play a preponderant part. One has only to open
his eyes to see the trend of our national policies,
and immediately grasp the growing importance of
our Western Provinces. The West is gradually
passing from the pioneer conditions and becoming
conscious of its importance. With the beautiful

qualities and unlimited resources of youth, it has also its dangerous shortcomings. Daring, venturous, over confident, the western mind is easily and frequently hasty and radical in its conclusions. Intoxicated with wealth and success, inspired and aroused by the great possibilities of his new home, the Westerner is ever tempted to experiment in legislation, make extreme views prevail and believe the newest is always the best. He will boast of broadmindedness, of love of freedom and at the same time will, under the deceiving tyranny of number, suppress the most sacred rights. Nowhere we claim in our Dominion, is Catholic leadership and therefore higher education, more needed at the present hour than in the West. Our Catholics there need indeed higher education, for, at this hour particularly, the nation's business is our business; they cannot remain an isolated factor in presence of the tremendous issues that stare the world and our country in the face. But if we wish to make our influence as Catholics felt, let our leadership come from *"Higher Catholic Education"* as from its fountain head.

Higher Catholic Education for Catholics in Western Canada.

There is a decided distinction between higher education for Catholics and higher Catholic education. This leads us to place before the reader the principles upon which rests the catholic ideal

in matters of higher education and to suggest
means of its speedy realization in Western Canada.
A friendly exchange of ideas on this most important and very interesting topic will be profitable
to all at this juncture, and help, we hope, to clear
up hazy notions and cloudy conceptions which
some may entertain on the subject.

.   .   .   .   .

In matters of Catholic education, the most
weighty argument is that of the authority of the
Church. Her views and practices, particularly on
questions of education, should be the views and
practices of every good Catholic. In the New
Canon-Law, in the Councils and Letters of the
Popes, is to be found the only authoritative direction in this momentous problem. The Church is
most emphatic and most precise in its pronounce-
ments on the matter of higher education. The
Canon 1379, paragraph 2, of the new Canon-Law,
is very explicit on the subject. "If the public universities are not imbued with Catholic doctrine
and surrounded with a Catholic atmosphere, it is
most desirable to found in that country or region a
Catholic University." The Plenary Councils of
Baltimore and of Quebec (Tit, VI-C, VII) command in the most pressing manner the Catholic
youth to frequent only Catholic universities.
When circumstances necessitate attendance at non-
Catholic universities, safeguards are exacted to
minimize the danger. These recent dispositions

of the Church's legislation reflect the stand the Church has always taken on this ground of higher education. Is She not *"Mater universitatum?"* Modern civilization owes its universities to the Catholic Church, as the very stones of Cambridge and Oxford still proclaim . . . *lapides clamabunt!* And in these days of religious indifference, after heroic efforts and great sacrifices, in spite of the allurement of our wealthy state and independent institutions, the Church counts in every country seats of higher learning, where her children may receive the benefit of university training without danger for their conscience or their faith.

This stand of the Church in primary, secondary and higher education is the logical conclusion of her doctrine. "The theory of life," said Father Little, S.J., "and the theory of education go hand in hand." As the Church has a definite teaching on life, its value and its purpose, She has necessarily fundamental principles upon which education must rest if it wishes to be in harmony with Christian life and Catholic belief. In her eyes education, in all its degrees, must be primarily and profoundly religious. "If indeed, the Catholic Faith which makes such tremendous and such confident statements about God and His ways with men, is true, then obviously it takes the central place in human knowledge, and all other knowledge groups itself round and is coloured by Faith." Therefore, the principle, "every Catholic boy and girl in a

Catholic college or university" should be to us as sacred as is "every Catholic child in a Catholic school." One is the consequence of the other; both are the practical conclusions of our faith. This close connection between theories of education and the attitude towards problem of life is evident in history.

The Pope, Benedict XV, in his recent letter to the American Hierarchy (March, 1919), writes: "The future of the Church and State absolutely depends on the condition and organization of the schools; there will be no other Christians than those whom you will have formed by instruction and education. . . . We have followed with joy," he adds, *"the marvellous progress of the Catholic University at Washington, progress so closely united to the highest hopes of your churches.* We have no doubt that henceforth you will continue even more actively, to support an institution of such great usefulness and promise as is the University."

The Most Reverend Dr. O'Dwyer, Bishop of Limerick, in 1904, vindicated for the Irish people not the privilege, but the right to a Catholic University. "For us Catholics," he wrote, "the Gospel as taught by our Holy Church, is our philosophy of life and we hold that any attempt to educate a youth in what we call secularism is a retrogression to a lower level than that of pre-Christian culture. For this reason we have withstood every attempt to force *secularism* on this country and we shall resist it to the last. We have equally withstood *mixed education*, which, false as it is in itself and pernicious, is in this country a specious pretext for Protestant educational ascendancy."   (University education in Ireland.)

If such is the case with Catholic Ireland, what should we not conclude as regards our Western Provinces?   Here, more than anywhere else in Canada, does the Church need staunch, genuine, Catholic leadership.   In it the future of Catholicity beyond the Great Lakes is involved.   Reason and experience prove that the training which makes for genuine Catholic influence is plainly out of question unless it be received in a college and university whose atmosphere, teachings, aspirations and ideals are thoroughly Catholic.   The recent foundations of a Catholic University in Milan and in Nimeguen, Holland, justify this claim.

.   .   .   .   .

Conditions existing in our modern neutral universities vindicate our stand and strengthen our position.   The tendency in these universities is, without doubt, towards infidelity or to say the least, towards diluted Christianity.—"The transformation from the old denominational education to the new undenominational education was in point of fact due to an antitheological—and even in some of its manifestations—anti-religious movement.   If it included a sense of the justice of equal treatment for all creeds and a sense of the liberty necessary

for science, it also included some of the anti-
Christian spirit of Continental liberalism.   The
undenominational movement was the practical expression of the liberal and scientific movement."
(Life of Newman—L 306.)

A few years ago there appeared in the "Cosmopolitan Review," under the glaring title "Blasting
at the Rock of Ages," an article which startled the
intellectual world.   It was a crude and biting ex-
posure of the intellectual license and unhealthy
moral atmosphere of the great American universities.   To follow the author of this powerful indictment in the proof of his facts and statements
would be beyond the scope of this paper.   Only we
would advise some of our near-sighted Catholics
who through that snobbishness which money often
gives them, have a sort of worship for non-Catholic
universities, to read this indictment.   In giving
them a glance of the "inside of the cup" it may
change their opinion.

Dr. James Henry Leuba, professor of psychology at the Bryn Mawr College, Pennsylvania, gave
out to the public the answers he received from
sociologists, biologists, psychologists and teachers
of universities and other institutions in the United
States, as regards their belief in the existence of
God.   More than fifty per cent. admitted that they
had no belief whatever in the existence of God;
forty per cent. denied the immortality of the soul.
The great majority, said Dr. Leuba, were univer-

sity teachers and none could compare with them in influence over the rising generation. (Cfr. Archeological Report 1917—published by Ontario Government.)

When subversive theories based on an absolute materialistic conception of life, and from which God, Divine Providence, Christ, Christianity are systematically excluded and ridiculed as myths of by-gone days; when, we say, such theories are rampant in the halls of our modern universities, should we be astonished to see outright infidelity, political socialism, religious anarchy, stalk the length and breadth of the land? "Impurity, obscenity, moral corruption in many forms, with the ever consequent cynicism and pessimism, forerunners of moral decadence, destruction of the original, creative, shaping, joyous, confident energies of society, come daily more boldly to the front of the stage and defy criticism or mock at the archaic sanctions of yesterday. One does not need to peruse the great modern historians of Roman morals to foresee the results of such an educational debauch, when allowed time enough and the working of its own, unholy but intimate and inexorable logic." (Mgr. Shahan—at the Catholic Educational Convention, U.S., 1919.) Sow the wind, you will reap the whirlwind.

Should not such atmosphere of infidelity or diluted Christianity in non-Catholic universities be for Catholic students a source of danger to the vigour and even to the integrity of their faith, to their constancy, in the full and faithful observance of their practical religious duties? Familiarity with error, at the age of youth principally, breeds contempt of truth and jeopardizes faith. The suppression of truth in its various forms, the concealment of religious profession and observance, necessarily lead to religious indifference. How many sad examples could we not give to back this statement? This danger which Catholic youth meets with in the very atmosphere of our neutral universities is still greater when we consider the method of teaching now in honour in these schools of higher learning. The tutorial method, still in vogue at Oxford, has given place to the *professorial*. The systematic lecture has replaced the exposition of texts. The professor, with his frame of mind, his views on facts and ideas, is the living book from which our youth read their daily lesson. His personality dominates the mind of the pupil. We all know what fascination the science, reputation and eloquence of a professor have on the unarmed and impressionable minds of youth. The *"Magister dixit"* is very often the supreme law, the last criterion of truth. President Garfield's ideal of a college, "Mark Hopkins on the other end of the log," recognizes the educative value of the contact with a master-mind.

Authority and reason militate in favor of higher Catholic education for Catholics in Western

Canada, this is the logical conclusion of our statements.

.   .   .   .   .

Yes, nice theories, some may say; but we are facing facts. How are we to contend with these well equipped, richly endowed, neutral institutions of higher education? Where shall we find the resources to pay efficient teachers, to establish the various faculties that go to form a university worthy of its name? Have we not a state-university marvellously well equipped and for which our Provinces are yearly spending fabulous sums? Why not take advantage of our own money that goes in taxes for the support of these institutions?

To argue along these lines is to concede to our enemies our position on the Separate School question. All these objections have been met with in other countries and other provinces, and the answer to them was the creation of Catholic colleges and universities.

The great fallacy of the age, and particularly in this part of the country, is State Monopoly in educational matters. This is looked upon as the great triumph of modern democracy and the palladium of liberty. The monopoly over the human mind by this monopoly of education is the most dangerous of all state-monopolies. It is the resurrection of the pagan ideal, the magnification of the state to the detriment and absorption of the individual and the family. Germany has given us an example of where "the standardization of thought and outlook" by the State education leads to. The Prussian ideal, in its last analysis, is nothing else but the pagan ideal.

But no country in the British Empire has pushed the policy of monopolisation of education so far as our Western Provinces. Under the specious plea of efficiency and absurd reason of uniformity, they will not even grant charters to independent institutions of higher learning. This policy surely does not reflect true statesmanship and makes British liberty a misnomer on the lips of many of our ultra-loyal Westerners. We would ask our Western Governments to take lessons in this matter from England. When some few years ago the question of converting the university colleges into Universities was before the English public there was much talk of the danger of Lilliputian universities and of low standards of teaching and examination. But this question was brought to trial by the State before a high tribunal and a firm decision was given in favour of the principle. A special committee of the Privy Council conducted a semi-judicial enquiry and gave sentence on Febr., 1903. The result of this decision was that the colleges of Liverpool, Manchester, Leeds, Sheffield, Birmingham, Bristol, Durham, blossomed out into teaching universities. This is the real British way of doing things.

The United States* have granted university charters to the various Catholic institutions of higher learning which dot that land of Liberty from coast to coast. And let us not forget,—facts and figures will bear us out,—the independent universities in the United States, in England and in Belgium, only to mention some, have been in many Faculties more efficient and more successful than the state institutions. The remarkable record of St. Louis University, a Jesuit institution, is illustrative of this point. A comparison of the respective medical and dental records of this institution with perhaps two of the greatest professional schools of the United States, John Hopkins and Harvard, gives proof of higher efficiency to St. Louis University. The official bulletins of the Medical Dental Associations give the statistics.

The right of Catholics to their own schools— primary, secondary, university, is a birthright we must always fight for. It is the elementary right of a civilized people to educate her sons as she sees fit. In the battle for this right the best strategy is to offer the accomplished fact of a college and

---

*Speaking of Publicly and privately supported institutions of learning in the U.S., Dr. Cappen, assistant commissioner of the United States Bureau of Education, stated that there are 93 of the former in the U.S. and 477 of the latter. About 62 per cent. of the college students in the country attend voluntarily supported colleges, and the private schools have about 68 per cent. of the educational funds of the country at their disposal. This includes of course such very wealthy endowed institutions as Harvard, Princeton, Yale, Cornell and Stanford,

a university which by their efficiency, their intellectual and moral value, impose themselves upon the community and win their way to acceptance. Let us blaze the trail and to-morrow, it will be the great highway of Catholic education for the coming generation in Western Canada.

But instead of this policy of *"isolation"* which in school matters is the ordinary policy of the Church, some Catholics, in view of circumstances, rather advocate that of *"permeation."* The presence of Catholics in State Universities will, they claim, create a better atmosphere, abate or soften prejudice, beget a better feeling among the future leaders of the community. In England, it is true, Catholics are allowed to attend Oxford and Cambridge; in Germany, they attend State Universities. The Catholics of Australia have since 1916 also a College in conjunction with the Melbourne State University. Student societies have been formed, Catholic halls opened, courses of apologetics are given to help the Catholic youth in the "steady daily pressure working against them in a non-Catholic university," and to influence religious thought in those centres of higher learning.

Has this *"modus vivendi"* brought about by various circumstances which it would be too long to analyze here, produced the desired results? In Germany it has not created a Catholic atmosphere in one single university. Have not, on the contrary, the German universities been the hot-beds of Modernism and many a young cleric has come from their halls inoculated with this virus.

As for Oxford and Cambridge, we all know the controversy which divided the Catholics for so many years. As Catholics have been allowed to follow the courses there for only a few decades, we are not yet, we believe, in a position to judge of the influence of these universities on the Catholic body of England as a whole. Time only will tell. But one thing is certain, no comparison can be established between our state universities and these colleges. Although in the halls of Oxford, Christianity "is often attuned to the outlook and temper of the age" as the book "Foundations" (a statement of Christian belief in terms of modern thought, by seven Oxford men) sadly reveals it, nevertheless, there is not to be found in the English Colleges that atmosphere which the absence of religion has created in our state universities. The presence of various denominational colleges on the grounds of our Provincial Universities only gives them a tint of Christianity. The teaching of history and philosophy will tell the tale. "It must be remembered that an Oxford scheme was never Newman's ideal. It was a concession to necessities of the hour. His ideal scheme, alike for education of the young and for the necessary intellectual defence of Christianity, had consistently been the erection of a large Catholic University like Louvain. This he had tried to set up in Ireland.

In such an institution, *research and discussion of the questions of the day would be combined* as in the middle ages with a *Catholic atmosphere,* the personal ascendancy of able *Christian professors* and directly *religious influence* for the young men." (Life of Newman)—by Ward.

Were there question only of postgraduate work, of some special course in agriculture, domestic science, there would be no difficulty, we believe, to see Catholic students take advantage of the marvellous facilities our state universities offer. The matter, the short term of these courses or the advanced age of the pupil would be in themselves sufficient guarantee. *But what we strongly object to is the Arts Course, and particularly undergraduate work,* even were the contentious subjects, such as philosophy and history, be given by Catholic teachers to Catholic students separately. The Arts Course, we must remember, is the real dominating factor in higher education. For we maintain with Cardinal Newman that a University is a place of teaching universal knowledge and that its object is primarily intellectual. It has in view the diffusion and extension of knowledge, rather than its advancement, which is reserved to Academies. It is the Arts Course of a University, particularly its Philosophy, that gives this general knowledge and enlargement of the mind. Its influence is most telling in the various Faculties where students specialize for their future career. For Philosophy plays such a large part in *human life, the movement of opinions and the direction of minds*. The Catholic student in those most plastic years, in that critical period of receptivity, wherein ideas are analyzed and synthesized for life time, cannot help but imbibe ideas and doctrines opposed to his belief. The élite alone, we believe, can resist in the long run the influence of that indefinable quality called atmosphere, and maintain among so many cross-currents, the right course. The ordinary and inexperienced mind will be, if not contaminated, at least weakened and this alone is disastrous in a leader. Many changes, many transformations, we know, take place in the mind of youth as it emerges "from collegiate visions into the rough path of real life." As Morley wrote, "We know after the event, the tremendous changes of thought . . . of conception of life, that coming years and new historic forces were waiting to unfold before the undergraduate when he had once floated out beyond the college bar." Yet, the solid teachings of Catholic Philosophy will remain to him as the charter and compass when his ship has taken to the high sea. This is the principal reason why we vindicate the right to our own higher education. To push the argument further, we would ask why should we be obliged to pay taxes to have doctrines opposed to our conscience propounded from the professorial chairs of our State University? The granting of a Charter by the State is but the minimum of our rights.

Dream or Reality?

A Catholic University for Western Canada! Is this but the dream of a far off future or can it be a reality within a few years?—-There is the problem which now faces the Catholic Church of our Western Provinces and upon which, in our estimation, rests the influence the Church is to have in the formation of the new and most promising part of our Dominion beyond the Great Lakes. A high conception of the duty of the present hour and the whole-hearted co-operation of every Catholic unit in the West, will without doubt bring its happy solution and make our dream a reality. To act on ideal principles with little or no attempt to forecast accurately what is practicable would be to court failure. We are gradually passing the mile-stone of pioneer life in the West, and the Church is slowly but surely being organized and entering into full possession of her normal life. The duties which Catholic solidarity imposes upon us as regards the Church and the community at large are growing apace with the status of the Church in these new Provinces. Among these duties none, we believe, are more important than that we owe to the cause of Catholic education. Naturally, the burden of the responsibility falls here upon parents whose bounden duty it is to see that the school, college, university, be, as much as possible but the extension of their Catholic home. *The rising generation in the West has a right to the benefits of a higher education; to this right corresponds in the community a duty imposed upon its members by Catholic solidarity.* For in the growing youth we see the Country and the Church, with whose future welfare it is necessarily united. A true Catholic must have his vision of what the Church ought to be in his Country and must work to make that vision come true.

Through a Catholic University, and through it only, will the Church give its full *contribution to the national life of Western Canada* by creating as we said, Catholic leadership. We have as Catholics, ideas to give to the nation, to its up-building, and to its prosperity. The sun of Canadian liberty is shining for our doctrines as it does for other ideals. And, strange to say, the most subversive theories seem to take the greatest and most frequent advantage of this freedom. We have no apology to make for our ideas. They stand on their own merit and have been vindicated by the acid-test of time. To bring our message to the country, to spread its beneficial influence is the mission of our Catholic leaders. Only a large number of truly educated Catholic men are able to make their influence felt on the life and thought of a country.

This identification of a Catholic university with our Western Provinces will be an asset to our public life and beneficial to the people at large, notwithstanding their aloofness and unreasoned opposition to our principles and methods. The evils of the times are the direct result of the secularization of education. Catholic higher education is the only antidote and remedy to this evil. Its principles are a vigorous protest against materialistic philosophy. We believe in the mastery of ideas and in the final victory of truth.

The Church also for her own benefit needs true Catholic leaders. Leaders in a Catholic Community, who are not thoroughly Catholic in their training, who have false notions, warped views, biassed conceptions of vital questions, are most detrimental to the cause of Catholicity. Distorted and confused ideas, in religious matters particularly, always lead to a compromise. After school days they fail to find their Catholic faith correlated with the *problems* and *experiences* which never troubled them before, and which now, lack of higher education will not allow them to solve and to face. Have we not indeed in Western Canada to guard ourselves against latitudinarianism in our Catholic life? Material prosperity, success in business or in farming, associations with men and women who have practically no belief whatever, erroneous conceptions of broadmindedness in religious matters, absence of traditions, lack of Catholic education, all these causes and many others have created especially in our cities, where such a large floating population is to be found, and in our country places where there is no resident priest, a compromising Catholicism, apologetic Catholics. How many Catholics in the West are always ready to cringe in presence of those who are not of our belief and to apologize for their faith. To react against this abiding danger we need all through the country well instructed and thoroughly educated Catholic leaders who will be in our world of agnosticism and irreligion, the protagonists and apologists of Catholicism. The fearless proclamation of the truth combined with a good moral public life is in itself a tremendous power. Indeed, we need in all the avenues of life men whose university training will give them influence in public life. But let it never be forgotten those captains of industry, those brilliant and successful professional men, those progressive farmers—valuable as they all may be—must count more as leaders of Catholic thought than as money-makers. If not, they will be found wanting when the Church needs them the most. We emphasize this point, for in the plea for higher education very often our attention seems to be more on the successful business man than on the Catholic thinker.

Love of Church and country will therefore inspire us with a high sense of duty in relation to the establishment of a seat of higher education in this promising part of our great Dominion. And this duty, let us not forget it, *is urgent*. Every decade means a new generation that should have passed from the halls of our university to the commanding

heights of the country's leadership. Our hesitancy
means a further postponement of the triumph of
the Catholic Cause.

This high conception of an urgent duty gives
the vision. From the clearness, breadth and depth
of that vision will spring the conquering spirit of
co-operation. Co-operation to be efficient and persevering demands a united plan of action and an
authoritative leadership.

The Catholic population of Western Canada
is yet very limited. We cannot afford to scatter
our forces and multiply our institutions. One university for all Western Canada would be sufficient
to meet the present requirements. The multiplica-
tion of inefficient universities is a calamity for
genuine higher education. This has been the contention of "Catholic" in a recent series of brilliant
articles in the "Casket." The policy would therefore be for all to agree on one college as the non-
Catholics have done in the different Western Provinces. This naturally requires the sacrifice of
parochialism and provincialism. But if the
Methodists, Presbyterians and Baptists have each
agreed on the establishment of one educational
centre for their students, surely the Catholics can
also sacrifice local interests to the welfare of the
cause. How many efforts our bigoted provincialism has neutralized in the past!

Authoritative leadership only can unite our
efforts on this unity of plan of action. Nothing in

this matter can be done without the direction and support of the Hierarchy of the West. The division among Bishops was, according to Newman, one of the main causes that made the Dublin Catholic University scheme a failure. Naturally this problem of higher education is one that overflows diocesan boundaries and remains common to all. "Boundaries of jurisdiction, as wrote so advisedly, Archbishop McNeil, of Toronto, are conveniences and means to an end." Beyond the responsibilities of each separate diocese there are other responsibilities which affect the Church of Canada as a whole. Let one man with vision, judgment, energy, and action, make the creation of the Catholic University in the West the work and ambition of his life, let him have the sincere approbation and efficient co-operation of all the Hierarchy . . . that man, we claim, will rally the Catholic forces around him and will give to the West and its rising generation the blessing so much needed of Catholic university training. Newman was fond of repeating that it is only *individuals* who do great things.

And what will, this Catholic university mean to Catholic life in Western Canada? Well established upon the highest academic level by its success in the competitive field of learning, it will stand out as the embodiment of Catholic intellectual life and the centre of Catholic activities. It will be the counter-ideal to the ideal of agnosticism and materialism so fostered and so prevalent in our neutral universities. Just as the cathedrals are the expression of the Catholic faith in Christ's abiding presence in the Sacrament of His love, so is a Catholic university the embodiment and accomplishment of the Church's ideal in education. By its extension work, summer courses, circulating libraries, correspondence courses, lectures, etc., the university would unite our activities, eliminate waste of energy and direct our combined efforts. Cardinal Newman believed that a Catholic university was essential for thorough health and efficiency in the Catholic body at large. To realize all that a Catholic university would mean one has only to know what Washington stands for in the life of the Church in the United States. In his beautiful letter to the American Hierarchy, Benedict XV said of it: "The University, we trust, will be the *attractive centre* about which will gather all who love the teachings of Catholicism."

What is the Conclusion?

We may summarize our argumentation in favour of our contention in the following statements:

1.—THE INTERESTS OF CHURCH AND COUNTRY, PARTICULARLY IN THE WEST, DEMAND CATHOLIC LEADERSHIP;

2.—NO GENUINE LEADERSHIP WITHOUT UNIVERSITY TRAINING;

3.—For Catholics Higher Education means Higher Catholic Education.

Now, Patient reader, allow us to conclude these already too lengthy pages, by this pointed question: *"Is a Catholic university for Western Canada within the possibilities of the near future,"*

Our answer will be simple, direct, conclusive, and, we hope, convincing. If all Catholics in the Western Provinces, under the direction and with the continued support of the Hierarchy, unite in one sublime and persistent effort, we have the utmost confidence in its immediate realization. Some Catholics, we know, will distrust its expediency, despair of its success or even feel an obligation to oppose it. Difficulties, most undoubtedly, we will have numerous and great. With time, patience, perseverance and self-sacrifice we will overcome them. Nothing succeeds like success. The establishment of a work of that kind is the work of years and even of centuries. There must be some day a start, a foundation to build on. The policy of nihilism leads nowhere. The frequentation of our State universities would indefinitely postpone all efforts for the Catholic ideal, and be a surrender of the whole situation. But let us not be carried away with the modern fallacy of materialistic grandeur. Spacious and beautiful buildings, nice grounds and attractive surroundings are not to be despised when the finances are good. But all these things are secondary; they do not give the intrinsic value to a university, they are not "the pulse of the machine." The great business of a university is to teach; the highest academic level should be its worthy ambition. The teachers are the real makers of a seat of higher learning, they pitch high or low the standard of learning.

This great work will demand from every Catholic a continued effort of loyal and generous support. The Canon-law, the Councils, the exhortations of the Pope insists on this support of Catholic universities. Particularly those who are blessed with the goods of this world and to whom Providence has been generous, should remember that "their wealth has a fiduciary character; a character that entails duties towards the Catholic community at large, none less obligatory because they are rooted in the virtue of *charity,* instead of the virtue of *justice."*

But experience tells us that our Catholic institutions are founded and supported more by the "widow's mite" than by the millionaires' donations. The support will come from the Catholic communities of Western Canada; it will indeed come with most gratifying results if *the appeal is lofty in its motive and proposal, concerted and systematic in its action.*

We are not to go to the Catholics of the West with an appeal in one hand and an apology in the other. A straightforward, self-respecting presentation of our cause will bring a no less straightforward and self-respecting response. To make this appeal an unqualified success there must be also concerted action. Intensive efforts alone bring results. This means the canvass of the West for this single purpose, at a stated time. But any canvass of this kind, to be effective, must be prepared by an educational campaign. Give the Catholics, we maintain, the vision of their duty, sound the call . . . and they will respond. For indifference, profound and widespread,—fruit of ignorance more than of ill-will,—would be the greatest obstacle to overcome. Arousing interest will be the initial task. In Australia, Archbishop Mannix organized a campaign, in co-operation with his suffragan bishops, for the purpose of the Catholic College of Melbourne and from June to December, 1916, half a million of dollars was collected. The Catholics of Western Canada are just as ready, we claim, to furnish such annual payment as would be wanted: if only they are properly called upon. But this proper calling involves first a systematic and periodical recommendation of its claims by the clergy and influential laymen.

System will avoid a conflict of claims for other great causes equally worthy of our generous support. The war has in this matter taught us at home a great lesson. There were appeals for the Patriotic Fund, the Red Cross, the Belgium Relief, the French Aid, etc., etc. They all came to us in rotation. No apology was made, every one felt in duty

and honor bound, and the money was always there
with an extraordinary readiness. Organization is
the first element of success.

  .   .   .   .   .

 Who will be the promoters of this great work?
Naturally the Hierarchy of the West will be its
inspiring and moving spirit. But, should not the
Knights of Columbus, that body-guard of Catholic
laity, be called to the honour of "seeing it through."
This great undertaking would be a most appropri-
ate background for all the activities of our valiant
Knights in Western Canada.

 A society, Catholic in principle and membership, must, to last, and be an asset to the Church,
have a definite programme of action in harmony
with its aim and constitution. If it keeps its
energies pent up behind the walls of the council-
chambers and only finds them an outlet in social
functions and friendly gatherings, it will soon go
to seed or die of dry rot. When on the contrary
an organization, such as the Knights of Columbus,
throws the full weight of its energies in the forwarding of a great cause, the possibilities of its influence are limitless. The war activities of the
Knights and their splendid results for the Church
and the nation are a tangible proof of it.

 Could there be a work more in harmony with
the aims of the great Catholic organization
than that of higher education. At the national
convention of 1912, held at Colorado Springs, the

committee on Catholic Higher Education ends its report by saying: "In the newer impetus that will come to Catholic education as the result of better understanding (its necessity and value), the Knights of Columbus must make themselves an important factor. We owe it to ourselves and to that special loyalty to both Church and State which we pride to claim as the special note of the order. It is often asked what are the Knights of Columbus doing that they should be so proud of their organization, and the best possible answer would be for all of us to be able to point to benefits that were conferred by Knights individually and in bodies upon our Catholic education. There can be no mistake about the benefit to be conferred on Church and State by progress in Catholic education."

The active and persevering co-operation of the Knights in the forwarding of the great cause of a Catholic University for Western Canada, would be their contribution to the great period of reconstruction which the world is now facing.

.   .   .   .   .

On one of those beautiful mellow autumn evenings, of which the Prairie alone has the secret, the traveller, as his train steams into one of our Western Cities, will behold a stately cupola tipped with a golden cross.—"What is that new building, yonder on the outskirts of the city?" will he inquire. The answer will be: *"That is the Catholic University of Western Canada."*

PART III

SOCIAL PROBLEMS

"The political and economic struggles of society are in the last analysis religious struggles; their sole solution, the teaching of Jesus Christ."—(John Stuart Mill.)

CHAPTER XII.

BEYOND BERLIN*

*After-War Problems from a Catholic View-Point
—Reconstruction, the Duty of the Hour.*

THE heavy clouds of war and the bloody mist
of battles are lifting; once more the sun of
peace bursts forth triumphant over a sad and weary
world. The storm has wasted its fury. the landscape is washed clear and bright, the atmosphere
is glowing and transparent; destruction and ruins
everywhere stand out in sharp and ghastly relief.
On the distant horizon, beyond the Rhine, the dark
clouds drag their tattered shreds; the angry lightning still flashes and thunder yet rumbles yonder—
on German and Russian soil.

The war is over. The muddy trench, the deadly shrapnel, the perfidious gas, the roaring cannon,
the forced marches on the slimy roads of Flanders,
the heroic dashes and agonizing retreats of struggling armies, the lurking submarines, the treacher-
ous, owlish zeppelins, the long-protracted vigil on
the deep—all these grim realities of four, long,
endless years have melted away in the blaze of a
glorious victory. Now the German Armada rides
at anchor, prisoner, in British waters, the armies

---

*A speech delivered in the Assembly Hall of the Knights of
Columbus, St. John, N.B., December 22, 1918. "The Catholic Mind"
of New York reproduced it in one of its issues.

of the Allies bivouac on the banks of the Rhine, and our Canadian boys, flushed with victory, come marching home.

The day of the German surrender, Clemenceau, Premier of France, made this significant statement: "Great have been the problems of the war, but greater will be the problems of peace." Nations, indeed, now face one of the most momentous periods of history. The world has struck its tents and is once more on the march. Never, we believe, have such tremendous responsibilities weighed upon a passing generation. The future will be greatly imperilled if at this critical juncture great questions are fought out between ignorant desire for change and ignorant opposition to change. The handwriting is on the wall, and our economic and social life, foreign to Christian morality, has been found wanting. Will a new and better social order rise from the ashes of this world-conflagration? There is the searching problem which presses itself upon the mind of every thinking man. "On every side," writes Father Plater, S.J., "there is talk of reconstruction, economic, political, social, educational. Government departments are hard at work gathering information, elaborating schemes. Numerous organized bodies, such as the Labor party, are putting forward their programmes. Conferences and lectures on reconstruction are multiplied and literature on the subject pours from the press."

"Great ideas," said Wilson, "at last have cap-

tured the hearts of the common people and directed into positive channels and constructive programmes the very energies which otherwise may
have spent themselves in the acts of retributive destruction." Reconstruction! This is now the
world's watch-word. It sums up the various problems with which nations will have to grapple in
every realm of human activity. It speaks of conditions that are no more and suggests new outlines
of the social order. Our present and pressing duty
then is to weigh the anchor, to swing out into the
middle stream and take our course on the permanent principles of Catholic Truth. These principles stand on the shores of History as the great
revolving lights that sweep the high seas in the
darkness of night.

Canada, after having bravely and generously
solved the problems of war, is now also facing "the
greater problems of peace." This period of reconstruction, more than that of the war, will test
our national fibre. The strain will be greater for
the conflict is being lifted to a higher plane, that
of ideas. But nowhere in Canada will this vast
work of readjustment be more tangible than in
our Great West. The youth of that part of the
country, and the dominating factors of the national
problem will, we believe, make the West the classical land of reconstruction. A gradual evolution
will bring our Eastern Provinces to readjust themselves to the changing conditions of political and

economic life. The West, on the contrary, has in such matters the beautiful qualities, the unlimited resources of youth, but also its dangerous short-comings. Daring, venturous, over-confident in democracy, the Western mind is frequently most hasty and radical in its conclusions. It has not been matured by time, that great teacher of patience and moderation; experience has not, as yet, tempered that feverish and progressive youthfulness, so prone to speedy and often drastic legislation. The heat of fever is often mistaken for the glow of health. And as legislation is in the minds of the Western people the panacea of all evils in society, will not the common tendency be to carry on the work of reconstruction by parliament bills and orders-in-council? Is there not here a great danger? "The danger of premature commitment is much greater than that of more cautious policy, proving a stumbling block in the way of future progress."

Moreover, the most vital factors of reconstruction in Canada will affect more particularly the Prairie Provinces. The back-to-the-land movement, demobilization, settlement of returned soldiers on the farm, intensive immigration policy, extensive agricultural production are indeed Western problems.

The choice of the Hon. J. A. Calder of Saskatchewan, as chairman of the Reconstruction Committee in the Federal Cabinet; the prominent part given to him and to the Hon. Mr. Meighen of Manitoba, in the formation and discussion of plans at the recent meeting of the Premiers of the Provinces; these are in themselves striking illustrations of our contention in the matter.

Although the West will, in the period of reconstruction command the attention of the country at large, there are, nevertheless, problems, particularly those affecting our social and economic life, which will weigh heavily on our Eastern Provinces. So reconstruction will be a nation-wide work.

The Duty of Catholics

What is, therefore, the duty of Catholics, at the present hour? Are we to fold our arms and let others rebuild the very framework of society according to plans which our faith, reason, and history disapprove of, and very often condemn? Our ideas in the matter may not prevail, but how would we be justified in deploring the consequences of a legislation which we did not even try, by our influence, to suppress or modify? To abstain as Catholics from this great work of reconstruction is profoundly un-Catholic. It is the act of a traitor to the Church and country. As Burke so gloriously said: he was aware that the age is not all we wish, but he was sure that the only means to check its degeneracy was heartily to concur in whatever is best in our time.

The Church depends upon her children to spread the beneficial influence of her social doctrines. "The great work of the Catholics, after the war, will be," said Father McNabb, O.P., "to bring the vision of the Bride of Christ, the Catholic Church, before the millions of our countrymen." "These countrymen of ours are blind and often bigoted," adds Henry Somerville.

There are Catholics who make this blindness and consequent bigotry an excuse for their own narrowness and selfishness, for their neglect to share in the nation's work, for their refusal to co-operate in patriotic, civic and social undertakings as if they were none of our business. The nation's business is our business. If we serve the nation efficiently, we serve the Church. We take then the best means to open the eyes of our fellow-countrymen to the fact that Catholicism is not uncivic. If we make ourselves valued, anti-Catholic prejudice will be dispelled.

Cardinal Bourne in his letter on "Social Reform" speaks very pointedly of the duty of every Catholic in this matter. His pronouncement and that of the American Hierarchy are the most notable declarations from Catholic sources on "Social Re-construction." "It is admitted on all hands," says the English Primate, "that a new order of things, new social conditions between the different sections in which Society is divided will arise as a consequence of the destruction of the formerly existing conditions.

"The very foundations of political and social life, of our economic system, of morals, of religion are being sharply scrutinized, and this, not only by a few writers and speakers, but by a very large number of people in every class of life, especially among the workers."

The nation's business is our business. The true love of country demands from Catholics at this critical stage of our history to throw all their energies into the various social activities. Society throughout the world is shaken in its very foundations. This universal unrest in the political, social and economic spheres is a decided mark of the birth-throes of a new social order. Therefore, we will conclude with Cardinal Gibbons; "The Church cannot remain an isolated factor in the nation. The Catholic Church possesses spiritual and moral resources which are at the command of the nation in every crisis."

The reform or remodelling of the social fabric, if it is to be effective and abiding, must ultimately rest on the definite and unchanging principles of morality. These principles constitute the moral law, as physical principles are the basis of the physical law. Ernest Fayle, in a very instructive article on "Reconstruction," in the October number of the *"London Quarterly Review,"* makes a statement very pertinent to this matter; "The economic, political and social factors in human life are so inextricably entangled that if we accept quality of life and not mere power or wealth as the touchstone of national success we dare not, even in the consideration of economic or political questions, lose sight of the moral issues."

The Catholic Church has always been the teacher and guardian of that natural moral law which stands as the foundation and buttress of the social edifice. Her plans of Reconstruction rest on the eternal principles of equity which God has engraved on the human conscience and which the teachings of Christ have sanctioned and perfected. In the light of Catholic doctrine moral laws are definite and unchanging, for they are the deliberate expression of the necessary and fundamental relations upon which rests human nature. They are the living, free expression of man's place in creation. The most elaborate schemes and powerful organizations are soulless without these basic principles of morality and have but an ephemeral existence.

Is it not, therefore, a great act of patriotism to try to throw into the scales of the nation's destinies the mighty weight of indestructible and tried principles? A growing respect is to be found for the soundness, the wisdom and the justice of Catholic social principles, even in circles where our beliefs have not yet found acceptance. True statesmen have always recognized the influence of the Catholic Church's doctrine in social matters, although they may not believe in the truth of her teachings.

They always looked upon her principles of social life as the ballast that steadies the ship on heaving seas. To make the Church a spiritual ally, to recognize her moral power and her far-reaching influence has always been considered good diplomacy and clear-sighted statesmanship.

Catholic's Patriotism in Public Life

Reconstruction is the great work of the hour; co-operation is a duty every Catholic owes to Church and country. What definite and concrete form of co-operation will that responsibility assume? There is the problem. Our first duty, in the matter, lies, we believe, in a greater participation in public life. Too long have we stood aloof from movements that aim at the social welfare of the community. A false timidity and an erroneous conception of our responsibilities have estranged us, to a great extent, from the various activities of national life. This isolation has been most prejudicial to our Catholic laity, for it has fostered in their ranks disinterestedness and often apathy. "With regard to the necessity of Catholics to obtain positions on public bodies, Cardinal Bourne stated that very often Catholics were urged to take part in public affairs, by becoming elected to public bodies in order that they might safeguard Catholic principles. That was a great good—a very laudable object—but it was not the highest object. The great object was that out of the fulness of their

Faith they might give to their fellow-countrymen the principles that flowed from that Faith, so that little by little there might be built up in the consciousness of the nation that belief in and use of those sound principles of the Catholic Faith which contained the only solution of the difficulties with which they were faced."

"Too long have Catholics lived in isolation, allowing others to think and act for them. It is indeed, high time that they felt the pulse of life that beats in the real statesman, as distinct from mere politician. Duty demands that Catholics add their power of intellect and will to the similar power of other citizens anxious to help the commonwealth. We are not aliens in this land, not aliens by birth or principle. As to the latter, I may say with all truth, that no one has given clearer expression to the basic principles of democracy than the Catholic theologians, Suarez and Bellarmine."*

This attitude of aloofness, during the coming period of reconstruction especially, would be profoundly un-Catholic. Our active participation in public life will give us occasion to dispel prejudice, to offset subversive doctrines, to advocate in spite of failures and bigotry the principles of Christian sociology. We are firm believers in the prevailing strength of ideas. They are indestructible; they

*R. H. Tierney, S.J., Editor of America, at the Catholic Federation meeting, Brooklyn, September 15, 1918.

rule sooner or later. They may take time to crystalize into convictions, but the force of mental gravitation must ultimately prevail. And after all, Reconstruction, as Dr. J. J. Walsh stated, is more a question of remaking the map of man's mind than that of remodelling the map of Europe.

The Catholics of England give us, in this matter as in many others, a beautiful example to follow. During the war they formed a "British Catholic Information Society," having at its service" the Catholic War News Office." The result of their aggressive policy is the public recognition of the value of the Catholic Church by the English people in the national work of Reconstruction. We would here refer the reader to Father Plater's letter on "Catholics and Reconstruction" for further details in this interesting matter. Like our Catholic brothers of England, let us also take our place boldly in the broad daylight of public life. We have ideas to give to the Nation, let us give them. Canadian liberty, without doubt, exists for our doctrines as it does for the subversive theories of State-Socialism. We have no apology to make for our ideas. They stand on their own merits and have been vindicated by the great acid test of time. Yes, we possess the great curative and creative forces for social Reconstruction; We have only to call them into play.

The Catholic Solution

In season and out of season, in the press and on the platform, in private gatherings and public meetings, through every medium of social control, let the people hear the Catholic solution of the problems now facing the nations of the world. We have a message to deliver. That message, if it comes to the people shining like a steel blade, sounding like the blare of a trumpet, if it wells up from a fiery heart and drops from burning lips— that message will be heard. In this period of strain and suffering the public mind is keyed to its highest pitch, ready to snap at any moment. Strong feeling has generated in many minds intellectual hysteria. "In war time," says E. H. Griggs, "there is a curious paradox of widening radicalism of thought, with constantly decreasing freedom of action and expression. When the discrepancy becomes too great, you have the explosion, —a revolution." Therefore in this time of intellectual ferment, the continued affirmation of truth, and the persistent statement of principles are in themselves a highly valuable service, which we are bound to give to the world. The thought of the human mind, like rays of sun-light, focused on one point, acquires the burning power of conviction.

Participation in public life develops conviction; conviction repeatedly asserts itself; continued assertion creates opinion; and public opinion is without doubt one of the most universal powers at work in the world. In every sphere of life you can feel the constant pressure of this tremendous influence. It may well be named the "current" of public opinion. Draining to its profit the latent and loitering powers of the individual thinker, silently, irresistibly it moves on; checked, it becomes an angry whirlpool of confused and gyrating waters; harnessed to the wheels of national life, it will transform its energies into light, heat and power.

The creation and the spreading of Catholic opinion in social matters should be in our mind, the ultimate goal of our activities, for it is the greatest asset we can contribute to the vast work of Reconstruction. As Lord Morley said, "great economic and social forces flow with tidal sweep over communities half conscious of that which is befalling them. Wise statesmen are those who foresee what time is bringing and try to shape institutions and to mould men's thought and purpose in accordance with the change that is silently surrounding them."

Time, you readily understand, will not allow us to dwell upon the various problems which Reconstruction will bring before the country. Our aim, now, is rather to awaken the sense of responsibility, stir the sleeping conscience into watchfulness, and give to our Catholic men and women the stimulating thought of co-operation. Our country is being re-created in its political, social and economic life; to be a living factor in that "re-creation" is the duty of the hour.

Before bringing these remarks of a rather general character to a close allow us to mark for your attention the leading problems. They will be as landmarks planted to guide you on the way. In the international order, the problem of resetting nations on a new basis by a "just and durable peace" now faces the world. Racial and language problems command our attention in the national order. In the political world ideas are to be readjusted as to the nature, powers and obligations of the State. Of late, the monopoly of the State has been asserting itself so strongly that one is led to believe the old pagan principle of the supremacy of the State will once more reign supreme. When nations have ceased to give to God what belongs to God, they give to Caesar alone what belongs to Caesar and what belongs to God.

The social order will witness demobilization and immigration. Who cannot grasp the importance of these great problems with their various and intricate issues? The greatest transformations are, perhaps, reserved for the economic order; capital and labor, efficient and greater production of industry and agriculture, the living wage, and uplifting of the workman's status, etc. In the educational order the battle will be greater, for there is a great tendency to centralize, to federalize education, under the plea of "national schools."

The religious order will see tremendous efforts for union among the various non-Catholic denominations; "social service" will be their center of unity, the common field of action.

Various and important, as you see, are the problems that confront us in the realms of human activity. Now, bear in mind, the Catholic doctrine has a solution for each problem and it is your duty to give it. Knights of Columbus, as you helped the Church to solve the problems of the war, so will you also help to solve the greater problems of peace. If you wish to be the body-guard of the Church, your mission is to lend your noble and generous efforts to your spiritual leaders in this great work of reconstruction. For, of this reconstructive period and its great opportunities for militant and active Catholics, we may say what Carlysle said of the period that followed the French Revolution; "Joy was it, in that age, to be living—and to be young, was very heaven." The task indeed is enormous, but the incentive most inspiring.

We are bound to meet with the fluctuations and uncertainties of the human mind, particularly in such times of readjustment and intellectual unrest. Let us then never forget that since the coming of Christ and the establishment of His Church on earth the principles of His teaching are for all nations. The sun of truth has its meridian in Rome, on the rock of Peter. There it stands at its zenith, in the permanent blaze of a perennial mid-day; there it sets the time for the Catholic world amid the ever-changing and conflicting problems of human history. *Stat Crux dum volvitur orbis.*

CHAPTER XIII.

WHOM DO MEN SAY THAT THE SON OF
MAN IS?   (MATH. XVI.-13.)—PUBLIC
OPINION AND THE CATHOLIC
CHURCH

*What is Public Opinion—Its Power—How is it
Formed—Public Opinion and the Catholic
Church—Our Duties to Public Opinion.*

NUMEROUS and strong are the influences at
play in human life.   Acting and reacting on
the free will of man they are ever at work moulding his character and shaping his destiny.   Like
the waves of an incoming tide they are beating the
shores of our heart; their triumph is to carry away
our liberty on their receding waters.

Surrounding influences for good or for evil are
indeed, to a great extent, the determining factors of
our moral life.   Day by day they write our history
and with it the history of the world; for, the life of
every man is but a line on the great page of his
nation's history and the history of a nation, but a
chapter in that of humanity.

Of all the influences underlying human activities in the moral, social, economic, and political
world, one of the most universal and most effective
is beyond doubt, nowadays, *Public Opinion*.   We
may well name it the *"current"* of Public Opin-

ion.   In every sphere of life one can indeed feel
the constant pressure of its tremendous power.
Like the waters of a mill-race constantly and irresistibly the stream of Public Opinion sweeps on.
It is very difficult to determine exactly where lies
its strength; it is nowhere and everywhere.   Unconscious of its swollen powers it spends its energies for the welfare of the community, or, unfortunately too often, loses itself in an angry torrent of
destruction.

You thwart its onward march: it will bury your
barrier under its laughing waters or . . . sweep it
away.   You ride with it: it will gladly carry you.
You check it: its troubled waves will rise angry
around you and engulf you.

Such is the *"current"* of Public Opinion.   To
direct this great power, to harness its tremendous
forces, to convert them into light, heat, and energy
and set the wheels of moral, social, and political
life running with greater smoothness, rapidity, and
strength, should be the noble effort and the great
task of every serious-minded man.

By no idle whim or sheer literary piquancy
have we coupled *Public Opinion and the Catholic
Church*.   The inevitable relations that exist between Public Opinion and the various predominating factors of a nation should necessarily interest
every true Canadian.   Among these factors the
Catholic Church stands pre-eminent.   Her beneficial influences and her ready solutions to the

various social and moral problems that confront the world, cannot, even to the most prejudiced, be passed unnoticed. So no matter what our spiritual allegiance may be, the relation of Public Opinion to the Catholic Church should be of the greatest interest to any one who has at heart the common welfare. In Western Canada particularly, where Public Opinion has such a sway, this subject, we presume, must be of service both to those of the Catholic Faith and to those of a different persuasion.

．　　　．　　　．　　　．　　　．

What is Public Opinion—Its Power—How is it Formed?

1. *What is Public Opinion?*

Ideas rule the world, but various are the effects ideas have on the minds of men. On some minds they exercise only a passing influence; they are then what we call *"Impressions";* variable as lights and shadows over a summer lake they come and go. Impressions are indeed only on the surface of the mind, like foot-prints on the sand washed away by the next tide.

When ideas take a stronger footing in our intelligence and are accepted with a certain confidence, on their face-value or on the authority of some leader, they become *"Opinions."* Loosely entertained and readily exchanged, opinions are the ordinary mental pabulum of the masses.

Few minds see their ideas crystallized into *"Convictions."* Convictions are permanent, unchangeable ideas: based on facts and supported by satisfactory evidence, they rest on the bed-rock of truth. Few minds indeed, particularly on the larger and fundamental issues, can claim the right to convictions. For, convictions demand a breadth of vision and grasp of detail which are given but to few souls. These minds, few in number, are the minds of leaders. Their noble duty and great responsibility is to *Awaken, Stimulate,* and *Organize* the thinking of the people. Their thoughts, their ideas, are on the unchartered sea of truth as the tossing buoy or lighted beacon from which the unthinking masses take their course. Rather than go to the pains of thinking for themselves the crowds leave this task to a few and content themselves with ready-made opinions, as these float by with the tide of the hour. Few make up their minds; they are made up for them.

The common opinion which reflects the mind of the great majority, embodies the prevailing idea, the universal sentiment, and directs the common action is called. . . *Public Opinion.*

2. *Power of Public Opinion.*

You readily see, by its very nature, the tremendous power of Public Opinion. It is the "reason why," the basis of appreciation, the norm of conduct of the great mass of the people. As we stated before, Public Opinion is like the stream that drains to its profit the loitering energies of the individual mind, and makes them tributaries that swell its volume and compress its course. Who can analyze the powers of this *"Organized Thinking"* of the people in a democracy? Who can measure the force of these sweeping currents, of these tidal waves of Public Opinion?

In fact, Public Opinion may be considered in our modern societies as the greatest driving power. For, Public Opinion is the vision of the unthinking multitude, and vision is the first and foremost of constructive or destructive forces. It lights the way and invites action accordingly. Marvellous indeed is the sweep of the tide of Public Opinion in various realms of human activities. Its ebb and flow—although frequently beyond analysis, are felt on every shore.

In the world of finance,—and this is the lowest in the scale of real values,—is not that fragile but mighty factor we call credit based on Public Opinion? For, credit is but the general opinion of the community on the possibilities of the industry or undertaking in which its capital is involved, and on the honesty and ability of the management.

What has weakened the moral fibre of our modern society so much that at times one wonders if we are living in the Christian era? If the home is now so often desecrated by theories of free love and trial marriages, if the cradles are empty, if the very sense of shame is a thing of the past, if the most elementary principles of morality are questioned, is it not because the public conscience is being warped, chloroformed, deadened by a frenzied propaganda of a corrupted Public Opinion?

Has not the politician and the legislator the ear to the wind, the eye on the running tides and cross currents of thought, to know and sound Public Opinion?   Like the skilful and watchful pilot, he counts with the set of the tide and catches it at its crest.   He knows the exact height of the rising tide that will float him and his cargo over the bar . . . of a coming election—.   This tide of public feeling has carried some to the high seas of success but left many stranded on the desert shores. Many public men indeed have set out on its angry waters to brave its fury . . . and have never returned.   "In our times of Democracy when the "competitive" principle has replaced the "hereditary," not the kings, princes and nobles, but bankers, merchants, railroad magnates, capitalists, politicians, editors, educators, writers and artists occupy the high seats, hold the baton and beat the time for the great social orchestra." (Ross-Social Psychology.)   "Power and influence," said Morley, "no longer reside in the Crown but in the strong, subtle forces called Public Opinion: and that Public Opinion is apt to involve fatal contentment with simple answers to complex questions."

In the great international life of nations Public

Opinion also holds the reins. This power manifests itself particularly at the great turning points of History, such as we are now witnessing. There is always then resistance between conflicting forces; and resistance, we know, strengthens the current. What power was at work for the last fifty years and marshalled, on that fatal August day of 1914, the formidable army that swept over Belgium, France and Russia? Public Opinion created by the military caste in Germany! What secret and growing force made of the Allies' contemptible army of yesterday the crushing victorious army of to-day?— The invincible power of Public Opinion!—It leaped from the very depths of the wounded heart and outraged conscience of nations, and created in a few months that unconquerable army of inexhaustible reserves upon which the Allies relied until their final triumph. It fired the morale of our armies and smashed the way to victory. For those who could not go to the battle-field, it kept the homefires burning and fringed with the silver lining of radiant hope the dark clouds that hung over our horizon for four long, dragging, weary years.

3. *How Public Opinion is Formed.*

You may ask how are the thoughts of the multitude so marshalled as to make the unit of Public Opinion. As we already remarked, the thinking power of the ordinary man does not go *far, wide,* nor *deep*. His facility of absorbing ideas is far greater than his power of valuating them. He generally accepts as real value any thing that bears the stamp of current opinion. His belief in the value and weight of number is without recall; his absolute trust in what Bryce calls "the fatalism of multitude" is beyond appeal. He lives and thrives on the *surrounding mental atmosphere*.

How is this atmosphere created? By the continued, persevering repetition of the same ideas; by the vesting of these same ideas in the attractive garb of self-interest, passion, fancy and vogue. On this process, we all know by experience, is based the ever youthful power of *Advertisement* . . . and of *Fashion*.

Advertisement! Modern business is built to a great extent on the mysterious allurement, the attractive invitation and innocent camouflage of the advertisement that you find sparkling everywhere, on the flashy poster, in the show-window, in the magazine, in the daily paper. Without willingness to admit our weakness, we fall victims to this wizard that we despised yesterday and court to-day, and line up at the counter . . . for a *Special Sale,* an *Astonishing Bargain.* "We are so thoroughly accustomed to the exploits of the advertiser that we take them as a matter of course, rarely pausing to appreciate the art, or at least, the artfulness with which we have been lured into the acceptance of his ideas."

Fashion! Who can analyze this power so great, so universal? Who can explain the psychology of this fact? Every spring and fall of the year Dame Fashion has an opening-ball—Paris plays the tune, New York wields the baton, the ladies of the world . . . keep time . . . and the gentlemen pay the piper.

We mention these facts of every day life to illustrate the permeating and driving force of an idea, when constantly kept before the mind. And what advertisement and fashion are in the commercial and social life, *Propaganda* and *Publicity* are in the world of thought. The policy of propaganda is to enlist the active co-operation of every vehicle of thought for the furtherance of an idea and to keep that idea ever before the public. One readily sees the tremendous responsibilities, and understands the flagrant abuses of those called to create and direct Public Opinion. "The supremacy of ideas," it was stated, "gives the greatest places of opportunity to those who awaken, stimulate and organize the thinking of the people and especially the thinking of a people in a democracy. The teacher's desk, the preacher's pulpit, the orator's platform, the writer and editor's sanctum—these are the places of true leadership, the thrones of real power."

This analysis of Public Opinion, of its power, of its formation will now make us better understand its relations with the Catholic Church.

Public Opinion and the Catholic Church.

Nowadays the relation of Public Opinion to the Catholic Church is, generally speaking, one of suspicion, frequently of silent contempt and very often of open hostility. This statement of fact may appear to many too sweeping; its broadness may trouble the peaceful faith of others. Yet, history and every day experience prove the truth of our assertion. We go further and claim that for the Church this condition will, and must exist. The Church, like Christ, her Founder and Master, is to be a *"Sign of Contradiction."* Her very name "Catholic" is a perennial witness to her sublime and admirable Catholicity, and thereby an abiding proof of her Divinity. A Church that modifies her tenets and adjusts her moral standards to accommodate herself to the conveniences and fancies of the world is not, and cannot be the Church of Christ. Now, as in the times of the Apostles, the Church *"Is a Sect that is everywhere spoken against"*—*"If ye were of the world?"* said the Saviour, *"the world would love his own; but ye are not of this world, therefore the world hateth you."* Yes, suspicion, contempt and hostility are the hall-marks of historic Christianity, for they are the realization of Christ's promises to His Church, the fulfilment of His prophesies. This fact for a Christian who has eyes to see, and ears to hear, is particularly noticeable when periodically a tidal

wave of bigotry or open persecution strikes the
Catholic Church, lashes itself into fury, washes the
Rock of Peter with ugly foam . . . and dies away,
ashamed of its own powerlessness and unfairness.

Viewing this relation of Public Opinion to the
Catholic Church—not as an evidence of that spiritual conflict, often unconscious but ever real—but
as a fact, a historic reality, some may ask the proof
of our rather bold statement. Even those who are
not of our Faith, and yet always wish to be fair
and broad in their dealings with the Catholic
Church, may question it.

The proof is very simple to give. Public
Opinion is against the Catholic Church, because
the powers that create and maintain Public Opinion are against the Catholic Church. Facts here
speak for themselves.

The Press—the Novel—the Periodical Literature—the Cinema—the Stage—the Public School
—the Academy and University Halls—the Legislative Assemblies . . . are without doubt the high
voltage-wires that receive, carry and distribute the
current of Public Opinion. Or rather, like the
wireless stations they gather those invisible and imponderable waves of thought and feeling that are
ever flashing through the intellectual and moral
atmosphere of nations, and translate their message
to the masses. Between these powers and Public
Opinion there is a continuous action and reaction.
They are at the same time the *moulders* and *mir-*

rors of Public Opinion. They are its *masters,* but with the condition of being first its *servants.*

Of all these creative forces none is greater and more universal than the *Press.* If Public Opinion is the king and master of the modern world, the Press is assuredly his faithful and most active Prime Minister. This chief executive has extended the kingdom of his master to the very confines of the civilized world. Nothing has contributed more to the rule of Public Opinion than the Press. With it ideas and opinions run through the public mind as rapidly as the dispatches that carry them. "Mental touch is no longer bound up with physical proximity. With the telegraph to collect and transmit the expressions and signs of the ruling mood, and the fast mail to hurry to the eager clutch of waiting thousands the still damp sheets of the morning daily, remote people are brought as it were into one another's presence." (Ross-Social Psychology.)

The ordinary man now sees the world through his newspaper. He absorbs facts and principles with the shades and variations the daily paper gives them. Reports of events and announcements of policies are colored to suit the aims and opinions of the editors and proprietors. Windy platitudes —at least for those who know facts and have studied principles—become gospel truth for the unthinking mass. Public Opinion is thus conscripted by an "irresponsible power." This irresponsibility of the Press is without doubt the greatest menace of the day. For, the opinions,—we mean to say—the propelling forces of the silent millions are at its mercy. . . . And these silent millions make and unmake the world.

This great power of the Press is inimical to the Catholic Church. By press, you will readily understand, we do not mean any particular paper, or a certain group of papers, but rather that formidable ensemble of tremendous financial backing, of world-wide information-services, of chains of papers that encircle the globe, of these various agencies that tap the telegraphic wires of every country and keep the cables hot. The Hearst papers alone reach simultaneously four or five million readers daily. From New York to San Francisco one man is leading the minds of these millions "to conclusions that he wants them to arrive at "—What Hearst is for the United States, Lord Northcliffe is for England.

This great press is against the Catholic Church. The total suppression of truths and of facts; the conspiracy of silence—often more dangerous than an open attack; the coloring of news with shades of thought suited to a definite purpose; the partial admission of truth and the maimed relation of facts; the bold assertion of deliberate falsehoods; the deceptive headlines—and the people live on headlines; the insinuating title which is often in flagrant contradiction to the dispatch it underlines:

—these are a few of its various strategies of attack. "The Pope and the War," "Quebec and the War," "The Guelph Novitiate Incident," are recent instances of what we refer to.

Some may object that the Catholics are of a rather susceptible nature and always expect "privileges"—No, we only want the privileges of truth, we mean fair play, equality, and justice.

What we say of the Press can also be said of periodical literature and modern fiction. "The very nature of periodical literature," says Cardinal Newman, "broken into small wholes and demanded punctually to an hour involves the habit of extempore philosophy . . . and that philosophy, we know is not Christian philosophy. The writers can give no better guarantee for the philosophical truth of their principles than their popularity at the moment and their happy conformity in ethical character to the age which admires them."

Any one who has kept in touch with the stream of modern fiction is well aware to what extent its waters are polluted and have contaminated the mind and heart of our present generation. When the world has been slaking its literary thirst at sources such as H. G. Wells, Galsworthy, Ibanez —only to mention a few—should we be astonished that public opinion is drifting to paganism? If theories of "Free Love" and Divorce are rampant in our society, the responsibility to a great extent lies with our modern novel. The novels that are written and read, indicate the mind and morals of a people.

What could we not write of the *Moving-Picture* and the *Stage?* Suffice it to state with Rev. R. A. Knox—then an anglican minister, and now a catholic priest: "When a nation has lost its hold of first truths and its love for clear issues, which has had its morality sapped by sentiment, thinks of Christian marriage in the light of the problem-play . . . the moral fibre of that nation is gone." For, the vision of life and the interpretation of its pleasures and sorrows, that come from the glare of the foot-lights, or the dimness of the Movie-Screen, are surely not that given by the Catholic Church. Over the screen of the movies and the proscenium of the stage could we not very often write what the author of the play "Enjoy Life," Max Hermann Neisse, said lately to a Berlin sensation-seeking audience that was underlying with frantic applause the unsavory remarks and filthy inuendos of the closing act: "Pardon me, I did not write this act.—You dictated it to me."

In pandering to the morbid curiosity and lustful passions of a pleasure-mad world, the stage, the moving-picture, the novel, the illustrated weekly are leading Public Opinion to depths before unknown. The abyss calls to the abyss. Ways of living always follow ways of thinking. Should we then be astonished that crime-wave after crime-wave is sweeping the shores of every country.

Existing conditions in our universities, **public
academies** and schools are not of a nature **to** conciliate Public Opinion with the Catholic Church.
We know perfectly well that in our seats of higher-learning the Church is looked upon as an effēte Institution, as something of the past that has kept a
certain air of respectability.   Her teachings and
her history are there viewed in the light of **the**
"evolution theory."   Who has not read, a few years
ago, that terrible indictment against the antichristian education of the American Universities, **as it**
appeared in a celebrated article, under the title:
"Blasting at the Rock of Ages?"

In our legislative assemblies, here and abroad,
do we not find the educational problem the burning problem for Church and State?   Over the
head of the child swords clash, for the child of today is the man of to-morrow.   The stand **the**
Catholic Church takes on the educational problem
—from which She never deviates—has always
stirred Public Opinion against her in political
and social circles.   We have only to mention
"separate schools" to awaken the memories of a
long and bitter struggle.

The same inimical relations dominate the International Order.   Rome and its world-wide
moral influence have been deliberately ostracized
in the recent and unhappy attempt to form a
League of Nations.

So the tide of Public Opinion sweeps upon tide. Everywhere its heavy waves break into a foamy froth on the Rock of Peter. We conclude: *Public Opinion is against the Catholic Church.*

Our Duties to Public Opinion.

The antagonism against the Catholic Church is an overt fact. What are the causes? *A distorted vision,* born of misrepresentation of facts and misrepresentation of doctrine and practice; the *blind prejudice* against which our refutation of facts and explanation of principles are of little avail: *these are the two main causes to which can be traced this universal opposition.* And indeed no one will tax us with exaggeration were we to repeat here what Tertullian wrote in his "Defence of the Church," a hundred years after St. John's death: *"They think the Catholics to be the cause of every public calamity, of every national ill."* Have we not in our own country, organizations that live and thrive only on enmity to the Church of Rome? They cannot meet without passing resolutions of condemnation of the Church, of the Pope, of separate schools, etc. We all know how often Public Opinion, in our country, has been inflamed by prejudiced appeals to racial and religious feelings. Racial antagonism itself is only a cover for anti-Catholic fanaticism.

Let us, by clear and sound thinking, by definite and bold expression *enlighten Public Opinion.*

To-day Public Opinion is shifting as the winds, swinging like a boat with the ebb and flow of the tide. These are days of loose thought, wild words, catchy phrases, especially in social and religious matters. Words and phrases are passed off as ideas, and fragments of an idea as the whole idea. Let ideas always be clear-cut, with a sharp, definite relief. Hazy notions are of no constructive value, and always full of danger, particularly in times of intellectual ferment, such as we are now going through. They are on the great sea of Truth as the smoke-screens, behind which lurk the destroyers of error.

Cardinal Newman concludes one of his letters on "The Position of Catholics"—which bears on the subject of Catholics making themselves known: "Protestantism is fierce because it does not know you; ignorance is its strength; error is its life; therefore bring yourselves before it, press yourselves upon it, force yourselves into notice against its will. Oblige men to know you. Politicians and philosophers would be against you, but not the people, if they knew you."

Create Public Opinion by *individual and concerted action,* that is our next duty. Truth spreads, not like the devastating torrent, but like the tide. From individual to individual as from pebble to pebble it slowly creeps in and spreads the silent power of its rising waters. "No one ever talks freely about anything without contributing something, let it be ever so little, to the unseen forces which carry the race on to its final destiny. Even if he does not make a positive impression he counteracts or modifies some other impression, or sets in motion some train of ideas in some one else, which helps to change the face of the world." Godkin "Problems of Modern Democracy." 221-224.

By the continued repetition of truth and the persevering refutation of falsehood we will help to create around us, in our limited sphere of action, a sane Public Opinion. But it is above all by the radiance of our moral life that truth, particularly religious truth, will spread. Religion, as we know, is of the moral order; its dogmas, precepts and sacraments reach out into that domain. Paul Bourget, the celebrated French writer sums up one of his most striking novels in this phrase: *"At Forty-three"* which he calls the noon hour of life—*"man must live what he believes or he will eventually believe as he lives."* To live up to our principles is always the best proof of our belief in them.

Concerted action will extend the benefits of this individual action to the creation of Public Opinion in the Community, in Society at large. As all great powers, Public Opinion is courted; this courtship is *"Propaganda."* Truth requires propaganda as life needs transmission. An efficient propaganda takes myriad forms but its purpose is always the same, i.e., give to others our ideas and through them organize the public mind. Distribution of literature, lectures, the press, the novel, the cinema, bureaus of information, active participation in public life are vital factors of an efficiently organized propaganda. The recent Northcliffe propaganda, followed by the Hearst propaganda are typical illustrations of how the public mind of a Country was swayed from a pro-British to an Anti-English attitude.

The Direction of Public Opinion is the ultimate triumph of propaganda. This is obtained when our principles pass into the warp and woof of the social textures which are always in the making on the great loom of our nation's life. Ideas have their full value when they are extended to social and political issues. It is only then that they influence a nation as such. For our lives are knitted with the lives of others, and their action and reaction upon them form our public life. "In the formation and guidance of the public opinion which ultimately determines public action, Catholics bear responsibility and must take their part." (Cardinal Bourne, at the Catholic Congress of England, 1920.)

As Catholics we have a contribution to make to the great upbuilding of our Country. There is in every problem an ethical side, an unchanging and unchangeable principle, the bedrock on which it rests. This principle, the Catholic doctrine possesses; we know it, we are sure of it.   Why not then have that aggressiveness of militant Catholics who take advantage of every opportunity, without being obtrusive?   Are we not too apologetic in our Public life?   We would not suggest in the least to be discourteously aggressive, although at times we are tempted to do so and seem justified in our retaliation.   But there is no reason why we should apologize for our principles, for the solutions we have to offer.   The sun of Canadian liberty shines also for us and for what we stand; we have our place under the shade of the "Maple Leaf."

May we add a word for our non-Catholic friends.   They also have duties towards Public Opinion in its relation with the Catholic Church.

Receptiveness of mind is, in our estimation, the first and most important duty of the non-Catholic. Open-mindedness was named by Confucius "mental hospitality."   It opens the door to truth by allowing ourselves to be convinced by the strength of argument and the weight of evidence.   This state of receptivity permits the mind to correct its distorted vision, and to see facts and principles as they really are.   Freedom of mind enables those who possess it to see things in their true proportions.

Fairmindedness will overcome prejudice, the great obstacle in matters of Religion.   Prejudice is made of a coarse and impenetrable fibre, of a close woven texture; it is the product of numerous and various influences. The ordinary causes of this pre-judgment or mental torsion are an habitual intellectual outlook resulting from education and surrounding influences, and a mental laziness which fails to question its own attitude and to pursue principles to their logical conclusions, and problems to their solution. This explains how reluctantly the mind, in religious matters particularly, will accept views contrary to those with which it has been familiar since early youth and which time and surroundings have but strengthened. A straight-forward appeal to *fairmindedness* is alone able to break down this barrier.

Duties are in proportion to the responsibilities they entail. Public Opinion, as we have seen, is a tremendous power but it is the power of a high explosive which misdirected and ill-used will spread disaster. Leadership is the spark that ignites the charge, is responsible for its driving force. In the days of real intellectual leadership the mastery of ideas prevailed and Public Opinion was considered as the triumph of an idea. But in our days of so called democratic equality the centre of gravity of this power has shifted from the leader to the multitude. De Tocqueville in his book "Democracy in America"* has a remarkable page, illustrating this point. "The nearer the people," he writes, "are drawn to a common level of

*Vol. II., Chap. II.

an equal and similar condition the less prone each man becomes to place implicit faith in a certain man or certain classes of men. But his readiness to believe the multitude increases and opinion is more than ever the mistress of the world. Not only is common opinion the only guide which private judgment retains among democratic people, but amongst such a people it possesses a power infinitely beyond what it has elsewhere. At periods of equality men have no faith in one another by reason of their common resemblance; but this very resemblance gives them almost unbounded confidence in the judgment of the public; for it would not seem probable, as they are all endowed with equal means of judging, but that the greater truth should go with the greater number. The public has therefore among a democratic people a singular power which aristocratic nations cannot conceive of; for it does not persuade to certain opinions, but it impresses them and infuses them in the intellect by a sort of enormous pressure of the minds of all upon the reason of each."

To this prestige of vast numbers Bryce has given a name. "Out of the mingled feelings that the multitude will prevail and that the multitude, because it will prevail, must be right, there grows a self-distrust, a despondency, a disposition to fall into line, to acquiesce in the dominant opinion, to submit thought as well as action to the encompassing powers of numbers."

"This tendency to acquiescence and submission, this sense of insignificance of individual effort, this belief that the affairs of men are swayed by large forces whose movements may be studied but cannot be turned, I have ventured to call it *"The Fatalism of the Multitude."* It is often confounded with the tyranny of the majority, but is at the bottom different though, of course, its existence makes tyranny by the majority easier and more complete. . . . In the fatalism of the multitude there is neither *legal* nor *moral* compulsion; there is merely a loss of *resisting power,* a diminished sense of personal responsibility of the duty to battle for one's own opinion, such as has been bred in some people, by the belief of an over mastering fate."*

One can readily grasp the dangers of Public Opinion at the mercy of blatant agitators and unscrupulous leaders. They have no idea to promote, but only a feeling to exploit. They flatter Public Opinion to gain it. They appear to consult it when in reality they are creating and directing it. They catch the restless and undirecting currents of popular feeling when they are seeking an outlet and swing them slowly at first but with a growing impetus in the channels of their own interest or of the party they represent. The people are deluded into thinking that they are their own leaders and masters. The feeling of unrest that now prevails is due to this abuse of Public Opin-

---

*Bryce—"The American Commonwealth," Vol. II., Chap. 84.

ion. Like children the leaders of nations have
been playing with this wire of high voltage.
Should we be surprised to see the world suffer
deadly shocks from whence it should receive light
and power?

We are now at one of the most momentous periods of history. Never have clear thinking,
earnest expression and concerted action been more
needed than now. The world is ringing with wild
words and dying from loose thinking. "The persistent statement of principles and the union of all
true conservative forces are absolutely necessary, if
we wish to bring the nation safe through this agonizing period and make the world safe for democracy," as President Wilson said.

Therefore we claim that it is for the greatest
benefit of the community at large to have Public
Opinion enlightened as to the value of the Church
as a reconstructive factor.

"Great have been the Problems of War!" But,
with Clemenceau, we also are realizing—and
some countries, with bitter deception and de-
pressing sorrow, *"That greater still are the Problems of Peace."*

CHAPTER XIV.

TRUTH SHALL MAKE YOU FREE*
(Jo. VIII, 32)

Facts—Principles—Policy of the Catholic Truth Society—Its value for the Church in Western Canada.

TRUTH and liberty, error and license are inseparable partners. The measure of truth gives the measure of true liberty, just as the degree of error tells the degree of bondage. This is a logical necessity, a natural consequence. The Master emphasized it when He said: "And you shall know the Truth and the Truth shall make you free." These pregnant words of Christ are the charter of Christian civilisation and mark the passing of expediency as the supreme rule of human liberty.

This explicit confidence in the abiding power of Truth and in its necessary relation with our moral and religious life has prompted the creation of the Catholic Truth Society and inspired its policy. Never was any Society more useful nor so well adapted to the conditions of present times.

The world nowadays is fast drifting from its Christian moorings and taking to the high seas of modern paganism. The outlook on human life is as in the days of Greece and Rome. The old cry:

*This Chapter was published in pamphlet form by the Catholic Truth Society of Canada.

panem et circeuses!—is to be found on the lips of our multitudes and reflects the aspirations of their life. In the social realm, State-monopoly is fast absorbing the individual and the family, and is heralded as the supreme ideal of human society. A speedy and complete return to Christian principles will alone re-establish the world on its proper axis. Christian Truth shall again make the world free and save it from the bondage of neo-paganism. For, history and experience prove that there is nothing more tyrannical than that bondage —let it be the bondage of Czardom or Bolshevism —which comes to man under the cover and name of liberty. In the present universal unrest, so widely and so emphatically voiced throughout the world, the mission of the Catholic Truth Society appears as most providential. The spreading of Catholic Truth will help the world to reconquer its liberties and, with them, true civilization.

To state facts, discuss principles and advocate policies, in connection with the Catholic Truth Society of Canada, particularly in the West, is the object of this chapter.

Facts.

The Catholic Truth Society was born in England; November 5th,, 1884, was its birthday; Mr. Britten,* its honored and devoted parent. The

---

*Cardinal Vaughan and Lady Herbert are the real Founders of the C.T.S. But Mr. Britten carried out the idea.—It was to be essentially a lay-movement.

activities of the Anglican Church inspired this
great Catholic layman to counteract the influence
of its propaganda.   Tract for tract, pamphlet
for pamphlet, lecture for lecture, advertisement
for advertisement was the plan of campaign of our
new militant leader.   To marshal all the tremendous forces of the "printed word" for the service and
defence of Mother Church was his noble ambition.
He had implicit faith in the everlasting vitality
which lies concealed in the divine seed of the Word
of God.   He knew that by spreading it broadcast,
it would necessarily fall on prepared and expectant
soil, germinate and produce a hundred fold.   With
the approbation of the Hierarchy and the generous
support of a few intelligent associates, the Society
issued devotional, controversial, historical and dogmatic pamphlets.   Small in form, compact in doctrine, living in expression, these messengers of
Truth winged their way through the world.   Little
by little the Society's influence has spread everywhere and proved beyond doubt to be a great factor of Catholic apostolate in our time.

For twenty-one years (1888-1909) the annual
meeting of the Catholic Truth Society was the outstanding event of Catholic life in England.   It
became the field on which Catholic forces—clergy
and laity—met yearly to exchange ideas, formulate
plans, co-ordinate purpose and concentrate activity.
This gathering gave rise to the "National Catholic
Congress"—which now stands out as the annual

review, the "mass-manœuvre," of the Church militant in England. These meetings have made of a
handful of Catholics, many but neo-converts of
yesterday, the aggressive body we all admire, and
from which we, in Canada, have many things to
learn.

The Editor of the "Universe" in his issue of
Sept. 22, 1919, on the occasion of the C.T.S. Conference in Nottingham, paid a beautiful tribute to
the Society.   "This summing up of its activities is
in itself an inspiration and incentive. We are re-
minded by this Conference of the debt and duty we
owe to the society under whose auspices it meets.
The debt is all-pervading. How many Catholics
in this country are there, teachers or taught, who
have not profited directly and personally by the
labour and enterprise, freely given, of the comparatively few who, since that memorable day of its
foundation, November 5, 1884, have maintained,
written for, and contributed to the expenses of the
Catholic Truth Society? It has provided the
apologist with an armoury and the teacher with
material; it has saved the scholarly many an hour
of troublesome research; it has given the unlearned
instruction suited to their needs; it has given the
masses of our people the popular Catholic literature they want; it has been a veritable sleuth-hound
on the track of traducers of the Church; it has explained and commended her cause to even greater
numbers outside her pale who were simply ill-

informed; it has helped more souls than anyone will ever be able to count, into the Fold. Moreover, it has been the fruitful parent of progeny (not always filially grateful) which extends today to the uttermost parts of the earth. And always it has maintained a standard—which, in fact, it created amongst us—of material high quality, of intellectual respectability and of religious solidity, the more worthy of grateful appreciation because not everywhere fully appreciated. Nor can we forget that the Society is in a real sense "the work of one man," though never has it been that very different thing, a "one-man work." No one layman (and very few ecclesiastics) has done a larger definite and objective work for the Catholic Church in our time than Mr. Britten."

Such a record should shame the faint-hearts among us who seem to think that no corporate efforts are of any use in the world now rushing on to its own destruction. That it should shame those who take no interest at all in the progress of their religion, would be too much to hope.

The mustard seed has become now a great tree; branches have been detached from the main trunk and transplanted in the various parts of the world. Ireland, Australia,* India,† America, Canada,

---

*Australian Catholic Truth Society.—At the annual meeting of the Australian Catholic Truth Society the report stated that during the year 1919 152,309 pamphlets had been put into circulation, while the total number published since the foundation of the Society was 1,837,947. The executive had decided to publish in future 36

each now has its own Catholic Truth Society.

In 1887, six years after the foundation of the parent Society in England, Canada had a first branch in Toronto. Halifax,* Montreal, Winnipeg, Regina, Saskatoon, Vancouver soon followed suit. Silent and powerful as the incoming tide, the Society in Canada is working its way into every diocese and parish of the land. The Society is now incorporated by act of Federal Parliament, with Head-Office in Toronto, 67 Bond St. Its noble and just ambition is to weld into one great efficient organization the various other branches that are in operation here and there throughout the Dominion. Organization means efficiency, strength and success.

The time has come for the Catholic Truth Society in Canada, to create its own literature, to issue its own pamphlets dealing with the needs and problems of our own Country. We have been importing from other countries and have lived until now on their mental activity. But this move demands unity of purpose and concentration of effort. Moreover, should not this Dominion-wide organi-

---

penny pamphlets each year, instead of 24, and trusted that their enterprise would be rewarded with a substantial increase in the number of subscribers.

†The headquarters of the C.T.S. of India are in Trichinopoly. They have already their own publications.

*Although the Halifax branch of the C.T.S. does not form a unit of the C.T.S. of Canada yet it is one of the most active branches in our Country.

zation serve marvellously to rally our dispersed and disunited forces? There is indeed a sad need of unity in our ranks to-day.

Principles.

The assured possessionof truth and the pressing obligation for Catholics to spread it: these are the two main principles upon which is founded and exists the Catholic Truth Society. As Catholics, we are absolutely sure that we have the Truth; as Catholics worthy of the name, we feel in conscience bound to give it to others.

The Catholic Church, like Christ, stands at the cross-roads of humanity and cries out to the passing generations as they come tramping down the avenues of time: *"Ego sum Veritas, Via et Vita—* I am the Truth, the Way, the Life." Her kingdom is that very same Kingdom of Truth of which the Master spoke to Pilate when the latter had asked Him so insolently: "What is Truth?" Faith gives to everyone of Her children the right to all the wealth of that Kingdom.

The self-assurance of the Catholic mind in matters of Religion is a noted and universal fact which implies necessarily the tranquil possession of Truth. This certainly is not a blind adherence dictated by fear or fatalism as some would lead the unwary to believe; but rather, as St. Paul states, the reasonable subjugation of the mind . . . *"Rationabile obsequium."* The universal unrest and chaotic condition of Christendom outside of the Catholic Church are in sharp contrast with the unity and tranquillity of the Catholic mind. This is not the place to prove for our own pleasure and benefit the security of our position. Christian Apologetics have vindicated it.

This security of the Catholic mind extends beyond the sacred domain of Religion. Catholic philosophy has been justly named the "scientific justification of common sense." Its principles do not rest on the capricious fancies of the versatile human mind, as is the case with the philosophy of the dreamer of Koenigsberg. We only mention here Kant, for his influence has in our days been tremendous and far reaching. In Catholic philosophy the mind indeed reflects the objective order of things and from that order evolves universal laws. This basic truth of our mental attitude is still more evident when considered in the moral order. For, when God becomes but a "pure abstraction," and the moral law solely dependent on the human will, one readily sees where such philosophy may lead. This *"ego-centric philosophy"* is responsible for the frame of mind which gifted the world with German "Kultur." Nietzsche taught Germany how to think, and Germany had set out to teach the world the lessons she had received. As some author remarked, Kant and Nietzsche are responsible for the firing of the Krupp guns. Thus the war has shown the fallacies of anti-Catholic philosophy.

From these serene heights of Philosophy, Catholic Truth flows into the political, social and economic fields of human life. Our principles on Authority and Liberty, on Capital and Labor, on Family and State, on Marriage and Education are as solid as the rock, and are recognized as such, even by leaders who have a different religious persuasion.

Yes, religious, philosophical, social, political, economic truth we do possess. But of what use to the world, to the laborer, to the patriot, to the inquirer, is this truth and the solutions to problems it offers, if they are not known? If we have the light we cannot hide it under the bushel. We must place it where it can be seen, where its beneficial rays can light up the way for those who are "sitting in darkness, in the shadow of death."

No Catholic is a Catholic for himself only. Christian Charity imposes upon us the duty to help our brother. The spreading of Catholic Truth is one of the great works of Mercy and is as binding as alms-giving for the relief of temporal want. The love of God and of our neighbour is the foundation of this obligation. This consciousness of Christian solidarity whereby the rich come to the rescue of the poor, the learned help the ignorant, is the driving force behind the Catholic Truth Society.

With the vision of the Truth and the conscientious impulse to spread it, the Society is bound to grow in a genuine Catholic soil. We say it frankly, there is something wanting in a parish where the Catholic Truth Society meets with no response, creates no interest. The sense of real Catholicism and the consciousness of the duties it implies are conspicuous by their absence. There, Christianity does not run deep enough. This also stands true where the Catholic Church Extension or other organization of its kind, has no hold. The same principle is at stake; in both cases deficiency reveals a negative, rather than a militant Christianity.

Policy.

The world nowadays, like Pilate, asks the Church: "What is Truth?" But like Pilate also, proud of its power, its wealth, and success, it will not wait for the answer. Yet the Church's mission is to give to the world that truth after which humanity thirsts. Her mode of dispensation will vary from age to age. New times, new duties. Her policy is often suggested by the change of front in the line of the enemy.

As the "printed word" is now the great vehicle of propaganda, the great message of Catholic Truth will be given more by print than by speech. This new apostleship has opened the doors to Catholic lay activity. The Catholic Truth Society is one of its many forms and should, to be faithful to its origin, remain a specifically Catholic laymen's movement.

The policy of the Catholic Truth Society is very broad and embraces a great variety of activities which all tend to the propagation and defense of Catholic Truth.

Pamphlets.—The printing and diffusion of pamphlets are characteristic features of the Society. These winged booklets have come to be most fruitful transmitters of Catholic Truth. Silent Messengers of truth, they steal their way into homes and circles where the priest, and even at times the catholic layman cannot penetrate. Eloquent Preachers, their voice is heard to the extremities of the earth. Perpetual Missionaries, they continue the work when the apostle has passed to another field. They keep the light of faith burning bright in many a lonely homesteader's cabin on the Prairies of our Great West. How often have we not seen farmers coming into the Regina Cathedral to fill their pockets with pamphlets from the book-rack before they returned to their farms often situated at thirty or forty miles from a Church! Silent Controversionalists, they give Catholic information and drive the argument home without offence to the pride of the reader; for, the personal element of the controversy is eliminated. Their unobtrusiveness is what the inquirer appreciates in matters of religious research particularly.

The *Circulation of Catholic Papers* and their *remailing* to those who live far from large centres and are out of touch with the Church are other forms of the Apostolate of the Catholic Truth Society. By these means Catholic printed matter is capital, bearing compound interest and more.

Free distribution of leaflets; the Mass register in the hotels and public places; the information bureau; the bill-board; information about Catholic Faith given by a Correspondence Guild; circulating libraries; reading and study circles; reference library; the introduction of Catholic literature into Public Libraries by creating the demand for it, . . . these are some of the means through which the Society pursues its policy. To every wind, we may say, it sows the good seed of truth.

To fully understand the principles and forward with energy and perseverance the policy of the Catholic Truth Society, demands an enthusiastic love of the Church and an abiding confidence in the conquering power of Truth and in its ultimate triumph. Only a zealous and aggressive Catholic can grasp this vision and walk in its light. But the example of the enemy's activities alone should be sufficient to give us that zeal and aggressiveness. The Dominion is flooded with the literature of the Methodist Social Service, of the Bible Society, of the Christian Science, of the Rationalistic Press Association. Their activities should act on our apathetic Catholics as the gust of wind that scatters the ashes and fans the smouldering embers to a flame.

Generous are the hopes founded on the future of the Catholic Truth Society of Canada. With its far-flung line, from coast to coast, great are the services it can render to the Church. But there is no field with greater possibilities for this apostolate of the "printed word" than our Western Provinces. There the pastors are yet few and the flock very scattered. The little pamphlet, the Catholic paper will keep the watch around the lonely settler's faith until the living contact with the Church's authority and sacraments be renewed. And in the great battle against religious indifference and profound materialism which are rapidly spreading over our West, the Catholic Truth Society will make us realize the saving power of Christianity. . . . *"And you shall see Truth and Truth shall make you free."*

CHAPTER XV.

A SUGGESTION*

Importance of the Catholic Press—Requisites for its Success in the West.

NOWADAYS the Press is assuredly the greatest factor of the public mind. For, if public opinion is "King" and "Master" of the modern world, the "Press" is his "Prime Minister." Between these two great forces there is a continuous action and reaction; the Press is at the same time the moulder and mirror of public opinion.

We all know how the world has turned this mighty weapon against the Catholic Church. To create an anti-Catholic opinion, to surround the Church—its authority, its practices—with an at-

*This Chapter was published as an article in the "North West Review," Winnipeg, June 1st, 1918, under the following caption—"Timely Suggestions on needs of Catholic Press in West—Constructive attempt to solve problem which has engaged attention for many years."

The following editorial remarks accompanied its publication.

"We are indebted to Rev. Father Daly, C.SS.R., of Regina, for a thoughtful contribution on the needs of the Catholic Press in Western Canada. This subject is by no means new. Most people have had a fling at it one time or another, and those have been most insistent as a rule who have known least about it. The article under consideration, however, which may be found upon another page, besides pointing out the difficulties which must be encountered and overcome, outlines a constructive policy which should engage the earnest attention of the Catholic public. A scheme of development is there in broad outline and it is with particular pleasure that we call our readers' attention to it. We

mosphere of prejudice and antagonism has always been the aim of the non-Catholic press. Of late this campaign has become so universal and so violent "that were St. Paul to live among us, he would become a journalist," said Archbishop Ireland. Repeatedly the Pontiffs of Rome have urged the faithful to contribute to the support of the Catholic Press. "In vain you will build churches," said Pius X, "give missions, found schools; all your works, all your efforts will be destroyed if you are not able to wield the defensive and offensive weapon of a loyal and sincere Catholic Press."

The Catholics of Western Canada should have these words of the beloved Pontiff continually before their minds. There is no place in Canada where this vital factor, the Catholic Press, is of such an absolute necessity. In our sparsely settled Provinces the Catholic paper is the greatest help

---

would ask them to study it—particularly those who have had some practical experience in newspaper work—and to give us the benefit of their thought and experience. A special invitation is extended to our staff of faithful correspondents and contributors who have stuck to their posts through fair weather and foul at considerable expense and inconvenience to themselves. They are in a position to realize in a very special manner the difficulties of the situation and their suggestions should prove invaluable. If everyone interested would expend a fraction of the energy wasted in destructive criticism in working out a scheme of practical operation along constructive lines much good would result therefrom. Suggestions need not necessarily be for publication. Any communication marked "not for publication" shall be, needless to state, regarded as private and confidential. But let all help. An old newspaper maxim is to the effect that the printer's devil has ideas that the editor or business manager would pay good money for."

of the priest. It prepares, keeps, and perfects his work and very often is the only silent messenger of the Church's teachings on the lonely prairie. Isolation from all Catholic life, from its teachings, its authority, its sacraments, has created through Western Canada a tremendous leakage in the Church. This leakage can be stopped to a certain extent by the active service of a good Press. The Catholic paper, indeed, reacts as an antitoxin against the virus of unbelief and indifferentism which a non-Catholic atmosphere is bound to spread. In its columns we find the answers to the misrepresentations and slanders which bigotry is ever throwing at the Church. But above all it is through the medium of the Catholic paper that the lonely Western settler enters into what we would call the larger life of the Church. We are too prone to think of and judge the Church by what we see of Her in our own nearest surroundings. We lose sight of Her Catholicity and forget that greater life which is ever pulsating throughout the world. The reading of the Catholic paper breaks down the narrow walls of parochialism, provincialism and nationalism, and introduces its readers into the more serene and more spacious regions of Catholic life. This is, in our opinion, the greatest benefit one can derive from the assiduous and intelligent reading of a good, active, Catholic paper.

Australia and New Zealand have understood the imperative necessity, the paramount importance of a Catholic Press. "The Freeman's Journal," "The Southern Cross," "The Catholic Press," "The New Zealand Tablet," are widely circulated weekly papers that keep Catholic life so intense in those distant colonies. What the Catholics of Australia have done, why can we not, in Western Canada, do likewise?

One cannot, indeed, over-estimate the value of a Catholic paper, especially in a sparsely settled country where the Church has yet but missions, where the visits of the priest and the teachings of the Gospel are intermittent, where the Catholics are lost among people of different faith and often of hostile feeling. But, if we wish our Catholic Press to fulfil its noble mission, it must be received as an expected and welcomed friend, and not, as often is the case, as an intruder, a sickly visitor who imposes himself more or less on our faith and generous nature.

What then are the conditions of genuine success for a Catholic paper? *Vigour in policy, extensiveness in circulation*: these are the two essential conditions of success. The Catholic paper in a community must be a live-wire of high voltage, carrying light, heat, and power, and not a mere telegraphic-cable repeating what others have already said, or serving as a safety valve for the overflow of local gossip. The news and issues of general interest should be so combined with local topics as to awaken and keep the attention of the reader.

Circulation is also fundamental in journalism as well as in the human system. It carries life into the whole organism and is the warrant of success. The moment circulation becomes stagnant and loses hold of the people, the paper is but a ghost. Poor circulation is what gives to so many Catholic papers such languid existence.

How can we create these conditions of success for the Catholic Press in Western Canada, where its need is so deeply felt? There is the crux of the present situation. Our scattered and comparatively small population, even in our cities, the extreme difficulty of securing and keeping managers and editors suited for this work, the indifference and spirit of commercialism which characterize Western Canada: all these factors tend to render precarious the life of a Catholic paper. And still the crying need is there; how are we to meet it?

This leads us to make a suggestion which would help to solve the problem of the Catholic Press in the West. The beautiful work of the Catholic Press in France has prompted it.

The society of "La Bonne Presse" issues a weekly paper, "La Croix." This paper has different issues for the different parts of France. At the central office, in Paris, exists a well organized "boiler-plate" service for general Catholic news and opinions. These "boiler-plates" are shipped to all the sub-stations, where, during the week are composed the pages of local news, editorials, advertisements, etc. This is the most economical and most efficient modern method of publishing several papers or different issues of the one paper.

Our circulation in Western Canada would not perhaps yet warrant such an organization. But working along the same lines, could we not have *one paper,* with *different issues* for the different Prairie Provinces? This would necessitate a chief editor for the editorials of general character, common to all—and a sub-editor in each Province who could also act as manager in his section of the country. To write editorials adapted to the ever-changing needs of his Province, answer those who attack the Church in our local papers, guide our Catholics in the various issues which are discussed in the Province, and control the correspondence for the different news centres, would be the duties of this sub-editor.

One central printing plant would be sufficient. Being a weekly paper, the printing and mailing do not matter much, provided the plant were not too far from the extreme points of circulation. With the exception of the composition of the specific pages of each issue, according to Provinces, the general overhead expenses of printing and re-mailing would be the same, and yet we would have a *local Catholic paper.* This plan of unification would allow us, without heavy expenses, to answer efficiently the local needs of each diocese and each Province.

We have the "Northwest Review." It possesses a splendid equipment and could easily duplicate its actual out-put. Why could we not take that paper, and have a Manitoba, a Saskatchewan, and an Alberta edition? The plant is there, and why could not all Catholics take full advantage of it, at a price with which no local or provincial Catholic paper could compete, at least in the present circumstances. It would require "a sub-editor-manager" in each Province to direct the provincial policy of his specific edition and manage its circulation in every Catholic community. This plan would be workable until the time when success would warrant in each Province a local printing plant, having at its service a "boiler plate" supply from the main office.

The possibilities and opportunities for the Catholic Press have never been greater than they are now. Never and nowhere has its need been more commanding than it is now in Western Canada. In this period of social reconstruction, efficient organization and combination of all energies are necessary. Organization implies leadership, and able leadership needs the support of publicity to create sane opinions, to spread and defend them.

CHAPTER XVI

THE NEW CANADIAN

Immigration!—Are We ready for It?

DEMOBILIZATION is over. Canada has settled down to the work of "Reconstruction." Already the eyes of every serious minded Canadian scan the horizon, wondering if these transatlantic liners now bound for our ports carry in their dark hulls hosts of new settlers. Immigration is the topic of the hour. Confronted as we are by a fabulous national debt, GREATER PRODUCTION is the only solution. This intense and extensive development of agriculture and industry necessarily involves immigration.—Immigration is therefore an economic necessity.

War-wearied nations of Europe are just waking up to the realities of conditions. The dark cloud has lifted only to show everywhere silent industries and desolate fields. Thousands and hundreds of thousands are turning their eyes to the "New World"—as to the *"Land of Opportunity."* They need Canada to break away from a gloomy past, just as Canada needs them to build a bright and prosperous future.

*Opinions may vary as to the time when immi-

---

*200,000 are expected to come to Canada in 1921 from the British Isles alone. Hon. J. H. Calder, Minister of Immigration, made this statement.

gration will be once more at its height, but all seem to agree on the certainty of the fact. Probably the British Isles will open the march in the onward rush to Canada; Continental Europe will follow in their wake. Already the various philanthropic and religious organizations are preparing to welcome the new-comer to our Shores.

Misdirected and unsupervised immigration has been for the Church in the past a great source of leakage. Here and there noble and zealous efforts have been made to prevent these losses; but they were local and spasmodic. It was only a few years previous to the outbreak of the war that a Catholic Immigration Society for the Dominion was formed. The Reverend Abbe Casgrain was its Founder and Director. Homes and agencies were opened in every large city. Let us hope that this Dominion-wide organization will once more soon become a reality. A priest in full charge of its organization and responsible for its efficiency is, we believe, the main condition of success. And indeed immigration is in Canada one of those problems that over-lap the boundaries of dioceses and provinces and call for the co-operation and co-ordination of all forces. A leader, with the sanction and backing of the Hierarchy, will be the binding link between the various helping factors and will prevent immigration becoming "nobody's business" just because "it is everybody's business." This method of an organized and responsible unity will alone straighten out our line of defence from Halifax to Vancouver, and pinch out the various salients of enemy forces that are always and everywhere at work.

But who will carry out this leader's policy, once thought out and approved of? As our Catholic Immigration Society is about to reorganize its forces to meet new conditions, may we be allowed to offer a suggestion? The Knights of Columbus have just finished the great work of their "Army Huts." During the war and particularly during the demobilization, they had trained secretaries, hotels, recreation rooms, for the welfare of our soldiers. This work has placed them in the field of "Social Service" and given them a standing in the community at large. Now why could not that organization be maintained and serve the purpose of Catholic Immigration?

The Knights of Columbus are indeed ready for the task. Their chain of huts from coast to coast link together our main centres; their trained secretaries who have enlisted the sympathetic co-operation of devoted ladies; the very nature of the Order, Dominion-wide in its organization and spreading beyond the boundaries of any particular Province, everything seems now to invite them to turn their efforts to the great Cause of Immigration. During the war they worked side-by-side with the Red Triangle (Y.M.C.A.) and the Red Shield (S.A.). As these organizations are now intensely taking up what they call "Canadianization" work in its various aspects, is it befitting, would you think, for our Knights to drop out of the field? Should they not, on the contrary, prepare to "carry on"—as their brother Knights are doing across the border? The example they are giving there to the Catholic laity is simply wonderful. It is an object lesson that has awakened the tremendous energies that lie dormant in the ranks of the Catholic laymen and only want the spark of "leadership" to ignite them. And indeed no work should appeal more to the Knights, for it places them in their true sphere of action. It opens up long vistas of "Social religious work," by giving them the consciousness of the religious solidarity and the feeling of their social and national responsibilities. With that vision, under that impulse, they walk from their Council Chambers into the very life of the Church and of the Nation. They assume in all reality their office of a *Loyal Body-guard*. For, in this matter, our contention is that where the Knights of Columbus' Order is not wedded to some definite programme of action, in harmony with its aim and constitution, it ceases to be an asset and will soon go to seed, or die of dry rot.

The following would be a summary of activities to be undertaken in connection with Immigration work. This is merely an outline that may help in drawing up a more exhaustive plan of action.

1. *Permanent Secretaries.*—In our estimation, a permanent, trained and well-paid secretary is the condition of genuine success. The time has passed to have to depend on voluntary and untrained service. Times have changed and methods also. The permanency of a secretary gives to our work stability and promise of intense life. This has been the secret of the success of other organizations that we could afford to imitate.

Moreover this secretaryship can become the mother-cell of various activities which eventually will branch off—*i.e.*,Welfare Bureau, Information Bureau, etc., etc. This therefore should be our first preoccupation, for on it depend the life and prosperity of our Immigration Work.

2. *Ladies' Auxiliary.*—Local Women's organization can be called upon to bring their sympathetic support to the carrying out of this work of Catholic Immigration. Generous and devoted women are always to be found to whom this work will appeal. Their natural sympathy and their great faith make them always the "Real Workers." The very same ladies who helped so wonderfully in our patriotic work could continue to place their kindness and devotedness at the Service of this great Catholic Cause. We only need, we are sure, to call on them, and organize their various forces. Why should not "The Catholic Women's League" have its branch from coast to coast and take up everything of interest to the Catholic

Womanhood of Canada, and thereby, to the Church also?

This would have a great bearing on various issues and offer a great medium for organized opinion and co-ordinated action. Has not the time come when our women forces have to organize and unite into one great Canadian Catholic Body?

3. *Literature, Publicity.*—We are living in an age when literature and publicity are the great vehicles of public opinion. We need, to carry on the work successfully, plenty of good literature and efficient, sane publicity. The hour has come to walk right out in the open and nail our sign to the post at every cross-way. Our Catholic Immigrants are entitled to this service which will offset the influences of dangerous agencies that meet them too often as they set foot on our shores.

A new map of Western Canada with designations of Churches and Missions, with resident or non-resident priests is needed. The map published before the war would have to be revised, for the growth of the Church has been wonderful—in certain dioceses particularly. Attractive booklets giving useful information and warning the incoming immigrants against the specific dangers he is liable to meet with; folders and cards with addresses of the nearest Catholic churches and rectories, with 'phone number of the Catholic Bureau, should be ready on hand. A list of the various offices of the Society and of other Catholic Social

Centres should also be now prepared.   This, we may remark, is very important and demands careful study and experience.   A short snappy leaflet very often goes further than a diluted booklet. What others have done or are doing in this line will be of great help.   Before the war the Catholic Immigration Society of Canada had such literature.   The Catholic Truth Society of Canada could co-operate in this matter.

To reach the Catholic immigrant and emigrant is very often a problem of *publicity*.   Posters on the docks, in the railroad stations and other prominent places, cards, notices on the bulletin-boards of the steamers and hotels, distribution of leaflets on boats and trains, copies of current activities in the newspapers, advertising in our papers and papers abroad, listing of the Catholic Bureau with other similar work in the city, are some of the means to keep our work before the public.   Let us not be afraid to place our name where it can be seen.   We cannot afford to hide our light under the bushel.   Let it burn bright, to attract and guide our Catholic brother as he comes to our shores and goes through our country.

4. *Co-operation.*—Co-operation of all our bureaus with our Catholic Societies of Emigration of England, Ireland, etc., with Canadian Government bureaus, Federal and Provincial and various other benevolent organizations in Canada, as Traveller's Aid, etc., will be a marked and appre-

ciated aid to our work. And when others will see us at "Our Father's work," they will refer our own to us. This is the ordinary experience of all engaged in Social Service activities.

The Catholic Emigration Society of England has been recently formed and is preparing for the exodus that will follow the inauguration of the Government schemes for assisting ex-Service men. This Society will work on national lines with international co-operation. The "Universe" of Sept. 26, 1919, gives us an account of the first meeting. The movement is endorsed by the Hierarchy and representatives of Catholic life in the British Isles, Canada, Australia and South-Africa.

5. *Finance.*—Naturally this work will demand funds. Catholic Charity will come to our rescue as this is certainly a work of preservation which should appeal to any zealous Catholic. And what others have been able to do, why could we not find means to do?

But in this work the Canadian Government will give a helping hand. The authorities in Ottawa will be the first to appreciate what we will do for our new Canadians. In a recent memoir submitted to the Premiers of our various Provinces the social welfare of the immigrants was one of the topics to which particular attention was given. We can see that the Government will be ready to subsidize social work in Immigration, provided there is no over-lapping. There will be subsidies for

our work, if we are organized and ask for them.
When looking over the amounts distributed to various Immigrations Societies, we see, for instance, in
1913-1914 the Salvation Army receiving a subsidy
of over $22,000, while all the Catholic Immigra-
tion Societies received only about $6,000. We con-
clude that it is simply because we did not ask for
our "Pound of Flesh."

.   .   .   .   .

Should not, therefore, the work of Catholic
Immigration with all its wonderful possibilities
for the welfare of Church and Country, appeal
to our Canadian Knights of Columbus? Many and
many a settler has been lost to the Church—he, his
children and future generations—because perhaps
no one was there to receive him on his arrival in his
new Country, to help him to settle where there was
a church, a priest, and a Catholic school. No one
needs more the help of his Catholic brother than
the immigrant, who has just broken away with a
past made up of customs, friendships, racial feelings, of all that is dear to man's heart, and faces
an enigmatic future.

The long procession which we have seen in the
years of intense immigration, winding its way
through our cities and losing itself on the plains of
the West, is about to start again.   Shall we be
there to welcome and direct it?

Knights of Columbus, what is your answer?

CHAPTER XVII.

UT SINT UNUM

*A Catholic Congress of the Western Provinces, the
Ultimate Solution of Their Problems—What
is a Congress?—Its Utility-—Its Necessity
—A Tentative Programme.*

TO know a problem, to probe its nature, and
to analyze its various factors frequently lead
to an easy and happy solution. But as Church
problems are mostly of a complex nature and cover
a wide range, they necessarily depend for their
solution on the co-operation of the various com-
ponent units. This explains why we would now
appeal to the Church of the West as a whole, for
the solving of the problems dealt with in this book.
Of their nature they out-distance the boundaries of
parish and diocese, for they affect the Church as
a whole. Without wishing to disparage the value
of parochial and diocesan activities, we claim that
the issues we have placed before our readers are
not confined within the imaginary lines of the parochial unit or the boundaries of jurisdiction. They
will not be met with rightly and successfully, if
the Church as a unit does not agree on a uniform
plan of action. For, to prevent a deplorable waste
of potential powers, of misdirected energies
and of overlapping work, to forward the great

cause of the Church and realize its Catholic aspirations, to present a united front to common dangers, the union and co-operation of all the parishes and all the dioceses are an absolute necessity.

Never has the Church in Canada felt so keenly the necessity of this union and co-operation. An acute sense of uneasiness has spread, far and broad, apathy and lethargy. Instinctively eyes turn to the heights from whence they have a right to expect direction and help. The necessity of some INTER-DIOCESAN ORGANIZATION, along the lines of the National Catholic Welfare Council of the United States, is the outspoken conviction of many and the unexpressed desire of all. We are weak in our divided strength. The criticism of both clergy and laity in this matter is widespread and very often justifiable. We could willingly endorse what Cardinal Newman wrote to a friend: "Instead of aiming at being a world-wide power, we are shrinking into ourselves, narrowing the lines of communion, trembling at freedom of thought, and using the language of dismay and despair at the prospect before us, instead of the high spirit of the warrior going out conquering and to conquer."—(Life, by Ward II, p. 127.)

"Ut sint unum!" "That they may be one!" This is the supreme solution of the weighty problems now facing the Church at this crucial period of readjustment and reconstruction. A general Congress would crystallize, we believe, our desires for unity into a concrete fact. It would help to group the various thoughts and workable schemes around a definite plan and stimulate activities in view of its realization. Some may find it rather presumptuous on our part to formulate such a proposal. Our sincerity and loyalty to the great Cause in view is our only excuse.

What is a Catholic Congress?

A Catholic Congress—be it provincial, regional, national or simply diocesan—is the meeting of Catholic clergy and laity under the guidance of the Hierarchy, for the *study* of various problems, the *development and coordination of energies,* the *unification and concentration* of purpose.

The members of the Congress are delegates from the various parishes, from social, mutual and diocesan organizations. It is of absolute necessity that the laity be well represented, for the Congress is the great school of "social action," the great medium of educating the Catholic body and developing the sense of Catholic social responsibility.

The guidance of our Fathers in Christ, the Hierarchy, ensures to the Congress its value, its authority—*Posuit Episcopos regere Ecclesiam Dei.*

The object of the meeting is to give to Catholic life, by the perfect organization and coordination of all its moral, social and religious activities, its maximum of efficiency. This necessitates the *study of the problems of the day* in their relation with Catholic principles. Therefore the Congress is a readjustment of our vision to the everchanging conditions of society; desuete methods are dropped and methods more in harmony with the necessities of the times are examined, approved of and adopted. It affords an opportunity to discuss public questions, to educate and crystallize public opinion on the Catholic view-point of pending problems. This readjustment is, in our estimation, one of the greatest benefits of a Congress, for without it there is waste of energies and danger of compromise on the part of the most zealous.

The *development* and *co-ordination of energies* will be the natural sequel of this general exchange of ideas, of this universal consultation of the Catholic body. When we shall have counted our resources we shall then easily marshal existing forces, create new battalions for the defence and peaceful promotion of Catholic doctrine, liberties, and influence.

To give unity of purpose to the various Catholic organizations, to direct the loyal active co-operation of every unit towards the greatest welfare of the Church, in one word, to create Catholic solidarity, is the ultimate aim and supreme triumph of a Catholic Congress.

This congress therefore, stands for the mobilization of the Catholic army for manœuvres, and does not mean a mere pageant, a complacent exhibition of our numbers, the platonic rehearsal of our past glories and great achievements. "We are here to do a work, and not to make a show," should we say with Cardinal Manning.

The *Golden Rule* that presides over, and directs this exchange of thoughts, this study of problems, this marshalling of our forces, has always been: *In necessariis unitas, in dubiis, libertas, in omnibus charitas—Unity in essentials; liberty in non-essentials; charity in all things.* There is no reason whatever why a Congress should be ever aggressive. Destructive criticism leads nowhere. But there is every reason why a Congress should be perpetually active and "destructively constructive."

Should We have a Catholic Congress of the Western Provinces?

The utility and necessity of a Catholic Congress will be an adequate answer to this question—

Utility of Catholic Congresses.

Benedict XV in his letter to the American Hierarchy, March, 1919, underlines very strongly the utility of these Catholic Meetings, "We learn," says the Holy Father, "that you have unanimously resolved that a yearly meeting of all the Bishops shall be held at an appointed place in order to adapt means most suitable of promoting the interest and welfare of the Catholic Church and that you appointed from among the Bishops two commissions, one of which to deal with *social questions,* while the other will study *educational problems,* and both will report to their Episcopal brethren. This is truly a worthy resolve and with the utmost satisfaction We bestow upon it our approval."

"It is indeed wonderful how greatly the progress of Catholicism is favored by those frequent assemblies of the Bishops, which our Predecessors have more than once approved. When the knowledge and the experience of each are communicated to all the Bishops, it will be easily seen what errors are secretly spreading and how they can be extirpated; what threatens to weaken discipline among clergy and people and how best the remedy can be applied; what movements if any, either local or nation wide, are afoot for the control or judicious restraint of which the wise direction of the Bishop may be most helpful."

"It is not enough however, to cast out evil; good work must at once take its place and so these men are incited by mutual example. Once admitted that the *harvest depends upon the method and the means,* it follows easily, that the assembled Bishops returning to their respective dioceses, will rival one another in reproducing those works, which they have seen elsewhere in operation to the distinct advantage of the Faithful."

Great indeed are the advantages that accrue to the Church, in its social influence particularly, from a Congress. And indeed, since on Catholic principles alone depend the solution of the social problem, the welfare of Church and State alike requires that Catholics in every condition of life should co-operate in the application of those principles. The influence of the Church in these matters depends not only on her official teaching, but greatly on the social activities of Her children. These activities translate into tangible facts Her doctrines on justice and charity, and thus spread the beneficial influence of Her teachings.

The specific end of the Congress is to develop, co-ordinate, and direct these social activities of Catholics and bring their influence to bear upon the community at large. *Instaurare omnia in Christo* . . . is the programme of such gatherings.

The Congress (1) establishes a Catholic platform and rallies our forces around it, by creating a social solidarity, (2) enables our existing institutions and societies to extend their activities by the co-ordination of efforts; (3) facilitates the creation of new organizations to meet specific needs. "We cannot," writes Father Plater, S.J., "stand aloof from secular movements, neither may we wholly surrender ourselves to them. We must by common study bring them to the test of Catholic principles and we must by common action bend them to the great issues of which the world is losing sight."

Moreover, once the Catholic laity has been lured into taking active part in social work, once it feels that it is no more a dead unit but a living factor, the Congress becomes a necessity, for it then serves as the mental background that throws its work in relief and keeps the fires of enthusiasm burning.

Necessity of a Catholic Congress at the Present Time.

The absolute *absence of unity and cohesion* in our various social activities; the momentous *period of reconstruction* with its far-reaching consequences in our national, political, social and economic life; the *examples* given to us by other *Catholic countries* and by our own enemies; these three and potent reasons urge, in our estimation, the calling of a Congress to get our bearings and to discuss ways and means of action.

The deplorable lack of unity in the Church of Canada is obvious and can be traced to many causes. Racial and language conflicts particularly, have divided our forces, absorbed our activities, narrowed our views and made us forget the Catholic view-point of greater problems. But times and ideas are changing. Never, we believe has the feeling of our divisions and dissensions been so acute; never has the demand for united action been so imperative as now. The distressing times through which the world is passing have forced upon us issues which will require the united strength of Catholic forces.

United action, so much desired and so desperately needed, requires a *uniform plan* and an *authoritative leadership*. A Congress will give us these two elements of a much desired unity.

Too long, we believe, have Catholic social activities been directed along purely parochial and diocesan lines. The isolated action of parishes, especially in our cities, is no longer able to grapple with and solve our modern complex problems. Parochialism is conducive to the enjoyment of the Church's beneficial influences, but often leads us to forget our responsibilities to the Church Universal. "Parochialism is the clog on the wheel of united Catholic Action in Canada." (Canadian Freeman, Nov. 13, 1919.) And even on a broader field have we not seen conflicting directions and abstinence of necessary interference, precisely because the issues were seen in different quarters from different angles. So, a united plan of action which is so absolutely necessary for efficient work cannot be obtained without consultation and exchange of ideas.

This unity of plan will bring the Catholic consciousness to a focus. It will create an intelligent interest in Catholic social work, and lead to the gradual formation of various specific social organizations. When luminous rays are brought to a focus their light and heat are most intense.

The best concerted plans, the greatest enthusiasm to execute them, will be of no avail without leadership. For the secret of the success and usefulness of an organization is to be found in the ability, character and ideals of its leader. Never perhaps in Canada, has the absence of authoritative leadership, especially among the Catholic laity, been felt so keenly as at the present trying period. Let us hear an authoritative writer on the matter:

"When the great buzz and stir of rebuilding comes and the interchange and counterchange of ideas begin, the newly awakened folk will begin to enquire what the Church has to say and to suggest on every ethical and religious problem that comes up in the course of planning and discussion. But they will wish to know, not in the terms in which great minds of the past have formulated Catholic teaching, but in the speech and with the illustrations of contemporary life. What we need is Catholic intellectual leadership to interpret in a way they can understand, the deep ethical truths of Catholic ethics, dogmas, which are a guide to the reconstructive activities of all time. Without changing a jot of the unchangeable truth, new series of interpretations can be given to Catholic dogma, morals, ethics, with explanations that will catch the ear of the intelligent non-Catholic, give him in his own idiom the solid gist of Catholic Doctrine and appeal to him with the simple eloquence that Truth always has, when presented in the proper way." (Father Garesche, S.J., America, Dec. 28.)   For, as the Editor of the Universe said, commenting on the death of Sir Mark Sykes, "The secret of ideal Catholic leadership lies in a passionate desire for the Catholic good inseparable from the common good, combined with a complete aloofness from any sectional interest."

Now, we may ask, what has given to Catholic France, Catholic Belgium, Catholic England, these eminent leaders who in public and social life, are by their fearless courage and ceaseless action, the very personification of Catholicism? It is without doubt their Catholic Congresses. There, the contact with the great problems of the day gave them the vision of things before unseen, made them emerge from the common mass, and marked them as leaders. There, they learned to think just, broad and deep. The great Congresses of Catholic Germany brought Windthorst to the foreground and made him the leader of the greatest Catholic organization. What the Congresses have done for Catholic Germany, Belgium, France and England, they will also do for Canada. They will give us true leaders, men of clear vision, of indomitable and fearless will, of patient and persevering action. For *mistaken leadership is still a greater calamity than the absence of it.* The Plenary Council of Quebec urges the Catholics of Canada to meet in Congress: *"Qui quidem in talium caetuum frequentia liberius poterunt et validius sui nominis professionem sustinere, hostiles impetus propulsare."* In the mind of the great Pope Leo XIII, whose words are here quoted, "a Congress is the most powerful offensive and defensive weapon." Quebec Plenary Council—No. 441, d.

. . . . .

We may then conclude with a French writer: *"A Congress is a sacrament of unity."* It will visualize to the modern pagan for whom unity of doctrine means nothing, the tremendous powers, the living influences that flow from that same unity on the world. And for the Catholics at large it will now answer to a widespread, deep-seated longing for a more effective national Catholic unity of action.

Yes, at all times, a Congress is a necessity for united action; but in the troubled periods we now face, after the war, it becomes a factor of supreme interest and of the most vital importance.

. . . . .

Reconstruction is the world's watch-word as nations rise from the ruins a long protracted and universal war has accumulated around them.

The period of reconstruction, more than that of the war, will test our national fibre. The problems we face are in extent, in character, in complexity greater than at any other period of history. The strain will be greater, for the conflict is being lifted to a higher plane, that of ideas. And ideas are the supreme realities, the dynamic forces that rule the world, the fulcrum that shifts the axis of the world's civilization.

In these momentous times, the isolation of Catholics would be *a calamity;* their participation, *a blessing,* for Church and country. To stand aloof from the solution of the problems that stare us in the face and insistently demand attention and solution, to confine our efforts solely to parochial institutions and not enter into the broader field of public life is for Catholics, at this hour, nothing short of a calamity. The consequences of this abstention will be to limit our action to mere protestation and often useless defence, when our principles are assailed and our positions in danger, when a leakage, through the social activities of others, is but too manifest. Let us on the contrary, turn the energies we lose in mere defence to constructive work, and our positions will be safer, and our principles better appreciated. *"Our liberties are best defended when Catholics throw themselves into the stream of public life."*

And does not Catholic doctrine stand essentially for constructive forces in the social, political and economic life of a country? We possess the foundation, the plans, the material of all true and lasting social reconstruction. The Gospel and the natural law form the rock-bottom foundation; the definite and unchanging principles of morality are its structural lines; justice is as the steel girders and charity the fast-binding cement.

"At the present day," wrote Professor G. Toniolo, the eminent Catholic Italian economist, "the great Encyclicals of Leo XIII, which, sustained by the common light of the Evangelical teachings of Christian philosophy and Revelation, have illuminated all the phases of social, civil and political knowledge in harmonious, logical connections. At the present day we possess a unified complex of sociological teachings, brought together in a system, which rests against the supernatural, which measures up to the problems of our age, which, absorbing everything, takes unto itself all that is true in modern science and is proven by experience, and thus is prepared to oppose successfully a positivistic, materialistic and anti-Christian sociology."

Yes, we possess the true solution of modern problems and . . . what are we doing to give it to the world, to the community in which we live? Why, the very fabric of social order is questioned, our working men are absorbing everywhere the most subversive doctrines; the relations between capital and labor are strained to a breaking-point; our industrial system is controlled by economic theories divorced from ethics, whereby the worker is a mere producer; the State-monopoly is gradually spreading its influences as huge tentacles, around our most sacred liberties; the equilibrium between liberty and authority—these two poles of Christian civilization—is being displaced; . . . and what are the activities of the Catholic body, as a whole, in Canada, to stem the rising tide? A ser-

mon, now and then, on Socialism or on the rights
and duties of labour, will not solve the problems
and extinguish the volcano upon which we are
peacefully living. In our cities, the housing problem, which involves to a great extent, the moral life
of the masses, is acute; the white slave traffic has
established its haunts and commercialized vice; the
moving picture-show has become everywhere the
most popular educational factor: at its school the
young generation, eyes riveted on the flickering
screen, is drinking in the alluring lessons of free
love, divorce and every anti-Christian doctrine;
our ports will soon see a new tide of immigration
invade our shores; the non-catholic denominations
are crumbling away under the very weight of their
destructive and disintegrating principle of private
judgment; we are surrounded with pagans to whom
the supernatural religion of Christianity is but a
name or a memory; from our great West comes the
urgent cry for help, for men and money; the
Church Extension, as the watchman in the night is
crying out to our uninterested Catholics—"the day
is coming, the night is coming"—meaning that the
faint streak on the eastern horizon may be the last
rays of a dying day or the first blush of a new
dawn; . . . and what are we doing? Here and
there, a spasmodic effort, a generous outburst of
zeal—the work of some society, parish or diocese.
While, what we need now is the combined effort of
all the Catholics. This will only be obtained

through a Congress.   What we need is *organized opinion*.   The modern world is very sensitive to *organized opinion*.—Let us get together!   We only need leaders to see our opinion become *"articulate and authoritative"* and make its weight felt in public life.   Never has a Congress been more necessary than now.   Without it, Catholics will not take part in reconstruction, for a Congress alone can unite us and give us the guarantee that our energies will not be "frittered away by overlapping and friction."

There is a great moral tide now running in the world, said President Wilson in his toast to the King of England . . . and that tide is the great opportunity for Catholic social principles to take the high sea of public life.   Let us therefore, like the skilful mariner, count with this set of the tide and catch it at its crest.   "There is a tide in the affairs of nations like that of men, which when taken at the flood leads on to glory.   If we do not direct the ideas that are awork in the seething mind of the world, they will spend their energies in retributive destruction," wrote the Philosopher President of the United States.

"The thrilling opportunities of the time, we will say with Father Garesche, S.J., should stir us to the depths of our souls' capacity with enthusiasm, energy and sacrifice. . . . Our realization of the needs and chances of the Church and the world, should stir us to the utmost of personal effort."

.   .   .   .   .

Exempla Trahunt.—The great benefits that have ensued from a general consultation or meeting of the *body Catholic in various countries* form the best standing proof of their value. In England the annual conference of the Catholic Truth Society and other federated Societies, is the leading event of Catholic life. It has developed among the English Catholic laity, a militant, virile Catholicism, most remarkable for its aggressive policy and wonderful for its array of social organizations, as one may readily learn from the "Hand-book of Catholic Charitable and Social work" published by the C. T. Society of London. Who does not know the wonderful results of the yearly Catholic Congresses of Germany before the war? We would refer the reader to the wonderful book of Father Plater, S.J., "Catholic Social Work in Germany." To the same source may be traced the great social activities of Catholics in France and Belgium. In 1919 the Catholics of Holland met at Utrecht, and in a national general convention, discussed the Catholic view-point of burning questions—political, social and spiritual. The results of their united efforts are already tangible. Legislation favourable to Catholic Schools has been enacted; a Catholic University is being founded; the Catholic press is a power; sane social legislation has been adopted.

An example that may strike home better, is one that comes from our brethren in the United States.

Federation has already accomplished wonders among our American Catholics and is welding into one great unit the various societies of the Church in that immense country. This federation is only in its infancy and already its action has created a mental attitude which makes united action, in various spheres, a reality. The annual meetings of the Catholic Education Association, of the Catholic Hospitals, of Catholic Charities, of Catholic Press make good our statement. These gatherings have broadened the outlook and sympathies of the American Catholics in general, and created the vision, the sterling Catholicism, the fearless energy and the fervent enthusiasm that characterize leaders. Has not the general meeting of the American Catholic Hierarchy opened a new era for the Church in the United States? Five Boards have been formed: Education, Social Work, Press and Literature, Lay Societies, Home and Foreign Missions. Through these channels the American Episcopacy will know the doings, the needs and the possibilities of the Church as a whole, and be able at any time, to throw, on a given point, on a new issue, the full weight of united forces.

"The Welfare Council begins its second year of life and activity. It has already, in a remarkable and effective way, shown the wonderful wealth of Catholic activity, and Catholic Service throughout the country; it has unified our Catholic organizations, leaving to all their autonomy; it has made Catholic faith a greater factor in American life; and under its leaders it will, without doubt, be a further source of strength, of help and co-operation to the entire Catholic body of the Country. It is the Catholic body expressing itself with one voice and one heart in the work and in the interests common to us all as Catholics."—The N.C.W.C. Bulletin, Oct., 1920.

Fas est ab hoste doceri. . . . Powerful is the example of a brother, but often, stronger and more pungent is the example that comes from an enemy. There are times indeed, when shame and honour are stronger than love. This brings us to speak of the tremendous activities of our separated brethren. Never have their efforts in view of organizing their social service departments been so persistent and so manifest, particularly in the mission field. Doctrinal lines are being lowered and various denominations absorbed gradually into a "Church-union" scheme from coast to coast. A *"social service programme"* is the only binding element which is giving to them a fictitious unity. Fabulous sums are placed at the disposal of these bodies for home and foreign mission work. The Methodist Conference of Canada (1918—Hamilton) has pledged itself to levy $8,000,000 in the next four years for mission work. In our own country, in our Western Provinces, the field secretaries are most active among our Catholic foreigners. On the landing stage of our docks they are found to welcome the immigrants to our shores. And what could we not say of their "press activities!"

This movement for co-operation has, since the end of the war, taken tremendous proportions. Here is a fact which speaks volumes. . . . "The fight between Protestants and Catholics," said a German Protestant minister, "will forthwith subside in the domain of dogma, but it will rise in the domain of social problems. No doubt truth in the social order will prevail as it has prevailed in the field of religious dogma. But we have to change our strategy, study new tactics, and in our plan of campaign turn from the defensive to the offensive." Never should the Catholics of Canada present a more united front. To sneer and snap our fingers at the energies and organizing powers of others is often but a poor excuse for our own inertia. It is certainly no argument. *Fas est ab hoste doceri.* The lesson has often a sting, but it is a lesson. . . . We need organization! . . . The Congress is the great medium of organization. What are we going to do? Changing a little the wording of one of Cicero's famous sentences, in his orations against Catiline, the arch-enemy of Rome, we shall say: *"The enemy is at our doors! . . . and we are not even deliberating!"*

. . . . .

Before giving a suggestive programme for a Congress may we answer some objections.

"The need for co-operation and co-ordination is indeed *admitted on all hands;* it is its *feasibility* that is doubted by so many good Catholics. It is admitted to be an ideal; the question that is raised is whether the difficulties are not too great to be surmounted otherwise than by a very slow and lengthy process of evolution. That such a gradual evolution would be in accordance with both nature and history we should be the first to admit. But, after all, there is such a thing as retarding or assisting the process of evolution. The valuable maxim that 'things are what they are and their consequences will be what they will be,' is after all but half the truth. No Catholic believes that we are carried helpless along a stream of circumstances. He believes that man is man, a free being whose free action can within limits mould circumstance; and he believes that God is God, the one free Being Who can and does overrule circumstance, and Who, when and where He pleases, gives efficacy to the endeavour of His free creatures to do the same." (Universe, Aug. 15th, 1919.)

Some may say that by coming together we shall awaken susceptibilities, our motives will be suspected . . . and the final result will be more prejudice, more bigotry. . . .

There is no reason why a Congress should be of an unfriendly aggressiveness. We have ideas to advocate, they stand on their own merit. They are in our belief, the only key of salvation; let us then get together and bring them by organization and team work, into the domain of realities. Moreover, our enemies are not so very particular in dealing with us and with our principles. The best policy is to meet in the open, as our Catholics are doing in England and stand on the value of our doctrine and our works—*"Ex fructibus cognescetis illos."*

"What about the autonomy of parish and diocesan units? Are they not supreme? Will not what we advocate interfere with these organizations? Will it not destroy the work of our parochial societies, etc., etc.?"

"Organization which would attempt to meddle with local autonomy would not only defeat its purpose, but would be chiselling its own epitaph." . . . The parish and diocesan units are and must ever remain supreme, each in its own sphere. We could never get a better working basis; more genuine Christian charity and self sacrifice could not be met with outside of our acting brotherhoods and charitable organizations. . . . But, what we need more is *co-operation* between these various units in view of solving the complex social problems, especially in our cities. This suppresses neglect and over-lapping, gives efficiency with the least waste of energies. "Blend organization and co-ordination with the greatest amount of local autonomy and individual initiative": this is the sole aim a Congress has in view. There, and there alone, lies the solution of our problems.

·   ·   ·   ·   ·

Tentative Programme of Congress.

I—*Preparation.*

The *remote preparation* for such a great and important undertaking, would consist in what we would term "an educational campaign." The initial difficulty, the greatest obstacle would be to overcome the general apathy, the want of interest, *vis inertiae.* This could be done by the Catholic press, lectures, sermons, etc. It may take time to wake up our people from their slumber, but the faith is there with its latent energies, and we can count on them. The forces are there; they only need an occasion to call them into play.

.　　.　　.　　.　　.

The *immediate preparation* would consist in the appointment of a *small but strong organizing committee.* Agitation without organization is useless. On the choice and activities of this committee depends the entire success of the congress.

The various activities of this committee would be:

1. *Decide on Name.*—Congress, . . . Conference, . . . Catholic Social Service Meeting, etc. . . . This seems of no importance; but, in fact, it often goes a long way in interesting the public and warding off prejudice.

2. *Decide on Place.*—Winnipeg—Regina— Edmonton—Calgary—Saskatoon—Vancouver.

3. *Decide on Delegates.*—Mode of selection,

—clerical,—lay.   It is very essential that a meeting of that kind should be thoroughly *popular* and *representative*.

4. *Decide on Speakers, Language.*—(One or several sections.)

5. *Decide on Programme.*—This is really the essential work of the organizing committee.   In drawing the agenda, emphasis is to be laid upon problems of immediate necessity:

Defence and *construction;* defence against the enemies' activities; *strong constructive policy* with a wide scope for all energies: these are the two poles on which revolve a good programme.

Racial—Language—Political issues are to be absolutely barred from the programme.

6. *Decide on Committees.*—Their *number* and *matters to be trusted to them.*

7. *Sub-committees* can be appointed for *publicity, information, reception* (ceremonies), *invitations, billeting.*

8. *Appointment of Permanent Secretary.* . . .

N.B.—In a work of this nature it is the quiet, silent, well-thought-out preparatory work that counts.   The distribution of the work (papers—speakers—leaders) is the secret of genuine success.

Therefore, to make a Congress a success, we need:

1. *Clearly defined programme.*—(What do we want to do?)

2. *Compact and efficient organization.*—(How is it going to be done?)

3. *Competent and reliable leaders.*— (Who is going to do it?)

Foresight, energy, decision—should mark out the leaders;

Foresight will give the *vision.*

Energy will give the *will.*

Decision will push to *action.*

II—*Suggestive Programme.*

1. Committee on "Education":

1. *Our Primary Schools.*—Their legal status—their efficiency? Our teaching staff? Bureau for Catholic teachers.

2. *Higher Education.* — Catholic Colleges: their standing—*Catholic University*—Affiliation to State Universities?

3. *Sunday School.*—Teaching of Catechism—in our separate schools—in sparsely settled countries? Lay Cathechists?

2. Committee on "Catholic Missions."

1. *Home Missions.*—Church Extension.—What co-operation are we giving? Needs of the West: Men and money.

2. *Foreign Missions.* — Propagation of Faith.—Holy Childhood.

3. *What are we doing for non-Catholics?*

4. *The Missions* (parochial).

5. *Priestly* and *religious vocations.*

3. Committee on "Press and Catholic Literature."

1. *Catholic Newspapers.*—(Their policy. —Their circulation.) *Vigour in policy* and

extensiveness in circulation: two essential conditions for success.

2. *Work and establishment of Catholic Truth Society.*

3. *Catholic circulating libraries* for cities, countries. (Example of same, under care of Saskatchewan Government.)

4. Committee on "Public Morality."

1. *Divorce—Race-suicide.*

2. *Theatres—Moving pictures.*—(More severe censorship.)

3. *Eugenics?*

4. *Venereal diseases?*

5. Committee on "Social Action."

1. *Immigration—Reception* and *direction* of Catholic Immigrants at ports of St. John and Halifax and intermediate points. *Care of foreigners* (leakage).

2. *Colonization?*

3. *Young Men's Association* — on Y.M.C.A. lines. Young Girls' Association—on Y.W.C.A. lines—Girls' homes.

6. Committee on "Public Charities."

Children's Aid—Orphanages—Free Kindergartens—Day-nurseries—Juvenile Courts—Preventive and curative work.

7. Committee on "Labour Problem."

Labour Unions — Living wage — Child labour—Care of girl-workers, etc.

N.B.—The great point to elucidate in these matters is: *Must we, and how far can we, co-operate with non-Catholic bodies?* This is a very important point, far reaching in its consequences.

8. Committee on "Resolutions."

"The resolutions are to embody the fruit of the collective experience and deliberations of the Congress. They will remain then as the profession of Catholic conviction and go far to create public opinion on the questions of the day." (Fr. Plater.)

And indeed, public discussion awakens new thoughts, gives various views of a topic, suggests practical conclusions, expedient measures. It is the crystallizing process of all the activities of the Congress.

III—*After the Congress.*

The good results of a Congress are made permanent by the establishment of:

1. *A permanent Committee of Clergy and laity* —who meet occasionally to stimulate or check activities of the body at large.

2. *A Vigilance Committee*:

(a) *On legislation.*—To watch and initiate legislation—for different Provinces.

(b) *On press.*

(c) *On social work.*

3. *Bureau.*—Clearing house—where "expert knowledge and effective presentation" are to be found. To this bureau should be attached a priest who would specialize in social work.

He could be helped by an efficient secretary. His would be the energy that would carry to the various organizations life and power. The "Volksverein" in Catholic Germany was a model in this line of work.

.　　.　　.　　.　　.

"Praesentia tangens . . . futura prospiciens" is a motto which translates well the lofty ideal Catholics should have before their eyes at this turning point of history. Although we stand amid the ruins accumulated during four long years of war and are confronted by distressing after-war problems in every order of human activity, still we raise our heads in hope and look beyond the crude realities of the present to a brighter day breaking on the horizon of time, a day tinted with the rising sun of Christian doctrine. . . .

Instaurare omnia in Christo . . . to re-establish all things in Christ, is the only reconstruction that will last.

CHAPTER XVIII.

ULTIMA VERBA

THE Canadian West offers to one who has never gone beyond the Great Lakes but a misty vision of boundless prairies that stretch over three immense Provinces and lose themselves in the foothills of the snow-capped Rockies. Conflicting are the impressions that assail the traveller's mind, various the feelings that crowd around his heart when leaving behind him the East, he faces, for the first time, the "great lone land" of the West. From the immensities of the fertile prairie comes to him an invigorating air of optimism which fires him with enthusiasm and confidence in the possibilities of the country and gives him the assurance of its future. From the vast horizon that melts away into the distant blue skies "he seems to hear the footsteps of Freedom treading towards him." This mysterious attractiveness of the boundless desert that the plough has just turned into restful and fertile meadows has at all times a peculiar fascination. But it is at harvest season that our glorious West it at its best. Then under the deep blue firmament, in the glorious sunlight and exhilarating atmosphere of the rolling prairie one can hear, as it were, "the song of the land." With the hum of the binder, it comes to him from the long rows of golden sheaves, it rises from the fields where yet waves the ripening harvest.

Nature indeed is then most beautiful in the West. But for the Christian soul to whom Faith "is the evidence of things unseen and the substances of things we hope for," the visible harvest leads to the thought of that spiritual harvest to which the Master so often points in the Gospel. Under all the feverish activities which characterize our Western communities lie deep in the consciences of men those unseen realities, those spiritual values and eternal issues which constitute the religious world. In the mysterious furrows of the human heart is ripening the harvest of eternity.

The Church of God ever stands as Christ by the mysterious well of Jacob, at the intersection of the highways of History. Now, as in the days of the Saviour, winter has set in; a cold blast of indifference and unbelief sweeps over the land. Yet with the Master's vision and boundless confidence, the Church, pointing to the Western plains, repeats to us all the divine challenge. "Do not you say there are yet four months and then the harvest cometh? Behold I say to you lift up your eyes and see the countries for they are white already to the harvest." (Jo. iv, 35.)

Before parting with you, kind reader, may we make ours this pressing invitation of the Master. Yes, the immense West is "white already to the harvest." There stand as immense fields of ripening wheat, the Catholic youth of Eastern Canada, the sturdy and thrifty Catholic settlers of the British Isles and continental Europe. There the rising generation of Catholic children, like the tender green blades of the future harvest, is springing into manhood. Staring us in the face, their eyes in our eyes, the children of foreign parentage wonder what account we will make of their faith, what protection we will offer it. They are the new Canadians, the nation of to-morrow.

To focus the Catholic mind of the nation on the great problems which the West with its scattered population has forced upon our attention, has been the object we have consistently pursued through the pages of this book. *For it is a fact of every day experience that problems are only solved by those who know them, who understand their full meaning, and grasp their vital importance.*

Our sole endeavour has been to point out the controlling forces, the spiritual issues that lurk behind these problems. In debatable matters we always have tried to find that higher level which lies undisturbed by the cross-currents of opinions. Naturally there are conclusions we draw or forms of action we propose which may not find favour with everyone. There are so many angles of vision from which moral problems can be viewed. But we will say with Cardinal Newman "nothing would be done at all if a man waited until he could do it so well that no one could find fault with it."

Were we, in our insistency on certain topics and suggestions, accused of undue repetition, the importance of the subject and our eager desire of immediate action would be our only excuse and defence.

The Western spiritual harvest is indeed great and now ready for the reapers. Never in our mind has a period in the history of the Church in Canada been more fraught with greater problems than the present one which the sudden increase of the West has created. The vastness of their proportion and their far-reaching consequences involve to a great extent the future of the Church in these new Provinces and, consequently, in the Dominion at large. Moreover this immense harvest is *now* white and calls for the reapers. To-morrow will be too late, for, there comes a critical stage in the maturing harvest, when the labours of past months and the most bright prospects melt away in an hour. If therefore action is not immediate, irreparable, we contend, will be the loss to the Church in the West. Only by a prompt and united action will the stern and burning realities of the present be converted into the bright visions that our Faith has a right to expect.

The harvesters are few. But were the Church at this critical hour able to count on all the spiritual forces that lie dormant in the souls of her children in Canada, the history of the future in the West would be different from that of the past. As

in times of emergency, the conscription of Catholic forces is the supreme duty of the hour. It is
the duty of our leaders to affect by a definite policy
the "indeterminate masses," just as it is the duty of
each individual of the masses to shoulder his share
of responsibility by an active co-operation. *Without a definite workable policy of united action, and
the awakened consciousness of the Catholic masses
at large, throughout the Dominion, the Catholic
problems in Western Canada will not be solved.*

The Church in Canada, we maintain, stands at
one of those critical periods when the sweeping
current of events give a decided bend to the course
of History. The hour is serious, for never was
the future so greatly involved in the present as it
is now. All depends, to a very large extent, on
how, within the next decade or so, the Catholics
will consolidate their forces and extend their energies to meet the religious issues of the West.
Were we to fail at this momentous period, our in-
activity and want of co-operation will be charged
against us, and in the eyes of the Church we shall
be marked as felons and traitors to her great cause.
The chapter of our times in the history of the
Church would then be fittingly headed with this
accusing caption: *"What should have been!"* For,
we are the makers of History; we prepare its
verdicts.

One last word before parting with you, gentle
reader. If you have followed us through the vari-

ous problems to which we have given our attention in this book you will have remarked that there is one idea which permeates, we would say, every page of it. It is the key-note of our work. This idea is that of *"responsibility,"* which a genuine and active Catholicism necessarily implies. This thought of Catholic solidarity has inspired our humble effort; in it we place the hopes of the future. There lies in one word the burden of our message.

THE CHURCH OF THE WEST IS IN OUR HANDS—ITS FUTURE WILL BE WHAT WE SHALL MAKE IT—THAT FUTURE, WHAT SHALL IT BE?—THE DIVINE MASTER, HIS CHURCH, AND CATHOLIC POSTERITY, AWAIT OUR ANSWER.

APPENDIX

W E thought it would be a benefit to our Canadian reader to republish here three thought-compelling and illuminating articles that appeared, the first in the "New York Times," the second in the "Century Magazine" and the third in the "Detroit News." As they deal with a similar problem that confronts Canada also, they will corroborate views we have expressed here and there in our book. Let the reader substitute "Canadianization" for "Americanization" and he will find that the statements made can be well applied to existing conditions in our own Country.

I. AMERICANIZATION

By L. P. Edwards in N.Y. Times.

The United States is suffering from one of its periodic attacks of Know Nothingism. It is seriously maintained in the public prints that our recent Eastern European, and particularly our Russian, immigration contains enormous numbers of murderers, thieves, counterfeiters, dynamiters, arsonists and other criminals of the most atrocious character. It is alleged that the lives and property of all of us are in imminent danger from these incredibly numerous blackguards, and that the only salvation lies in what is called the Americanization of the foreigner.

Now, it is known to every respectable sociologist in America that our recent Eastern European immigrants, including the Russians, are just as peaceable and law-abiding people as native Americans or native American ancestry. This is a fact about which there is not the slightest doubt in the mind of any competently informed person. It has been repeatedly established by careful studies made by the United States Bureau of the Census; by various State boards and by highly qualified private foundations.

Furthermore, the most honest, thrifty, industrious, upright, God-fearing and conservative portion of our foreign population is precisely that portion which has clung most stubbornly to its native ways of life and has been least influenced by American customs. Our immigrants upon changing their foreign languages, customs, beliefs and ideals upon becoming "Americanized," deteriorate profoundly in moral character; deteriorate to a degree that shows itself in the criminal statistics.

It is very fortunate for the moral welfare of millions of our foreign population that the present furore for "Americanization" is destined to fail in its object. Its failure is in its own nature. The fundamental social virtues, honesty, industry, thrift, truthfulness and the rest, are the same for all societies on the same general level of development. They are not promoted by the custom of saluting any particular flag nor advanced by the ability to read any particular Constitution.

The very complete and profound change of character implied by the phrase: "The Americanization of the Foreigner" can be wisely and safely accomplished only if spread out over at least three generations, while four or five would be better. Every year less than three generations, that the progress is hastened, means moral and spiritual breakdown for thousands—means domestic tragedy and congested criminal calendars. There is only one foreigner who is really a menace to American society. He is the foreigner who is in rapid process of "Americanization." The danger point is the foreign-born child and the American-born child of foreign parents.

The danger from these classes is real and serious, perhaps the most serious presented in the whole range of immigration questions. Here again we have very reliable statistics which leave no room for reasonable doubt. America needs protection, needs it urgently, against the foreigner of the second generation, particularly against the youthful foreigner who goes through our Public school system. The father who stubbornly refuses to learn English or to adopt American ways is commonly a man of admirable moral character. The son, often quite as American as young men of our old stock, is equally commonly a youth of vicious and unprincipled character.

Public opinion in this matter is grievously at fault. There is danger to American institutions, and that danger is real, but it is just the opposite of what is popularly feared. The danger lies precisely in the process of Americanization itself, particularly in the endeavor to hasten that process. If, as is commonly maintained, the present need in America is peace and safety, security and conservatism, then the Americanization of the foreigner should be slowed down in every way possible. No encouragement should at this time be offered to the foreigner to abandon his native language or religion or to change his ethical or cultural standards.

On the other hand, every possible assistance should be given to Roman and Greek Catholic priests, Orthodox rabbis and other such leaders in maintaining and strengthening the traditional loyalties of their various groups. Our Mohammedans—no negligible element in recent immigration—should be encouraged to build mosques, to read the Koran and to obey the various other requirements of their faith. Our public libraries should provide themselves more liberally with books in foreign languages. Foreign language lectures and speakers of all sorts should be much encouraged. By such means and only by such means can the spirit of unrest and disquiet be stilled and the spirit of conservatism and contentment with the *status quo* be developed among our foreign population.

It is a most curious popular misconception that peace and quietness and respect for law and order can be developed in the foreigner by suddenly and violently disturbing his mental life. Changing a man's language, upsetting his moral and social conventions, altering his inherited traditions of conduct, unsettling his ancestral faith—these are the very best means possible for making him a disbeliever in all established institutions, including those of the United States. Yet this is precisely what "Americanization" aims to do with the best intentions.

Let us take a specific illustration. It may perhaps be theoretically desirable to bring our new immigrant to a realization of the crudity and superstition of his Eastern Orthodox faith, and to be a lively recognition of the superiority of American Protestantism. Practically, it can be seldom done and the reason is simple. When a person has been brought to realize the faults, imperfections, and limitations of a traditional system of belief in religion, government or what not, he inevitably applies his new critical attitude towards whatever system of belief is offered to him as a substitute for the one he has been encouraged to cast aside.

Most commonly the alternative system, being human, has serious faults, imperfections and limitations of its own, which are easily enough discoverable. The net result of very much conscientious missionary work in America is that the foreigner ceases to believe his traditional faith, refuses allegiance to any American substitute and becomes an infidel agnostic or atheist. The same thing is just as common in the realms of social, ethical and political faith as in that of religious belief.

Respect for Government and law is not a natural instinct. It is an artificial attitude slowly built up in the individual by all sorts of direct and indirect social pressure. The breakdown of old habits of thought in any one of the great departments of social activity very rapidly affects the other phases of conduct. The whole moral life of the individual tends to become unsettled. Nothing is held firmly except the selfish determination to obtain material wealth. Ideas and ideals which stand in the way of this are cast aside. The Americanized foreigner possesses all the native Americans' ruthless greed without possessing his social ethical, religious, or political idealism.

No man can learn a language perfectly who learns it deliberately, and social ideals are harder to learn than language. They can never be learned naturally and completely except when they are learned so gradually and imperceptibly that the process is unrecognized and largely unconscious. This can never be possible in the case of the foreign born, and is only very partially attainable in the case of the children foreign born. Its complete realization is possible only in the case of children born and reared in an entirely American environment. That is to say it cannot be accomplished before the third generation at the earliest, and often not then.

II. THE FAD OF AMERICANIZATION

By Glenn Frank in the "Century Magazine," June, 1920.

We are a nation of confirmed uplifters. We are never happy except when we are reforming something or saving somebody. It doesn't matter greatly whom we are saving or what we are reforming; the game is the thing. This uplift urge expresses itself in the "movement" mania, the endemic home of which is United States. The American cannot live by bread alone; he must have committees, clubs, constitutions, by-laws, platforms, and resolutions. These things, the machinery of uplift, are his meat and wine. The American society women takes to "social service" and the American business man to "public work" as a bird takes to the air or a hound to the trail. It is in the blood.

Just now the most popular social sport is "Americanization." It is in many ways an ideal movement. It fully satisfies the passion of the comfortable classes for uplift, and is a Godsend to the candidate who wants something to grow fervent about in lieu of a frank facing of fundamental issues of *politics* and *industry*. Above all, Americanization work gives one the righteous feeling of a defender of the faith. The epidemic faddist character of much Americanization work was pointedly stated in a recent article by Simon J. Lubin and Christina Krysto in "The Survey." They said:

"Every social organization, every religious society, every large industry, every woman's club has been busy for months mapping out its own particular program. The study of Americanization has been used to stimulate interest in organizations which were dying a natural death; Americanization has been used as a pretext for sudden improvements in industrial management when the attitude of labor has made sudden improvements imperative; Americanization has been used to give employment to social workers out of jobs."

This article further points out the inevitability of innumerable perversions of Americanization in such an orgy of organization. The article says on this point:

"Every political party has its hangers-on who, consciously or unconsciously, discredit the fine principles of that party by their erroneous expounding of these. Every new phase in industrial progress has its profiteers—men who capitalize the advanced ideas of their field for their own interest, regardless of the harm which they bring to the whole by their methods. Every scientific discovery has its charlatans who mix enough of the truth with their lies to undermine the whole truth when their lies become known. Every religion has its false messiahs, and many a man has been made an unbeliever because he has followed these too easily and been disappointed too grievously."

It should be said that the profiteers, charlatans, and false messiahs of Americanization are not, in the main, men and women of bad intentions so much as they are men and women of half-ideas of fractional and incomplete conceptions of Americanization. The title of false messiahs fits them better than either profiteers or charlatans, for false messiahs are usually profoundly sincere, although profoundly misguided.

No straight-thinking person disputes the need of a fundamentally sound program of Americanization, a vast collective effort toward the stimulation and spread of sane principles of national life among all sorts and conditions of men and women who make up our population. But anything and everything that goes by the name of Americanization is not necessarily an effective move in that direction. There is slowly growing up a body of incisive criticism dealing with the current epidemic of Americanization work that is sweeping the country on the wings of clever catch-words and generous emotions. It may be of interest and value to attempt an analysis and statement of the main points of that body of criticism. Here are a few plainly valid criticisms.

First, it is psychologically bad to approach Americanization work through a *super-organized and much-trumpeted movement, because such a policy warns the foreigner in advance that a crowd of superior* persons have set out to improve him. That is generally resented. The fact is that hardly a thing has been proposed as desirable in an Americanization program that is not the duty or function of some existing institution of our country, the church, the school, the industry, the press. Education, hygiene, and a decent inter-class courtesy are necessary features of any sound Americanization program, but they can be more effectively applied by calling them what they are and promoting them in normal ways than by branding them Americanization and cursing them with the blight of paternalistic uplift.

But it is probably useless to quarrel with a long established national habit. It is a habit of ours to create a new organization for every new task. Not only does that practice have the drawbacks just mentioned, but it robs our established institutions of the habit of doing creative work, leaves our established institutions as homes of the routine and the regular. There is a fundamental difference between England and the United States in this matter. In England the few men who have caught an idea or envisioned a need, do not, as a regular practice, create a new propagandist organization instanter, but in most cases set quietly to work to get the machinery of established institutions going on the task. An increasing number of clear-minded folk are becoming convinced that Americanization would proceed much faster and more soundly through the increase efficiency of the existing machinery of school and church and press and industry, without any fanfare of trumpets, than through any propagandist "drive" for uplifting the foreigner.

Second, it is a *fallacy* to suppose that Americanization *is a process needed by the foreigners only.* Much Americanization work proceeds upon the assumption that what is needed is to make the foreigner "like us." The fact is that Americanization is sorely needed by many of "us," Americanization does not mean merely getting an immigrant ready for his citizenship-papers. It means the continuous fostering of the American spirit of liberty, justice, and equality of opportunity in every man and woman and institution and policy. Americanization should be looked upon as the inspiring goal of both native born and foreign born, not as a missionary enterprise among the foreign born alone. To single out the foreign born as the exclusive objects of an Americanization effort is organized tactlessness. If, on the other hand, the foreign born feel that they are being invited to join with the native born in a vast collective effort to build a better nation in which liberty, justice, and equality of opportunity shall increasingly prevail, they will go out of their way to acquire the English language, a knowledge of our institutions and ways, and all the instruments necessary to the task of collaborating with us in the improvement of the republic.

Third, serious danger lies in *the over-simplification of the* problem of Americanization by propagandist organizations. We are in constant danger from too simple analysis of problems and too simple as the epigrams that grow up about it. Panaceas usually touch only a part of a problem. It is interesting to watch various types of minds approach the problems of Americanization in committee discussion. Here are a few simple solutions that the writer has heard from time to time:

Teach the foreigner to stick to the job and produce. We need to teach the foreigner that Americanism means patriotic production for the relief of the world's present peace-time plight, just as it meant patriotic production for the necessities of war-time. A great drive for industrial patriotism is the supreme need.

Teach the foreigner to respect our forms of government. Make the foreigner understand that we have settled the question of government forms and that criticism is disloyalty. We must discourage the practice of biting the hand that feeds.

Teach the foreigner the English language. There is no room in this country for more than one language. Alien intrigue could be killed if we turned the United States into a country of one language.

Make every foreigner take out citizenship-papers within a specified time or deport him.

Now, it is inevitable that when Americanization is made a popular "drive" by a vast propagandist organization that the army of men and women of one idea, apostles of simplicist solutions, will flock into the ranks of the propagandists. Even when the official program of the organization is well rounded, the army of simple-solutionists will do irreparable damage in their work as servants of the movement.

The problem cannot be dismissed by preaching to the foreigner that he should stick to the job and produce. The problem of maximum production has a thousand ramifications that run throughout the whole industrial problem. The preaching of industrial patriotism is a waste of breath unless it goes hand in hand with a far-reaching liberal program of industrial justice and efficiency. The industrial program is more important than the industrial preaching. Put the program into effect and the preaching of loyalty to the job may be unnecessary.

Far from being Americanism, it is fundamentally anti-American to urge an uncritical deification of any form of government. Americanism involves an invitation to continuous constructive criticism in behalf of a bettering of our machinery of government. It is no solution of the foreign-born problem to preach loyalty to the *status quo*. We shall get further by saying to the foreigner, "We are engaged in a great democratic experiment on this continent. We have settled a few principles in our minds. We believe in popular rule through political action, but as to details we are on a search for improvement. We ask you to learn our language and our institutions and then give us the benefit of your best thought on ways and means for the improvement of our machinery for democratic government. The bars are down for the frankest criticism from men and women who have the democratic patience to trust their proposals to peaceful procedure."

Learning the English language is only a means to an end. It is too frequently made an end in itself. There is no more virtue in talking English than in talking Hottentot. We shall not get far by the mere exaltation of a language. The only lasting results we shall achieve will be through the making of participation in this national democratic experiment of ours so attractive to the foreigner that he will burn with the desire to master our tongue, that he may better play his part and appreciate his privilege. A man can plot the downfall of the republic in English as easily as in an alien tongue.

Nor is there magic in the legal assumption of citizenship. It is the man behind the papers that counts. If anything, we have made citizenship too easy a privilege in the past.

Now, all this is said not to suggest that there is no room or need for special consideration of the Americanization problem by groups of public minded citizens. It is not intended to suggest that Americanization may not properly be made the subject of considerable propaganda. This comment has indulged in rather severe and unqualified strictures upon the Americanization "drive" in the hope of capturing attention for three manifest dangers that may prove the undoing of the real Americanization work that cries aloud for administration. These three dangers are; first, the danger of making the Americanization movement so plainly a conventional uplift movement that the foreigner will resent what he might, with a more tactful approach, request; second, the danger that, by thinking of Americanization as something needed by the foreigner alone, we shall miss the opportunity of making Americanization a vast national effort of self-education in the nature and application of the principles of liberty, justice, and equality of opportunity that, theoretically at least, comprise the American idea; and third, the danger that the propagandist's passion for simple solutions will further postpone the day of a broad and well-balanced program of national development.

We do not want "Americanism" to degenerate into a mere "protective coloration" for politicians who want to hide their reaction and their lack of ideas.

III. AMERICANIZATION WORK MUST PROCEED SLOWLY

By Rev. D. P. Tighe, "Detroit News," Aug. 23, 1919.

There are two methods of Americanizing the immigrant, says Fr. D. P. Tighe in the August number of the Catholic Light. One of them is *revolutionary,* the other *evolutionary.* To Americanize means to take the immigrant and remake him. Teaching him to write and speak the language of the country is a mere detail of the process. One cannot be awake to the industrial and social needs of the country without co-operating in every movement calculated to discourage the diversity of language, and to give to the foreigner every facility for the quick and easy mastery of English. But Americanization is a different proposition. Trotzky, when he lived in East New York, could speak and write English fluently, but he was not an American. He had neither understanding of, nor sympathy with American institutions; and, so, instead of setting himself to remedy the abuses in our industrial and political life as a good American citizen would remedy them, he became an anarchist and evisioned to himself a millennium of destruction that involved the good as well as the evil.

"Americanization is more than a mere matter of language. It involves stripping the immigrant of much of what he has inherited from the centuries. He is the finished product of those centuries His speech, his manner, his dress, his ideas along social and political and industrial lines have been fashioned upon the distaff of time. He lands upon American soil and at once there is a strangeness in the atmosphere that awes him, it is a new world in truth and the newness of it repels him and drives him back upon himself. The faintest link between the new world and the old is a Godsend to him. It gives him courage, it robs him of that feeling of aloneness. It tells him that after all, maybe he is wanted. In other words it creates an atmosphere of sympathy and understanding. Now any educator can tell you that this very atmosphere of sympathy is of the very essence of the class room, it's a condition of education, and Americanization is an education in nationalism.

"And here is where the revolutionary idea of Americanization falls down. Are you going to prove to the immigrant in one lesson that he is all wrong? Are you going to undo with a single jerk what it has taken centuries to do? Are you going to take this man and by a sort of patronizing coercion, yank him out himself and leave him, high and dry—nowhere? Or are you going to give him a reasonable time to learn the things of the new world, time to be influenced by the new environment? It took centuries to make him just what he is. Can't you spare him one generation to shed the crust of those centuries? Can't you be satisfied with making him the solid groundwork of the citizenship of his children?

"Do we favor Americanization? By *revolution, no; by evolution, yes*. The lasting kind of Americanization comes, not through a quick jerk, but through a long pull. First make the immigrant feel at home. Let him get his feet on the ground. Let him get rid of his suspicions and his distrust and his shyness by finding out the links that bind the new order with the old, the things that make for the broader kind of brotherhood. Don't rush him; lay emphasis upon the things that are common; from them he'll learn confidence, and confidence is a great big step in the transforming of an European immigrant into an American citizen."

Warwick Bro's & Rutter, Limited,
Printers and Bookbinders, Toronto, Canada.

Featured Titles from Westphalia Press

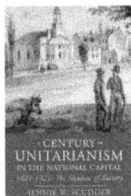

A Century of Unitarianism in the National Capital, 1821-1921
by Jennie W. Scudder

Jennie Scudder's work traces the sometimes controversial history of Unitarianism in the District of Columbia, centering on All Souls Unitarian Church. The account includes the development in the District and surrounding towns in northern Virginia and Southern Maryland.

Boston Unitarianism 1820-1850
by Octavius Brooks Frothingham

From the author, "Many years ago I proposed writing something in memory of Dr. Frothingham, but abandoned the project on account of the meagerness of the biographical material. Within the twelvemonth, a warm friend and admirer of his asked me to prepare a memoir."

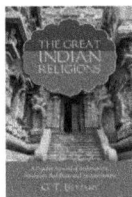

The Great Indian Religions
by G. T. Bettany

G. T. (George Thomas) Bettany (1850-1891) was born and educated in England, attending Gonville and Caius College in Cambridge University, studying medicine and the natural sciences. This book is his account of Brahmanism, Hinduism, Buddhism, and Zoroastrianism

The Bahai Movement: A Series of Nineteen Papers
by Charles Mason Remey

Charles Mason Remey (1874-1974) was the son of Admiral George Collier Remey and grew up in Washington DC. He studied to be an architect at Cornell (1893-1896) and the Ecole des Beaux Arts in Paris (1896-1903), where he learned about the Baha'i faith, and quickly adopted it.

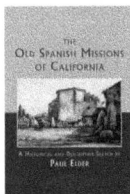

The Old Spanish Missions of California
by Paul Elder

This work only portrays a partial and sanitized tale of the Spanish missions in California and their impact. The missions relied on agriculture to fund themselves, and sought to convert and colonize the Native people and their land. Rebellions against the missions occurred since the missionaries sought to destroy native culture.

www.ingramcontent.com/pod-product-compliance
Lightning Source LLC
Chambersburg PA
CBHW072337090426
42741CB00012B/2823